MW01715619

Message from the Author

Becoming the Leader You Always Needed

If you're like me, you've been told more times than you can count that you should become an administrator. But still, you hesitate. Maybe it's because those quiet doubts keep sneaking in. Maybe you've convinced yourself you won't get hired because someone you know struggled to find a position. Or maybe you tell yourself that your students still need you.

The truth is, your students needed you yesterday, they need you today, and they will most certainly need you tomorrow. But do you know who may need you even more? Teachers, teachers who are waiting for a leader like you: someone who leads with compassion, empowers with wisdom, shares knowledge with clarity, and ignites motivation.

You've already helped students recognize strengths they didn't know they had. You've inspired those who had nearly given up. You don't lead through fear; you inspire through purpose and presence. Too often, we underestimate the quiet power of simply showing up.

Leadership isn't about holding a title; it's about living your purpose. And you already do that, every single day. You are uniquely gifted, and no one else brings exactly what you do.

If the cost of the exam is holding you back, consider this: you've already spent more on your students year after year. Now it's time to invest in yourself.

You never know how life will unfold in the next few years. Opportunities often arrive when we least expect them, and sometimes the only thing standing between you and the next chapter is a license.

After taking the sample test from ETS, I recognized the importance of becoming more familiar with the leadership standards that guide the exam. When I searched for study guides, every resource I found provided test questions without giving the opportunity to truly learn the standards and apply them. That's where this guide is different. That's why I designed two guides using real-world scenarios. You'll gain not only practice but the deeper conceptual understanding that allows you to transfer knowledge to any situation. Instead of memorizing answers, you'll build the confidence to think like a school leader.

The first guide was inspired by the Professional Standards for Educational Leaders (PSEL), I developed this guide to speak directly to teachers by a teacher using real-world scenarios that bridge what you already know with what the test requires. The second guide was inspired by The Praxis Study Companion for the School Leaders Licensure Assessment (SLLA – Test Code 6990).

This isn't just a study guide. It's a journey that helps you learn, reflect, and step confidently into leadership. You already have everything you need to succeed. Now, give yourself the time and space to grow. You're not just preparing to pass an exam; you're becoming the leader you always needed. Invest in yourself because your growth as a leader will always reach your students.

With you in purpose and practice,

Ingrid Fullerton
Certified Supervisor | Curriculum Specialist | Instructional Leader
NJ Learning for All, LLC

Copyright

This study guide was developed by NJ Learning For All, LLC, a registered business in the State of New Jersey, to support aspiring school leaders preparing for the School Leaders Licensure Assessment (6990). It is intended solely for educational and instructional use.

Every effort has been made to ensure the accuracy and alignment of the content with publicly available educational standards and testing frameworks. This guide draws from and references the following public sources:

- **Professional Standards for Educational Leaders (PSEL),**published by the National Policy Board for Educational Administration (NPBEA) Titled: Principal Exam Based on the Professional Standards for Educational Leadership (PSEL) ISBN 979-8-9930033-0-6
- **The Praxis Study Companion for the School Leaders Licensure Assessment (SLLA – Test Code 6990),** published by Educational Testing Service (ETS), (https://www.ets.org/pdfs/sls/6990.pdf)

Neither NPBEA nor ETS has reviewed, endorsed, or sponsored this guide. All instructional content, explanations, and interpretations are the original work of the author and NJ Learning For All, LLC.

For permissions or licensing inquiries, please contact:
NJ Learning For All, LLC
New Jersey, United States
Email: NJlearningforall@gmail.com

Printed in the United States of America.

Table of Content

Organization of the Guide

This study guide is designed to help you master each section by applying real-world examples that bring clarity and depth to every concept. The seven domains are listed below. For each of the first six domains, this guide includes:

- Three real-life scenarios with problems and solutions
- Unpacking of the essential questions with outlines and examples
- Twenty ETS-style knowledge checkpoint questions with solutions
- 50 short answer questions with solutions

The final domain consists of the Constructed Response (Essay) section. This domain includes annotated sample essays illustrating what a 3-point, 2-point, and 1-point response looks like, helping you recognize the differences and aim for top-tier performance.

I. Strategic Leadership

- 20 Questions; 13% of the exam
- Focuses on developing and sustaining a shared vision and school improvement plan
- PSEL Standard 1: Mission, Vision, and Core Values
- PSEL Standard 10: School Improvement

II. Instructional Leadership

- 27 Questions; 17% of the exam
- Emphasizes effective teaching, learning, curriculum, and assessment practices
- PSEL Standard 4: Curriculum, Instruction, and Assessment
- PSEL Standard 6. Professional Capacity of School Personnel
- PSEL Standard 7: Community for Teachers and Staff

III. Climate and Cultural Leadership

- 22 Questions; 13% of the exam
- Address's school culture, inclusivity, equity, and responsiveness to diverse student needs
- PSEL Standard 3: Equity and Cultural Responsiveness
- PSEL Standard 5. Community of Care and Support for Students

IV. Ethical Leadership

- 19 Questions; 12% of the exam
- Centers on integrity, legal and ethical responsibilities, and the professional norms of school leadership
- PSEL Standard 2: Ethics and Professional Norms
- PSEL Standard 9: Operations and Management (Legal responsibilities component)

V. Organizational Leadership

- 16 Questions; 10% of the exam
- Focuses on staffing, resources, scheduling, and school operations
- PSEL Standard 6: Professional Capacity of School Personnel
- PSEL Standard 9: Operations and Management

VI. Community Engagement Leadership

- 16 Questions; 10% of the exam
- Measures the leader's ability to communicate and collaborate with families and community partners
- PSEL Standard 8: Meaningful Engagement of Families and Community
- PSEL Standard 3: Equity and Cultural Responsiveness (communication across cultures)

VII. Analysis: Constructed Response (CR)

4 Essays 25% of the exam

- Measures the leader's ability to communicate and collaborate with families and community partners
- PSEL Standard: May draw from any of the 10 PSEL standards.

VIII. Train Your Brain Refresher

50 short answer questions with solutions

Domain I: Strategic Leadership

This section focuses on the principal's role in setting a clear mission, vision, and core values for the school. Strategic leadership provides the foundation for decision-making, school improvement, and long-term success.

Strategic Leadership

Real-Life Scenario A: Mission, Vision, Goals, and Core Values

When Ms. Fullerton became the new principal of Lincoln Middle School, she quickly realized the school's mission statement hadn't been updated in over a decade. Teachers worked in isolation, and schoolwide goals felt vague and disconnected from classroom realities. Student achievement data revealed widening gaps in reading and math, and family engagement had declined sharply.

Ms. Fullerton began by analyzing multiple sources of data from student performance reports, staff surveys, parent feedback, and classroom observations. She noticed inconsistent expectations across grade levels and limited alignment between instruction and the school's original vision. With this information, she assembled a visioning team of teachers, support staff, parents, and student representatives.

Together, they crafted a new mission and set of core values focused on equity, student voice, and academic rigor. From this, Ms. Fullerton led the team in developing SMART goals (Specific, Measurable, Attainable, Results-driven, and Time-bound), aligned not only to their new mission but also to district priorities.

For example, one goal was:
"By June, increase the percentage of 6th–8th grade students meeting or exceeding grade-level benchmarks in reading by 15%, as measured by district assessments."
The goal included regular progress monitoring checkpoints and professional development tied directly to literacy strategies.

As the new mission and goals were rolled out, Ms. Fullerton made sure they were visible and actionable, featured in every newsletter, referenced in staff meetings, and posted in classrooms. Staff began to take ownership, tracking progress toward goals and celebrating small wins. Within a year, Lincoln Middle had made measurable gains in both student achievement and teacher morale.

Strategic Leadership

Real-Life Scenario B: Shared commitments to implement the vision and goals

At Brookside Middle School, Principal Alvarez introduced a plan to implement a daily intervention block as part of the school's vision to ensure that every student receives timely, targeted academic support. While some teachers welcomed the initiative others, particularly from elective departments, expressed concern that the revised schedule would reduce instructional time for their courses. The disagreement quickly escalated, creating visible division among staff and breaking down communication between departments.

Recognizing the growing tension, Principal Alvarez anchored the conversation in the school's shared mission to improve student outcomes. She began by facilitating small group listening sessions where teachers from all departments could express their concerns in a respectful and structured environment. These sessions revealed a range of perspectives and surfaced a few common values: commitment to student growth, the need for adequate planning time, and a desire for fairness in scheduling.

To build consensus, Principal Alvarez led a schoolwide decision-making process grounded in collaboration and transparency. She used a protocol that included:

1. Identifying non-negotiables (e.g., protecting planning time, ensuring equity for electives),
2. Brainstorming multiple solutions as a staff,
3. Narrowing options based on agreed-upon criteria (e.g., alignment with student needs, sustainability),
4. Voting or ranking proposals to reach a final decision.

When an elective teacher shared that she felt marginalized in the process, Principal Alvarez met with her one-on-one to reaffirm that all staff voices were valued and clarified how her feedback was being integrated into the decision-making process. This meeting led to a creative compromise resulting in a rotating schedule that ensured elective time reductions were shared evenly, rather than disproportionately affecting a single subject.

Throughout the process, Principal Alvarez reinforced the school's vision by clearly communicating the purpose of the intervention block in staff meetings, emails, and newsletters. She regularly connected scheduling decisions to school goals and student data, helping staff see the broader impact of their collaboration.

Once implemented, the new schedule is launched with broad staff support. Teachers felt more ownership after influencing the final result. The intervention block allowed struggling students to receive consistent academic support, while teacher morale improved due to the transparent, inclusive process. Alvarez continued to monitor the program's effectiveness through feedback loops and data reviews, adjusting as needed.

Strategic Leadership

Real-Life Scenario C: Continuous improvement toward the vision and goals

When Dr. Patel took over as principal of Jefferson High School, the school was struggling with low graduation rates and declining community trust. The existing school improvement plan had strong goals on paper, but there was little buy-in from staff or families. Many teachers felt excluded from decision-making, and community members, especially from underrepresented groups, said their voices weren't valued.

Dr. Patel began by holding listening sessions with faculty, parents, and students. She made sure these forums reflected diverse perspectives, including multilingual families, students with IEPs, and community-based organizations. Through this outreach, she learned that while most people supported the school's goals, they didn't feel part of the process.

To address this, Dr. Patel launched a Vision Implementation Team that included teachers, students, parents, and community partners. Together, they broke down the school's goals into action steps, assigned clear responsibilities, and created shared commitments, such as holding monthly goal review meetings and hosting parent-led workshops on college readiness. She also trained team leaders to build consensus using protocols that encouraged all voices.

To measure progress, the school used data dashboards shared at monthly staff meetings and community town halls. These included real-time updates on attendance, grade distribution, and progress toward college application completion. Feedback loops were built in, allowing staff and stakeholders to adjust strategies as needed.

For communication, Dr. Patel adopted a multichannel approach: weekly newsletters, robocalls, translated updates, Instagram videos, and informal "coffee chats" with families. All messaging connected back to the vision college and career readiness for every student and emphasized how everyone's actions contributed to the larger mission.

As a result, staff ownership increased, parent engagement doubled, and by the end of the year, graduation rates rose by 9%. The school's success was not just due to the quality of the goals, but because everyone believed in them, understood them, and saw their role in making them happen.

Why Is It Important to Develop and Implement a Vision and Goals?

Creating and implementing a school vision and goals is like renovating a house. Before you start tearing down walls or painting rooms, you need a blueprint. That blueprint (the vision) tells everyone specifically contractors, electricians, designers what the finished home should look like. But a blueprint alone doesn't get the job done. You also need step-by-step tasks, deadlines, and tools (the goals) to make the vision a reality. Without either, the renovation becomes chaotic, expensive, and misaligned.

In the same way, a school needs a clearly defined vision to articulate its desired future, and measurable goals to guide daily decisions, allocate resources, and track progress. A strong vision and well-implemented goals ensure that everyone, especially teachers, students, families, and leaders can work toward a shared purpose with clarity and commitment.

Outline

1. Vision Acts as the School's Blueprint

- It defines what the school aspires to become.
- *Example*: A school's vision to "empower all learners through innovation and equity" shapes everything from curriculum to culture.

2. Goals Break the Vision into Measurable Steps

- They outline clear, time-bound objectives aligned to the vision.
- *Example*: A literacy-focused school sets a goal: "Increase Grade 3 reading scores by 10% by June."

3. Implementation Turns Words into Action

- A vision without action is meaningless.
- *Example*: Teams use goal-tracking tools, PD sessions, and data analysis to ensure progress.

4. Daily Decision-Making Guides

- Help leaders prioritize what matters most.
- *Example*: Choosing an SEL curriculum aligned with the school's commitment to student wellness.

5. Promotes Unity Across Stakeholders

- Builds a shared sense of direction for staff, families, and students.
- *Example*: Teachers collaborate around shared academic goals; parents support homework aligned to vision.

6. Provides Accountability and Measurable Results

- Make it possible to evaluate whether the school is moving forward.
- *Example*: Quarterly progress reviews tied to goal metrics.

What Types and Sources of Data Can Be Used to Determine or Support a School Vision and Goals?

Using data to shape a school's vision and goals is like checking a car's dashboard before a long road trip. The fuel gauge tells you how far you can go, the tire pressure warning helps you avoid a blowout, and the GPS shows your starting point and route options. Without this information, you're making blind decisions and risk breaking down along the way.

In the same way, schools need multiple types of data, academic, behavioral, demographic, and perception-based to make informed decisions about their future. These data sources help leaders understand where the school is starting, what its strengths and needs are, and where support is most urgently required. Vision and goals that are grounded in data are more realistic, equitable, and impactful.

<u>Outline</u>

1. Academic Performance Data

- Standardized tests, formative assessments, report cards, progress monitoring
- *Example*: If state reading scores reveal that only 40% of third graders are reading on grade level, the goal should be to focus on early literacy.

2. Attendance and Discipline Data

- Absentee rates, tardiness patterns, suspension/expulsion records
- *Example*: If chronic absenteeism is identified in Grades 6–8, the goal should be to develop a vision centered on engagement and belonging.

- **3. Demographic and Enrollment Data**
- Subgroup performance (e.g., ELLs, students with disabilities, low-income), mobility rates, enrollment trends
- *Example*: If there is an increase in multilingual learners, the goal should be to develop a vision for multilingual inclusivity and language equity.

4. Perception Data (Climate and Culture)

- Surveys from students, staff, and families; focus group input
- *Example*: If parent surveys show families feel disconnected the goal should be to focus on building community engagement.

5. Program Evaluation Data

- Data on effectiveness of academic interventions, extracurriculars, PD, or curriculum pilots
- *Example:* If data shows math intervention improved scores by 12%, the next step is to analyze which strategies were most effective.

Why Is It Necessary to Use Data When Planning to Implement a Vision and Goals?

Using data to plan the implementation of a school vision and goals is like organizing a cross-country road trip. You might have a dream destination in mind (the vision), but you can't set out without first checking your GPS, traffic reports, gas level, and weather. Data tells you where you're starting, what detours to expect, how long the trip might take, and whether you're heading in the right direction.

In the same way, data allows school leaders to move from inspirational vision to practical action. It identifies where the school stands, what barriers exist, and how progress can be measured. Without data, goals may be vague, irrelevant, or inequitable. With data, goals are targeted, measurable, and responsive to the real needs of students and staff.

Outline

1. Data Establishes a Baseline

- Determines current performance levels, gaps, and needs
- *Example*: Current data reveals that 58% of Grade 4 students are reading below grade level. This information provides a clear starting point for setting targets and monitoring growth.

2. Data Ensures Equity in Goal Development

- Highlights subgroup disparities (e.g., by race, language, IEP status)
- *Example*: Data shows MLL students score 25% lower in math, guiding goals for inclusive math instruction

3. Data Guides Prioritization and Resource Allocation

- Helps leaders decide where to focus attention, funding, and PD
- *Example*: Chronic absenteeism leads to investing in family liaisons and attendance monitoring tools

4. Data Provides a Framework for Monitoring Progress

- Allows for mid-course corrections based on evidence
- *Example*: Benchmark assessments track whether an ELA goal is on track or needs adjustment

5. Data Strengthens Stakeholder Buy-In

- Transparent data builds trust and shared ownership of goals
- *Example*: Sharing family survey results builds support for a new school culture initiative

What is meant by "data-driven decision making"?

Data-driven decision making is like using a fitness tracker to improve your health. You don't just guess how active you've been, you track your steps, heart rate, and sleep patterns. The data helps you decide whether to change your diet, exercise more, or get more rest. Your decisions are smarter because they're based on facts, not feelings.

In education, data-driven decision making works the same way. School leaders use facts such as test scores, attendance trends, and perception surveys to monitor school health, identify challenges, and take informed action. If math scores are dropping or absenteeism is rising, leaders don't rely on assumptions. They examine the evidence, ask meaningful questions, and implement targeted solutions. Just like a fitness tracker alerts you when your steps are low, school data alerts leaders when progress stalls, so they can adjust before long-term harm occurs.

Outline

1. Collecting Reliable Data

- **Academic**: NJSLA, I-Ready, classroom assessments, ACCESS for ELLs
- **Behavioral**: Attendance, suspensions, discipline referrals
- **Perception**: Stakeholder surveys, classroom walkthroughs
- *Example*: Weekly math checks highlight gaps in multi-digit division.

2. Analyzing Patterns

- Disaggregate by subgroup (ELLs, SPED, low-income, race/ethnicity)
- Identify trends and root causes
- *Example:* Identifying that chronic absenteeism is highest in 6th grade boys, helps to supports targeted intervention

3. Setting SMART Goals

- Specific, Measurable, Achievable, Relevant, and Time-bound
- Must align to school's mission and data findings
- *Example*: "Increase Grade 3 reading proficiency by 15% by June."

IV. Taking Evidence-Based Action

- Adjust instruction or professional development
- Implement targeted interventions
- Allocate resources strategically
- *Example*: Launching Tier II interventions after benchmark screening data

V. Monitoring and Refining

- Use continuous improvement cycles
- Review progress through data teams
- Adjust strategies and celebrate growth
- *Example*: Reviewing mid-year data in PLCs

What types of data are valuable for developing or revising a vision and goals?

Creating a school vision without using data is like planning a dream vacation without checking your bank account. You might picture luxury hotels, first-class flights, and five-star dinners, but if you don't know what you can realistically afford, that vision quickly turns into disappointment. Likewise, school leaders may envision equity, excellence, and innovation, but without data, they don't know what's possible, where the gaps are, or what needs urgent attention.

Data is your reality check. It reveals strengths, challenges, and patterns across students, staff, and the school community. It helps leaders decide where to invest effort, whether it's boosting math achievement, strengthening climate, or increasing family engagement. When school goals are based on data, the vision becomes achievable, strategic, and community-focused, not just a wish list.

Outline

1. Academic Achievement and Growth

- **Standardized tests (e.g., NJSLA, I-Ready, ACCESS for ELLs)**
  Example: NJSLA math scores show 5th grade ELL students performing 30% below state average which prompts goal to strengthen math instruction with language scaffolds.
- **Report cards, unit assessments, growth percentiles (mSGP)**
  Example: A teacher with an mSGP of 3.5 demonstrates strong student growth despite low starting points. The school recognizes effective instructional strategies for replication.
- **Class-level mastery and progress data**
  Example: If PLC data review shows Grade 3 students consistently struggling with fractions, the vision revision includes a focus on foundational numeracy skills.

2. Demographics

- **Student enrollment by subgroup (ELL, SPED, economically disadvantaged)**
  Example: If 68% of students are economically disadvantaged and 22% are ELLs, the school should commit to equity-based access and culturally responsive teaching in its vision.
- **Attendance, chronic absenteeism, and student mobility**
  Example: If 1 in 5 students are chronically absent, especially in Grades 6–8, the school should set a goal to improve engagement and implement attendance interventions.
- **Participation in programs (e.g., bilingual, gifted, special services)**
  Example: If data shows underrepresentation of Latino students in gifted and talented programs, the school should revise its vision to include equitable access to advanced learning.

3. Stakeholder Feedback

- **Parent, student, and teacher surveys**
  Example: If parent survey shows only 35% feel well-informed about their child's progress, the school should add a communication goal to its improvement plan.
- **Town halls, focus groups, community feedback**
  Example: If during a community town hall, families express concerns about school safety and student voice. The vision statement should be updated to include a safe, inclusive environment.

- **Family engagement data (event attendance, communication logs)**
  Example: If event data reveals strong K–2 family turnout but minimal middle school engagement, the school should set a goal to improve parent partnerships across all grade levels.

4. Behavioral and Climate Indicators

- **Suspension and referral data**
  Example: If 80% of suspensions involve Black boys in Grades 4–6, the school should commit to restorative practices and anti-bias training in its vision and goals.

- **PBIS, SEL, or school climate results**
  Example: If SEL screeners show high rates of anxiety and low self-efficacy among students, the vision should include social-emotional development as a top priority.

- **Student perception of safety and belonging**
  Example: If only 40% of middle school students report feeling "safe and accepted", the school should set measurable climate goals and updates the vision to prioritize inclusion.

5. Staff and Organizational Capacity

- **Walkthrough trends and instructional alignment**
  Example: If walkthrough data shows inconsistent use of learning objectives and checks for understanding, the school should set a goal for improving instructional coherence.

- **Teacher credentials, turnover, and support needs**
  Example: If the science department has lost 3 teachers in 2 years, and 40% are teaching out-of-field, the school should focus on retention and capacity building in STEM.

- **Budget and resource availability**
  Example: If analysis reveals a technology gap of only 1 device per 5 students in upper grades, the vision should include digital equity and expands tech integration.

Why would it be valuable for a school leader to poll key stakeholders about the purpose of education when developing a vision and goals?

Imagine you're hired to design uniforms for a dance group. But instead of asking questions, you immediately start designing the uniform without finding out the dancers' sizes, their ages, or even what kind of fabric is needed for the type of dance they're performing. You proudly deliver the finished product, only to find the costumes are too tight, too long, or too stiff for movement. The dance class refuses to wear them or pay for them. Now you must remake the uniforms from scratch, using your own time and money, just to fix a mistake that could have been avoided with simple conversation.

Leaving students, families, and staff out of the visioning process is no different. It's the same costly misstep. A school leader might create a bold, inspirational mission statement, but if it doesn't reflect the voices and values of the school community, it won't be embraced or implemented. And worse, it may need to be reworked after time and effort have already been spent pushing an idea no one believed in.

Polling stakeholders is how school leaders take measurements before cutting the fabric. It ensures the school's vision reflects the students and community it serves academically, culturally, emotionally, and socially. When leaders design with the community's interests in mind, rather than their own, they avoid waste, build trust, and create a shared sense of pride.

Outline

1. Introduction: The Importance of Stakeholder Voice in Vision Development

- School vision and goals must reflect shared values and priorities.
- Engaging stakeholders ensures buy-in, relevance, and alignment with community needs.

2. Defining "Key Stakeholders"

- Teachers and staff
- Parents and families
- Students (age-appropriate input)
- Community members and local partners
- School board members and district leadership

3. Reasons for Polling Stakeholders

A. Ensures the Vision Reflects Shared Beliefs

- Captures diverse perspectives about what education should accomplish.
- Avoids a top-down approach that may alienate the school community.

B. Builds Trust and Ownership

- Stakeholders feel heard and valued.
- This leads to greater commitment in implementing shared goals.

C. Identifies Gaps in Understanding or Priorities

- Reveals differing expectations among groups (e.g., college readiness vs. life skills).
- Help align resources to address varying needs.

D. Strengthens Equity and Inclusion

- Amplifies voices from underrepresented groups.
- Promotes culturally responsive and community-centered practices.

E. Supports Data-Informed Decision Making

- Poll results offer qualitative and quantitative insight.
- Data can be used to set measurable, meaningful goals.

4. Methods of Polling and Engagement

- Online surveys, town halls, focus groups, parent-teacher forums.
- Translating materials and offering multiple formats ensures accessibility for all families.

5. Long-Term Benefits for Vision and Goal Development

- Vision becomes a living, shared blueprint rather than a compliance document.
- Goals are more likely to be implemented and sustained when stakeholders are co-authors.

Essential Question #7 — Strategic Leadership

What goals are measurable? What goals are non-measurable?

Setting non-measurable goals is like mixing chemicals in a science lab without labels or measurements. You might hope for the best, but you won't know what worked, what failed, or how to repeat success. It's unpredictable, un-trackable, and ultimately ineffective.

On the other hand, measurable goals are like carefully controlled experiments. Each step is documented, each ingredient is measured, and outcomes are tracked. You know what caused success, and you can do it again or improve it next time.

Measurable goals are specific, quantifiable, and include clear criteria to track progress and determine success. They often answer the questions: How much? How many? By when? Example of a measurable goal: Increase 3rd grade reading proficiency from 60% to 75% by June.

Non-measurable goals are vague, subjective, or lack concrete criteria for evaluation. They often rely on general intentions rather than specific outcomes. Examples of non-measurable goals: Improve student behavior.

Outline

1. What Goals Are Measurable?

Characteristics:

- Clear, specific outcome
- Data can be collected
- Has a timeline or deadline
- Progress can be tracked

Examples:

- Increase 5th-grade math proficiency from 48% to 65% by June
- Reduce chronic absenteeism by 20% this academic year
- Host 6 family events with 50+ attendees each
- Ensure all new teachers receive two coaching sessions per quarter
- Raise student perception of safety on climate surveys from 60% to 80%

2. What Goals Are Non-measurable?

Characteristics:

- Vague or abstract language
- No data source
- No deadline or timeframe
- Difficult to evaluate

Examples:

- Improve school culture
- Foster academic excellence
- Build stronger parent relationships
- Promoting student success
- Strengthen instruction

3. Converting Non-Measurable Goals Into Measurable Ones

Non-measurable	Measurable
Improve school culture	Increase positive responses on climate survey by 20% by May
Foster parent relationships	Increase parent-teacher conference attendance to 90%
Promote student success	Raise school-wide GPA average from 2.7 to 3.2 by year-end
Strengthen instruction	Conduct 3 walkthroughs per teacher each semester with feedback
Build equity	Reduce achievement gap in math between subgroups by 15%

Why Is It Important for a School Leader to Have Effective Oral and Written Communication Skills?

Effective communication for a school leader is like running a group text for a family reunion. If the organizer sends vague messages, doesn't respond to questions, or forgets to include a few relatives, the whole event becomes chaotic. People will show up at the wrong time, bring the wrong food, or don't come at all. But if the leader sends clear, timely, inclusive updates and checks in along the way, everyone feels valued, knows what to do, and shows up prepared.

School leadership is no different. Whether speaking to staff, emailing parents, or presenting to the school board, strong oral and written communication ensures shared understanding, builds trust, and moves the school forward. When communication breaks down, confusion spreads, misinformation takes root, and the learning environment suffers.

Outline

1. Builds Trust and Clarity

- Transparent communication fosters credibility and reduces speculation.
- *Example*: Weekly updates to families about student progress, upcoming events, and school safety.

2. Aligns Staff with Instructional Goals

- Clearly articulated goals and expectations keep teachers unified.
- *Example*: A principal presents schoolwide data, explains its meaning, and invites staff to co-plan the next steps.

3. Prevents Misunderstandings

- Vague or inconsistent messages lead to conflict or confusion.
- *Example*: A poorly worded email about student dismissal causes chaos at the school entrance.

4. Ensures Inclusivity Across Languages and Backgrounds

- Language-accessible materials show respect for diverse communities.
- *Example*: Parent letters available in the top three home languages spoken at school.

5. Resolves Conflict and Reduces Tension

- Thoughtful, responsive dialogue prevents problems from escalating.
- *Example*: A leader listens actively during a parent complaint and follows up with a written action plan.

6. Sets the Professional Tone Schoolwide

- The leader's communication style sets the tone for all others.
- *Example*: A principal who speaks calmly and clearly during a crisis encourages staff to do the same.

Why Is It Necessary to Involve Others in Developing and Implementing a Vision and Goals?

Creating a school vision without involving others is like planning a group road trip and choosing the destination, route, and playlist without asking anyone else in the car. Sure, the leader might think they know what's best but if others feel excluded from the planning process, they are less likely to be excited, committed, or helpful when detours and obstacles arise.

In schools, shared vision-building isn't just symbolic, it's strategic. When school leaders involve staff, families, students, and community members in developing and implementing the school's vision and goals, they create a deep sense of ownership. People are more likely to contribute ideas, support initiatives, and work through challenges when they feel their voice shaped the direction. Collaboration builds buy-in, builds trust, and makes the vision more relevant to the community it serves.

Outline

1. Builds Trust and Ownership

- Involving others makes the vision feel shared, not imposed.
- *Example*: A leadership team invites teachers and parents to help define the school's top priorities for the year.

2. Encourages Diverse Perspectives

- Inclusive planning reflects the needs of the whole school community.
- *Example*: Students are surveyed about school climate before setting behavioral goals.

3. Improves Implementation and Sustainability

- People support what they help create, leading to better follow-through.
- *Example*: Teachers who helped write a new literacy plan are more likely to implement it in classrooms.

4. Enhances Equity and Responsiveness

- Engaging different groups ensures that goals do not overlook marginalized voices.
- *Example*: Multilingual parents are invited to a goal-setting night with translated materials and interpreters.

5. Models Collaborative Leadership

- Involving others shows a leader values shared decision-making.
- *Example*: A principal forms an advisory committee of staff, students, and families to monitor progress on school goals.

What Are Some of the Key Strategies for Involving Community Members in School Planning?

Imagine planning a neighborhood block party. If the host makes all the decisions alone, chooses the date, food, music, and activities, some neighbors may not show up because the date conflicts with their vacation time. However, if everyone is asked for input early on like voting on the theme, offering dishes, or organizing games. They feel invested, show up ready to contribute, and help make the event a success.

School planning works the same way. When leaders intentionally invite community members, families, local businesses, nonprofit partners, faith leaders, and civic organizations into the planning process, they build authentic partnerships, ensure diverse perspectives are represented, and create plans that reflect the unique needs and strengths of the community. The result is a stronger, more sustainable plan that the whole community supports.

Some key strategies for involving community members in school planning include establishing advisory committees that include parents and local stakeholders, and hosting community forums to gather input and feedback. Schools can also distribute surveys and need assessments to understand what is important to the community. Maintaining two-way communication through newsletters, websites, and social media helps keep families informed and engaged. Partnering with local organizations, such as businesses and nonprofits, provides additional resources and support. Including community members in decision-making processes builds trust and shared ownership.

It is also important to provide translation services and accessible materials to ensure all families can participate. Lastly, recognizing and celebrating community contributions encourages ongoing involvement and strengthens school-community relationships.

<u>Outline</u>

1. Establish Advisory Councils or Planning Committees

- Creates diverse committees that include families, students, and community members.
- *Example*: A school improvement team includes a local nonprofit leader and a parent from the neighborhood association.

2. Use Surveys, Forums, and Listening Sessions

- Collect broad feedback before decisions are made.
- *Example*: Hosting a bilingual community forum to gather ideas before writing the school's strategic plan.

3. Leverage Community Expertise

- Invite professionals to contribute ideas based on their knowledge.
- *Example*: A local health agency helps plan a student wellness initiative.

4. Provide Transparent Communication and Follow-Up

- Share timelines, drafts, and decisions clearly, and show how input shaped the plan.
- *Example*: After a planning forum, the school emails a summary of key takeaways and next steps to all participants.

5. Make Engagement Culturally Responsive

- Ensure all voices are welcomed, especially underrepresented groups.
- *Example*: Materials are translated, and meetings are held at accessible times in community centers, not just at school.

6. Invite Ongoing Feedback During Implementation

- Don't stop involving the community after the plan is finalized.
- *Example*: Monthly "Coffee and Conversation" sessions allow families to offer feedback on progress.

How Can School Community Members Learn More About the Importance of Having a School Vision and Goals?

Understanding a school's vision and goals is like joining a group fitness class: If everyone shows up with different objectives, some want yoga, others expect weight training. There's confusion and frustration. But if the instructor clearly explains the program, shares the desired outcomes, and checks in with participants, everyone moves together, motivated and aligned toward the same target.

School communities function the same way. When families, staff, and partners understand the school's vision and goals, they can contribute more meaningfully. They know what the school values, how success is defined, and how their role supports that success. Leaders must intentionally create space through meetings, visuals, storytelling, and outreach that explain not just what the goals are, but why they matter. This empowers the entire school community to work together with shared purpose and clarity.

Outline

1. Host Vision Nights and Community Conversations

- Create accessible forums to explain the school's mission, vision, and goals.
- *Example*: A principal invites families to a "Vision and Values" evening with food, translators, and student performances.

2. Share Clear, Concise Messaging

- Use newsletters, flyers, infographics, and classroom posters to reinforce key goals.
- *Example*: Each classroom displays the school's 3 goals in age-appropriate language.

3. Integrate Vision into Daily School Life

- Make vision and goals a visible living part of the school culture.
- *Example*: Morning announcements highlight how students are demonstrating core values like respect or responsibility.

4. Empower Students to Be Messengers

- Teach students to understand and share the school's vision.
- *Example*: Student ambassadors give school tours and explain the school's goals in their own words.

5. Involve Families in Goal-Based Activities

- Connect school events and volunteering with common objectives
- *Example*: A math night focuses on the school's academic growth goal and shows how families can support themselves at home.
- Provide Regular Progress Updates

What Processes Are Involved in Consensus Building and Conflict Resolution?

Consensus building and conflict resolution are like planning a family vacation with multiple relatives. Everyone has different ideas. Some want the beach, others the mountains. If one person pushes their plan without listening, tension grows. But if the group sets ground rules, shares ideas openly, and looks for overlapping interests, they may end up agreeing on a scenic lake house that offers both sun and hiking. No one gets everything, but everyone feels heard and that's what makes the trip successful.

In schools, consensus building and conflict resolution follow the same philosophy. They require inclusive dialogue, active listening, clear goals, and a willingness to compromise. School leaders who follow these processes foster stronger relationships, build shared ownership, and resolve disagreements in ways that keep the focus on what matters most: students.

Outline

Processes for Consensus Building

1. Define the Shared Goal Relevant Stakeholders

- Invite teachers, staff, families, and community members.
- *Example*: Including paraprofessionals and parents in school discipline reform talks.

2. Establish Norms for Dialogue

- Use protocols for respectful communication.
- *Example*: "One mic at a time," using talking sticks or timers during forums.

3. Facilitate Structured Dialogue

- Use tools like brainstorming, affinity grouping, or SWOT analysis.
- *Example*: Vision setting using gallery walks with feedback stations.

SWOT analysis is a strategic planning tool used by leaders, organizations, and schools to evaluate their current position and guide decision-making.
SWOT stands for:

Strengths – Internal advantages or assets the organization has (e.g., skilled teachers, strong community support, effective curriculum).
Weaknesses – Internal challenges or limitations (e.g., high teacher turnover, limited technology, low test scores in a subject).
Opportunities – External possibilities that could benefit the organization (e.g., grant funding, new community partnerships, innovative programs).
Threats – External factors that could pose risks or challenges (e.g., declining enrollment, budget cuts, competing charter schools, changing policies).

4. Identify Common Ground

- Highlight areas of agreement before negotiating disagreements.
- *Example*: All staff agree that equity should guide policy, even if strategies differ.

5. Build Agreement Through Transparency

- Document discussions and keep participants informed.

- *Example*: Posting meeting notes and drafts for public review.

II. Processes for Conflict Resolution

1. Acknowledge the Conflict Respectfully

- Don't ignore or minimize disagreement.
- *Example*: Acknowledge staff tension over new lesson planning expectations.

2. Gather Perspectives Privately if Needed

- Allow stakeholders to share without judgment.
- *Example*: Conducting 1-on-1 listening sessions before group mediation.

3. Use a Neutral Facilitator if Appropriate

- Third-party support can reduce power dynamics.
- *Example*: A guidance counselor helps facilitate a teacher-student issue.

4. Clarify Misunderstandings

- Focus on facts, not assumptions.
- *Example*: Resolving a miscommunication between a parent and teacher about accommodations.

5. Explore Solutions Together

- Invite both parties to suggest next steps.
- *Example*: Two team leaders agree to alternate facilitating meetings.

6. Document the Resolution and Follow-Up

- Ensure there is clarity and accountability.
- *Example*: A principal sends a summary email confirming the new plan.

How Can a School Leader Distribute Responsibility Effectively?

Distributing responsibility as a school leader is like running a well-orchestrated restaurant kitchen. The head chef doesn't cook every dish, serve every table, or wash every plate. Instead, they rely on trusted sous-chefs, line cooks, and servers, each with a defined role, clear expectations, and ownership of outcomes. The kitchen only runs smoothly when each person knows their responsibility and feels empowered to carry it out.

In a school setting, effective distribution of responsibility builds leadership capacity, increases ownership, and fosters a culture of trust and collaboration. Rather than trying to "do it all," strong school leaders delegate intentionally assigning roles aligned to staff strengths, providing the right balance of support and autonomy, and clearly communicating goals and expectations. When done well, distributed leadership leads to stronger performance, more innovation, and higher morale.

Outline

I. Identify Talents, Interests, and Strengths

- Get to know staff members' professional passions and capabilities.
- *Example*: Assigning a data-driven teacher to lead a data team or a passionate SEL advocate to run the climate committee.

II. Align Responsibilities to Strategic Goals

- Ensure every task or leadership opportunity supports school improvement goals.
- *Example*: A math department leader is given autonomy to align instruction to state standards and monitor progress.

III. Provide Clear Expectations and Resources

- Make roles, timelines, and outcomes transparent and accessible.
- *Example*: A teacher leading a PD series receives a template, timeline, and coaching on adult learning.

IV. Build Leadership Capacity Through Mentoring

- Pair experienced staff with new teacher leaders to provide ongoing guidance.
- *Example*: A veteran assistant principal mentors a new teacher leading the student council.

V. Monitor and Support Without Micromanaging

- Check in regularly, offer feedback, and course-correct if needed.
- *Example*: Weekly check-ins with team leader to reflect on progress toward goals.

VI. Celebrate Contributions and Results

- Publicly recognize leadership efforts to build morale and encourage initiative.
- *Example*: Highlighting team successes in staff meetings or newsletters.

Strategic Leadership Quiz

1. **A principal wants to ensure that school goals are aligned with district priorities and student needs. What is the BEST first step?**
   A. Review current district goals and disaggregate school performance data
   B. Create a vision statement with the administrative team only
   C. Hold a celebration to motivate staff
   D. Ask parents to suggest goals at the next PTA meeting

2. **What is the MOST effective strategy for a principal to monitor progress toward school improvement goals?**
   A. Rely on quarterly report cards
   B. Use walk-through data, assessment results, and stakeholder feedback
   C. Compare the school to national averages
   D. Host an end-of-year celebration for staff

3. **During a strategic planning meeting, staff express conflicting views about a new grading policy. What should the principal do FIRST?**
   A. Implement the policy immediately
   B. Delay the change until next year
   C. Facilitate a structured discussion to gather all perspectives
   D. Remind staff of the administration's authority

4. **A principal is forming a school leadership team to oversee improvement planning. What is the MOST important consideration when selecting members?**
   A. Choose only veteran teachers
   B. Ensure representation from diverse roles and backgrounds
   C. Select staff based on seniority
   D. Include only administrators and department heads

5. **What is the BEST example of a SMART goal in strategic planning?**
   A. Improve student attendance over time
   B. Raise student math scores
   C. Increase Grade 4 reading proficiency by 15% by June as measured by state assessments
   D. Help students become better readers

6. **To ensure equity in access to academic opportunities, what should a strategic leader do?**
   A. Require honors teachers to refer more students of color
   B. Randomly assign students to advanced classes
   C. Analyze enrollment trends and remove barriers to advanced coursework
   D. Promote the honors program during morning announcements

7. **What action demonstrates effective strategic alignment of resources?**
   A. Hiring additional coaches without assessing student needs
   B. Allocating professional development funds based on staff requests
   C. Assigning staff based on availability rather than expertise
   D. Investing in literacy coaches to support low reading scores identified in school data

8. A school leader notices that the instructional technology being used is outdated and inconsistent across classrooms. What is the BEST next step?

A. Purchase new devices for all classrooms immediately
B. Ask teachers to use personal devices
C. Conduct a technology audit and involve staff in selecting upgrades aligned to instructional goals.
D. Wait for the district to provide a solution

9. When communicating a new schoolwide initiative, what strategy is MOST likely to build shared ownership?

A. Send an email detailing the plan
B. Post a video explanation on the school website
C. Engage stakeholders early and allow for feedback before implementation
D. Announce the plan during morning announcements

10. Which strategy would MOST effectively ensure that strategic planning is informed by evidence?

A. Consult staff opinions informally
B. Use current school data and research-based practices to drive decision-making
C. Rely on past years' plans
D. Imitate the strategic plan of a successful neighboring school

11. A principal notices that students in the upper grades are consistently underperforming on state math assessments. What should be the principal's first step in developing a strategic improvement plan?

A. Replace the current math curriculum with a new vendor
B. Assign all math teachers mandatory weekly coaching
C. Increase test preparation sessions before state testing
D. Conduct a root cause analysis with teacher teams using assessment data

12. During a leadership retreat, the principal shares new school-wide priorities, but staff appear disengaged. What strategy best ensures shared ownership moving forward?

A. Require teachers to submit alignment plans with the new goals
B. Invite teacher leaders to revise the priorities collaboratively
C. Email the strategic plan to all staff for future reference
D. Hold individual conferences with each teacher to explain the plan

13. After analyzing attendance trends, the leadership team discovers chronic absenteeism is concentrated among 9th graders. What is the most strategic next step?

A. Create targeted intervention plans for the 9th-grade cohort
B. Develop a school-wide attendance reward program
C. Assign teachers to call home for all absent students
D. Focus on improving attendance policies in the student handbook

14. A new strategic goal is to improve instructional rigor across content areas. Which action best supports this goal?

A. Require teachers to submit lesson plans weekly
B. Observe classrooms and provide feedback focused on Depth of Knowledge (DOK)
C. Increase student homework requirements
D. Eliminate elective courses that don't align with state standards

15. The principal wants to ensure strategic initiatives are implemented consistently. What is the most effective tool to support this?

A. Public recognition for compliant staff
B. Monthly staff newsletters
C. A shared implementation timeline with checkpoints and responsibilities
D. Hiring additional support staff to monitor classrooms

16. The district expects each school to develop a three-year strategic plan. Which step should come first?

A. Draft a list of potential school-wide priorities
B. Set specific targets based on available district data
C. Review other schools' strategic plans for comparison
D. Identify stakeholders and conduct a needs assessment

17. The principal is preparing to allocate the school's budget to support strategic goals. What principle should guide the process?

A. Divide funds equally across departments
B. Increase funding for programs with the most students
C. Align spending with prioritized instructional goals and data
D. Avoid making major changes from the previous year

18. Midway through the year, progress monitoring shows that the school is not meeting its strategic goal for reducing behavioral referrals. What is the principal's best response?

A. Abandon the current goal and select a new focus
B. Increase consequences for student misbehavior
C. Analyze current strategies and revise the action plan with stakeholders
D. Remind staff to implement the original plan with fidelity

19. A school's strategic plan includes improving family engagement, but attendance at events remains low. What is the most effective next step?

A. Cancel the remaining family events due to lack of interest
B. Survey families to identify barriers and preferred formats for engagement
C. Require teachers to follow up with parents who don't attend
D. Hire a speaker to increase attendance at the next event

20. The school improvement team proposes a new literacy initiative. What should the principal do before approving the plan?

A. Ensure the initiative is backed by research and aligns with school goals
B. Implement the initiative immediately to test its impact
C. Present the initiative at a school board meeting for feedback
D. Ask all staff to vote on whether to adopt the initiative

Answer Key Strategic Leadership #1-10

Question Number	1	2	3	4	5	6	7	8	9	10
Correct Solution	A	B	C	B	C	C	D	C	C	B

Answer Key Strategic Leadership #11-20

Question Number	11	12	13	14	15	16	17	18	19	20
Correct Solution	D	B	A	B	C	D	C	C	B	A

Domain II: Instructional Leadership

This domain focuses on the principal's role in ensuring high-quality teaching and learning for all students. Instructional leadership involves aligning curriculum, instruction, and assessment with rigorous standards, supporting teachers through professional development, and using data to drive continuous improvement. By prioritizing effective instruction, principals create the conditions where students can thrive academically, and teachers can grow professionally.

Instructional Leadership

Real-Life Scenario A: Professional development and building capacity (PSEL Standard 6)

At Happy Grove Elementary School, the principal, Ms. Haye, recently received mid-year benchmark assessment results indicating that only 38% of students in Grades 4 and 5 met or exceeded expectations in reading comprehension, compared to 61% the previous year. Further data analysis revealed inconsistent instructional practices across grade levels, and classroom walkthroughs showed limited student engagement in higher-order thinking tasks.

Ms. Haye convened the instructional leadership team (ILT) to identify underlying causes and determine how to support teacher growth. Through disaggregated test data, student work samples, and teacher self-assessments, the team noticed:

- Teachers varied widely in how they planned and delivered close reading lessons.
- Several teachers lacked confidence in designing scaffolded tasks for multilingual learners (MLLs) and students with IEPs.
- Professional development had been delivered in one-size-fits-all formats without job-embedded follow-up.

Recognizing the need to rebuild instructional consistency and deepen teacher practice, Ms. Haye led the ILT in creating a targeted professional development plan anchored in student and teacher needs. The plan included:

- Job-embedded PD cycles focusing on small-group reading strategies and text-dependent questioning
- Peer coaching partnerships, where strong reading teachers modeled lessons and facilitated post-observation debriefs
- Monthly PLCs focused on analyzing student work and progress monitoring
- Individualized PD plans aligned to each teacher's growth areas, tracked quarterly using classroom walkthrough evidence

Additionally, Ms. Haye scheduled biweekly co-observation rounds with the instructional coach, ensuring that feedback was timely, specific, and actionable. Each walkthrough was followed by brief reflective conversations and support resources tailored to the teacher's next steps.

By the end of the semester, teacher survey results showed increased confidence in using scaffolded reading strategies, and formative assessments indicated a 22% gain in student performance across the focus standards.

Real-Life Scenario B: Rigorous curriculum and instruction (PSEL Standard 4)

At Riverstone Middle School, Principal Dr. Gregory noticed that while the school had made modest gains in reading and science, math proficiency scores had declined for two consecutive years, especially in 7th grade. Teachers expressed frustration over students' inconsistent background knowledge and uneven pacing across classrooms. During classroom walkthroughs, Dr. Gregory observed a wide range of instructional materials being used and varying degrees of alignment with the district's curriculum standards.

After reviewing the School Improvement Plan, Dr. Gregory realized that although professional development had been offered on math strategies, it lacked follow-through, coherence, and a connection to classroom practice. Moreover, vertical alignment with feeder elementary schools had never been formally established, and teachers were not routinely analyzing student work together or using data to inform instruction.

Dr. Gregory launched a schoolwide initiative called "Raising the Bar: Math for All", reinforcing the expectation that all students receive rigorous, standards-based instruction. In faculty meetings, he reviewed data that showed the equity gap in math achievement and framed it as a shared responsibility.
He invited instructional leaders from local elementary schools to begin vertical articulation meetings, reviewing pacing guides, key standards, and performance tasks to ensure a smoother transition between grades. The result was a joint math curriculum map that addressed common learning gaps and clarified instructional expectations.

Grade-level math teams began meeting twice a month to analyze student work, disaggregate benchmark data, and discuss instructional strategies for subgroups especially English learners and students with IEPs. Dr. Gregory provided time in the master schedule for this collaboration and rotated through meetings to offer guidance and resources. he instructional coach modeled lessons using Universal Design for Learning (UDL) principles and evidence-based strategies for teaching math concepts to diverse learners. Teachers received choice boards, digital tools such as Desmos and Khan Academy, and scaffolded math journals tailored to student needs. Dr. Gregory also developed bank of formative assessment strategies that teachers could implement with minimal prep.

Dr. Gregory committed to weekly classroom walkthroughs, using a feedback protocol centered on three guiding questions: (1) Is the instruction aligned to the standard? (2) Is the cognitive demand high? (3) Are all students meaningfully engaged? He met briefly with each teacher afterward to offer 1:1 feedback, coaching suggestions, and highlight "bright spots" in practice.

The school invested in adaptive math platforms, and Dr. Gregory partnered with the district tech coach to provide training on how to use the data dashboards to personalize instruction. Teachers learned how to assign follow-up tasks based on student performance and use digital tools for formative checks during lessons. After one marking period, the leadership team reviewed classroom walkthrough trends, teacher implementation data, and interim assessment results. They made mid-cycle adjustments, providing targeted support for teachers who were struggling with pacing or differentiation.

By spring, the school saw a 12% increase in math proficiency, and subgroup performance for multilingual learners and students with disabilities had narrowed. Teachers reported greater clarity around expectations, stronger collaboration, and more confidence using differentiated strategies. Student engagement in math measured by participation in problem-solving and feedback surveys also improved significantly.

Dr. Gregory presented the initiative at the district's leadership conference as a model of how rigor, alignment, collaboration, technology, and data use can drive systemic instructional improvement.

Instructional Leadership

Real-Life Scenario C: Assessment and accountability

At Oakcrest Elementary School, Principal Mr. DeSoto became concerned after reviewing the school's district writing assessment results. While 4th and 5th grade students performed near proficiency in grammar and mechanics, their scores in organization, elaboration, and clarity of ideas were significantly below district expectations, particularly among students in inclusive classrooms and those with developing English proficiency.

During classroom walkthroughs, Mr. DeSoto observed that while students were writing regularly, teachers were using generic prompts and rubrics, and student feedback often focused on surface-level corrections rather than deeper writing skills. Additionally, some teachers were creating their own writing assessments that were not aligned with the school's writing curriculum or the district scoring rubrics.

Realizing the need for a strategic shift, Mr. DeSoto collaborated with the literacy coach and grade-level teams to strengthen assessment practices through targeted instructional leadership actions.

Mr. DeSoto facilitated professional learning sessions where teachers analyzed writing samples across subgroups, using district rubrics to identify common weaknesses in organization, idea development, and use of text evidence.

Teachers conducted a review of their current writing assignments and rubrics. They discovered misalignment between classroom tasks and the writing standards assessed at the district level. With support from the coach, they redesigned assessments to match the rigor and format of the district writing expectations.

Mr. DeSoto implemented monthly "writing calibration labs", where teachers across grade levels scored anonymized student work using a shared rubric. This built consistency in expectations and deepened teacher understanding of high-quality writing.

The principal and coach conducted focused walkthroughs during writing instruction and gave immediate feedback using a three-part protocol: one strength, one area of focus, and one instructional resource. Teachers were also encouraged to bring student writing to PLCs for group discussion and feedback. Students began keeping writing portfolios and reflecting on growth using checklists aligned to the school-wide rubric. Teachers guided students in setting personalized writing goals and tracking progress over time.

By the spring district writing benchmark, students in inclusive and multilingual classrooms improved an average of 1.5 rubric levels in idea development and organization. Teachers reported stronger clarity in how to teach and assess writing, and student engagement in the writing process increased. Mr. DeSoto celebrated these gains with a schoolwide writing showcase, sharing annotated samples of growth and hosting a family literacy night to reinforce home-school connections around writing development.

The process demonstrated how valid, aligned assessment practices supported by consistent data use and instructional leadership can drive improvement in both teaching quality and student learning outcomes.

What are some strategies that would ensure that professional development is job-embedded and standards-based?

To ensure that professional development is job-embedded and standards-based, schools can implement several key strategies. First, scheduling regular collaborative planning time allows teachers to align their instruction with curriculum standards and analyze student data together. Providing on-site instructional coaching supports teachers in applying standards-based strategies directly in their classrooms. Establishing professional learning communities (PLCs) gives educators structured time to review student work, discuss instructional practices, and reflect on outcomes all within the context of the standards.

Classroom walkthroughs paired with standards-based feedback help identify instructional gaps and inform future PD sessions. Modeling effective teaching strategies and co-teaching with instructional leaders reinforces learning in real-time, making professional development more relevant and practical. Additionally, aligning PD goals with student performance data ensures that learning opportunities are targeted and impactful.

Curriculum mapping sessions are also effective in helping teachers ensure that lessons and assessments are fully aligned with required standards. Grouping educators by grade level or content area during PD sessions ensures relevance to their instructional roles. Providing time for post-PD reflection and follow-up helps reinforce new practices, while using evidence-based instructional strategies ensures that the professional learning is grounded in research. These approaches together create a system where professional development is continuous, relevant, and directly connected to student learning.

<u>Outline</u>

1. Align PD with Teaching Standards and School Goals

- Use frameworks like:
  - Danielson Framework
  - InTASC Standards
  - State-specific teaching standards
- Link PD to the school's vision, student data, and improvement plan.
- Ensure every session answers: *"How does this support our instructional goals and student outcomes?"*

2. Embed PD into Daily Practice

- Coaching and mentoring cycles where teachers get real-time feedback and support.
- Instructional rounds or peer observations followed by reflection aligned to standards (e.g., questioning techniques from Danielson 3b).
- In-class modeling and co-teaching with instructional leaders or coaches.

3. Use Collaborative Professional Learning Communities (PLCs)

- Structure PLCs around data analysis, lesson design, and standards-aligned outcomes.
- Engage teachers in action research or lesson study cycles tied to classroom instruction.
- Ensure PLCs meet regularly and have clear protocols and goals.

4. Leverage Student Data to Drive PD Topics

- Use formative and summative data (e.g., benchmark tests, student work, exit tickets) to identify instructional gaps.
- Tailor PD around what students need, not just what teachers prefer.

- Example: If students struggle with textual analysis, they should offer PD on close reading strategies aligned to literacy standards.

5. Provide Time for Application and Reflection
   - Allow time during the school day or staff meetings for teachers to apply new strategies, reflect, and revise.
   - Use teacher journals, exit slips, or portfolios to track growth over time.

6. Incorporate Standards-Based Walkthrough Tools
   - Conduct informal walkthroughs using rubrics aligned to teaching standards.
   - Use this data to design follow-up PD sessions that respond to patterns seen in practice.

7. Connect PD to Evaluation Systems
   - Aligning PD with the language and focus of the teacher evaluation system.
   - Help teachers see PD not as "extra" but as a tool to grow in specific performance areas (e.g., Domain 3a: Communicating with Students).

8. Include Micro-PD and On-Demand Learning
   - Offer short, targeted PD sessions during grade team meetings, planning time, or virtually.
   - Use videos, articles, or podcasts focused on one high-leverage strategy.

9. Involve Teachers in PD Design and Delivery
   - Tap teacher leaders to co-facilitate sessions or share best practices.
   - Encourage "teachers teaching teachers" through demo lessons, video analysis, or content-specific workshops.

What sources and types of data can be used to provide feedback to teachers so that they can improve student learning?

When school leaders aim to support teachers in strengthening instruction, they shouldn't rely on just a single snapshot such as one test score or one classroom observation. It's much like how a doctor doesn't diagnose a patient based on one symptom or a quick glance; instead, they gather information from many sources like blood work, scans, vital signs, and the patient's own story to form a clearer picture of what's really going on. In education, effective feedback works the same way: multiple data points help paint a full, fair, and actionable view of teaching and learning.

One vital sign in this "instructional check-up" is student achievement data, such as results from state exams, district benchmarks, or classroom assessments like I-Ready or MAP. If students across a grade level are consistently missing the mark on writing strong summaries, it signals something deeper to explore, like how the skill is being taught or how students are practicing it. This data becomes the starting point for conversations that sharpen instruction and support student growth.

Classroom observations are another tool similarly to listening to a patient's heartbeat. Whether it's a formal evaluation or a brief walkthrough, observations give leaders a real-time sense of classroom rhythm: They answer questions such as, "Are the learning goals clear? Are students engaged? Is the pacing effective?" When paired with a teacher's own reflections, these observations should become less about judgment and more like a meaningful dialogue between colleagues.

Student work samples act like lab results. A writing assignment, a math solution, or a project presentation reveals what's going on "inside" student thinking. Are students applying skills? Are they reasoning deeply or just repeating steps? Examining this work helps both leaders and teachers calibrate expectations, adjust scaffolds, and enrich the learning experience.

Engagement data, such as how often students participate, log into online platforms, or complete self-assessments is like monitoring a patient's energy and mood. If students seem disconnected or only a few are contributing, it might signal that instruction needs more relevance, voice, or variety. These insights help educators fine-tune the learning environment.

Feedback from students and families is like the patient speaking directly to the doctor. Surveys or reflections provide personal, sometimes surprising insights into how students feel; what is helping or hindering their learning; and how well supported families feel from home. This human element adds depth and heart to the data. Planning documents such as lesson plans, unit maps, or curriculum pacing guides are like medical history. They show the structure behind instruction and help leaders determine whether the instructions are aligned to standards and inclusive of all learners' needs. Supportive feedback in this area often leads to clarity, coherence, and better instructional flow.

And just like patients benefit from coordinated care, teachers grow through peer collaboration and coaching. Watching videos of one's own teaching, reviewing student work with a colleague, or co-planning lessons creates a supportive, growth-focused culture where feedback feels less like a prescription and more like a partnership. In the end, just as doctors rely on a range of data to support patient health, school leaders who gather a variety of instructional data are better positioned to support teacher growth. This well-rounded approach turns evaluation into encouragement building a culture where feedback is a tool for reflection, empowerment, and continuous improvement.

Outline

1. **Student Achievement Data**
Purpose: Shows how well students are mastering standards.
Types & Sources:

- State assessments (e.g., NJSLA, STAAR, MCAS)
- Benchmark assessments (e.g., I-Ready, MAP, STAR)
- Common formative/summative assessments
- Classroom performance data (quizzes, tests, exit tickets)
- Student growth data (e.g., mSGP, value-added models)
- Help identify patterns of instructional effectiveness by standard, skill, or subgroup.
- Guides conversations about pacing, reteaching, and targeted interventions.

2. **Classroom Observation Data**
Purpose: Assesses instructional practice in real-time.
Types & Sources:

- Formal and informal walkthroughs
- Use of evaluation rubrics (e.g., Danielson Framework)
- Observable Indicators aligned to high-impact teaching strategies
- Provides direct evidence of teacher-student interactions, instructional clarity, questioning techniques, differentiation, and engagement.
- It can include scripted notes and teacher reflection for a two-way dialogue.

3. **Student Work Samples**
Purpose: Reveals depth of learning and instructional impact.
Types & Sources:

- Writing samples, problem-solving tasks, science notebooks, projects
- Performance tasks aligned to standards
- Rubric-scored assessments
- Help teachers see if students are transferring skills, applying concepts, and meeting expectations.
- Provides a concrete way to talk about rigor, scaffolding, and misconceptions.

4. **Student Engagement and Participation Data**
Purpose: Reflects student involvement and learning environment.
Types & Sources:

- Engagement trackers during lessons
- Participation data from online platforms (e.g., Google Classroom, Nearpod)
- Student self-assessments and reflections
- Promotes teacher's reflection on classroom culture, equity in participation, and use of student voice.

5. **Student and Family Surveys**
Purpose: Gathers perception data on teaching, communication, and support.
Types & Sources:

- School climate surveys (e.g., Panorama, NJDOE)
- End-of-unit feedback forms

- Parent/guardian input on communication and accessibility
- Helps teachers understand the student experience and make adjustments to better support engagement and relationships.

6. **Instructional Planning and Curriculum Alignment**
Purpose: Ensures instruction aligns with standards and goals.
Types & Sources:
- Lesson plans and unit plans
- Scope and sequence pacing guides
- PLC collaboration logs and data protocols
- Provides insight into whether lessons are standards-aligned, scaffolded, and designed for all learners.
- Supports feedback on rigor, differentiation, and vertical alignment.

7. **Peer and Instructional Coach Feedback**
Purpose: Encourages professional growth through collaboration.
Types & Sources:
- Peer observations or co-teaching reflections
- Instructional coaching logs and goal tracking
- Video analysis of recorded lessons
- Promotes reflection and refinement in a low-stakes, supportive environment.
- Allows teachers to see themselves through another lens.

What are some qualities common to effective professional development?

Professional development (PD) is most powerful when it moves beyond a single workshop and becomes part of the ongoing fabric of a teacher's everyday work. The most effective PD is job-embedded, meaning it happens in the context of real classrooms through coaching, collaborative planning, or a literacy expert modeling a lesson right alongside the teacher. It's also standards-based and student-centered, always pointing back to one central question: "How will this help students learn better?"

Rather than one-and-done events, strong PD is sustained and ongoing, giving teachers time to reflect, try new strategies, and receive support over time. It's also collaborative, built on teamwork and shared learning through professional learning communities (PLCs), peer observations, or co-planning sessions.

Effective PD is also data-driven not just based on trends, but grounded in tangible evidence from student performance, classroom observations, and teacher feedback. It's also differentiated, acknowledging that new and veteran teachers have unique needs. A first-year teacher might benefit from classroom management tools, while an experienced educator may dive deeper into assessment design or culturally responsive practices.

What makes PD truly stick is active engagement. Teachers learn best when they can discuss, model, experiment, and reflect just like students do. This kind of PD also aligns to the school's larger vision and goals, ensuring everyone is moving in the same direction. It fosters reflective practice, inviting educators to think deeply about their instructional choices, beliefs, and impact on students.

Outline

1. **Job-Embedded**
   - It happens within the context of teachers' daily work, not apart from it.
   - Includes coaching, co-teaching, PLCs, and collaborative planning.
   - Tied to real classroom challenges and immediate application.
   - *Example:* A literacy coach models a comprehension strategy in a teacher's classroom, then helps the teacher implement it in a lesson the next day.

2. **Standards-Based and Student-Centered**
   - Aligned to teaching standards (e.g., Danielson Framework, InTASC) and student learning standards (e.g., NJSLS, Common Core).
   - Focused on improving student achievement and equity.
   - Effective PD always answers: "How will this help students learn better?"

3. **Sustained and Ongoing**
   - Occurs over time, not as isolated workshops.
   - Involves follow-up, reflection, and continuous support (e.g., coaching cycles or PD series).

4. **Collaborative**
   - Encourages teacher collaboration through learning communities, peer observations, and shared inquiry.
   - Builds a culture of collective responsibility and reflection.

5. **Data-Driven**
   - Uses student performance data, classroom observation data, and teacher feedback to identify needs and measure impact.
   - Help teachers connect instructional strategies to evidence of student growth.

6. **Differentiated and Responsive**
   - Tailored to teacher experience levels, subject areas, and instructional challenges.
   - Provides choice and relevance based on individual and team needs.

7. **Active and Engaging**
   - Involves interactive learning modeling, hands-on practice, peer feedback, and discussion.
   - Moves beyond lectures to engage teachers in meaningful problem-solving and reflection.

8. **Aligned to School and District Goals**
   - Supports the larger strategic plan of the school.
   - Reinforces a shared vision and common instructional priorities (e.g., literacy across content areas, culturally responsive teaching).

9. **Promotes Reflective Practice**
   - Encourages teachers to examine their own beliefs, practices, and impact on student learning.
   - Often includes journaling, lesson analysis, or video reflection.

10. **Led by Knowledgeable Facilitators**
    - Facilitators have deep content and pedagogical expertise, credibility, and understanding of adult learning principles.
    - It can include coaches, teacher leaders, administrators, or external experts.

What types of student data might be used to identify areas for professional development?

Understanding where to focus on professional development is like being a doctor diagnosing a patient. You wouldn't prescribe medicine without first running tests. In schools, student data is a diagnostic tool. Achievement scores from state tests or classroom assessments are like a student's vital signs. They give school leaders a snapshot of overall academic health. If the "pulse" of reading comprehension or math problem-solving is weak, it signals a need for targeted treatment. Professional Development, PD that strengthens rigor, supports better use of formative assessments, or improves differentiated instruction.

Looking at student work samples is like examining X-rays or lab results. They reveal what's happening beneath the surface whether students truly grasp complex ideas or are just memorizing. If their work shows shallow thinking, then PD might focus on building students' reasoning and analysis and training teachers to give more effective, actionable feedback. Exit tickets and quick checks are like a daily temperature check: they help teachers respond quickly if something isn't right. If teachers aren't using these tools effectively, PD can help them learn how to adjust instruction in real time.

Subgroup data is like checking a patient's individual medical history. If English Language Learners or students with disabilities consistently show signs of struggle, it points to systemic gaps. In response, PD might offer strategies for scaffolding, language development, or inclusive practices. Attendance and behavior data act like emotional and social wellness indicators. If students are frequently absent, disengaged, or acting out, it suggests deeper needs. In that case, PD in trauma-informed care or relationship-building might be the right prescription.

Finally, surveys and student reflections are like hearing directly from the patient. When students seem lost or disconnected, make it a priority to listen attentively and respond with meaningful support. Just like good medicine treats the whole person, effective professional development is guided by multiple data sources to support the whole learner by equipping teachers with what they need to help every student thrive.

In short, when leaders use data not just to diagnose problems but to guide meaningful, personalized PD, they empower teachers to meet students where they are. The goal isn't just to improve test scores but to help every child grow through stronger, more thoughtful instruction.

To identify meaningful areas for professional development (PD), school leaders must analyze a wide range of student data. These data sources help pinpoint where instructional gaps exist, where students are underperforming, and which teaching practices may need support or enhancement.

Outline

1. **Achievement Data**
Purpose: Identify academic strengths and weaknesses.
Examples:

- State assessments (e.g., NJSLA, MCAS, STAAR)
- Benchmark assessments (e.g., MAP, I-Ready, STAR)
- Unit and classroom assessments

- Course grades and failure rates

PD Implications:

- If students consistently struggle with reading comprehension, offer PD in close reading or literacy strategies.
- If math scores are low in problem solving, provide PD on multi-step word problem instruction or math discourse.

2. **Growth Data**

Purpose: Measure academic progress over time, not just achievement level.

Examples:

- mSGP (Median Student Growth Percentile)
- Value-added models (VAM)
- Pre- and post-assessment comparisons

PD Implications:

- If students show low growth despite passing grades, the school should schedule PD that focus on rigor, formative assessment, or differentiation.

3. **Student Work Samples**

Purpose: Assess depth of understanding, skill application, and rigor.

Examples:

- Writing samples
- Performance tasks or portfolios
- Rubric-scored assignments

PD Implications

- If student work shows shallow thinking or incomplete mastery, the school should schedule professional development focused on higher-order questioning, feedback strategies, and task design.

4. **Formative Assessment and Progress Monitoring**

Purpose: Track ongoing student understanding and inform real-time instruction.

Examples:

- Exit tickets
- Do Now's/Bell ringers
- Checks for understanding

Formative Assessment and Progress Monitoring (cont.)

- Running records (in literacy)

PD Implications:

- Inconsistent formative assessment use → PD on formative assessment techniques and data-driven instruction cycles.

5. **Disaggregated Subgroup Data**

Purpose: Identify equity gaps across demographics.

Examples:

- Performance by subgroup (ELL, SPED, race/ethnicity, gender)
- Discipline, attendance, and participation rates

PD Implications:

- If ELLs underperforming. Recommend PD in sheltered instruction or language scaffolds.
- Discipline disproportionality. Recommend PD for restorative practices or culturally responsive teaching.

6. **Attendance and Engagement Data**
Purpose: Understand patterns in student presence and participation.
Examples:

- Chronic absenteeism reports
- Tardy and disengagement logs
- Participation in remote or blended learning platforms

PD Implications:

- Engagement issues. Recommend PD in student-centered strategies, classroom culture building, or relationship-building practices.

7. **Behavior and SEL Data**
Purpose: Understand emotional, behavioral, and social development.
Examples:

- Office referrals and suspensions
- SEL screeners (e.g., DESSA, Panorama)
- Teacher behavior tracking tools

PD Implications:

- High behavior incidents. Recommend PD on trauma-informed teaching, PBIS, or de-escalation techniques.

8. **Survey and Perception Data**
Purpose: Gain insights into student voice and learning experience.
Examples:

- Student engagement or climate surveys
- Student reflections or course feedback

How do standards or changes in standards impact curriculum development and revision?

Think of academic standards like a GPS for learning. They set the destination for what students should know and be able to do by the end of each grade. Now imagine the school's curriculum as the route planned out to get students to that destination. When standards change, it's like the GPS rerouting you. The destination remains the same, but the route now includes new twists, changes, and obstacles. Just like a driver needs a new map to follow, schools must revise their curriculum to reflect the new directions. That means rethinking the order of lessons (scope and sequence), picking better tools and materials for the journey (like new books, tasks, or technology), and checking that students are on track through meaningful assessments with deeper tasks that show real understanding.

Teachers, in this analogy, are the drivers; and they can't follow a new route if no one shows them the map. That's why professional development is so important: it helps teachers understand what's changed and how to guide their students with confidence. And just like GPS ensures every car, no matter where it starts, can reach the same destination, academic standards help make sure all students regardless of their academic levels are aiming for the same high expectations. Updating the curriculum based on new standards isn't just a technical fix, it's a systemwide effort to ensure every child is on the right road to success.

Standards and changes in standards have a direct and powerful impact on curriculum development and revision because they define what students are expected to know and be able to do at each grade level. The curriculum is then built to ensure these outcomes are achieved.

Outline

1. **Define Learning Expectations**
   - Standards serve as the foundation for curriculum development, outlining the essential knowledge and skills students must master.
   - When standards change (e.g., from content-based to skills-based), the curriculum must be realigned to reflect those new priorities.
   - *Example:* A shift to Next Generation Science Standards (NGSS) required schools to move from memorization of facts to inquiry-based, phenomenon-driven instruction.

2. **Influence Scope and Sequence**
   - Changes in standards often require curriculum teams to reorganize the pacing of instruction across the year and across grade levels.
   - This ensures vertical alignment, so concepts are built logically and aren't repeated unnecessarily or skipped.

3. **Drive Instructional Materials and Resource Selection**
   - Curriculum must be reviewed and revised to ensure all lessons, texts, tasks, and assessments are aligned to the new standards.

- This includes adopting or adapting instructional materials that reflect the new expectations (e.g., performance tasks, real-world applications, or new text complexity levels).

4. **Require Professional Development and Capacity Building**
    - Teachers need training to understand the standards and how to design instruction that support them.
    - Effective curriculum revision includes ongoing PD to support instructional strategies aligned with the new focus (e.g., modeling, critical thinking, conceptual understanding).

5. **Impact Assessment Design**
    - Standards-aligned curriculum must include assessments that measure the depth and complexity required by the standards.
    - When standards emphasize higher-order thinking or application, assessments must shift from simple recall to open-ended, performance-based tasks.

6. **Promote Equity and Consistency**
    - Standards provide a common academic framework that helps ensure all students regardless of background or zip code have access to the same expectations.
    - Curriculum revisions aligned to standards help close opportunity gaps by ensuring instruction is focused, rigorous, and aligned.

7. **Trigger System-Wide Review and Coordination**
    - When standards change, it often requires collaboration across departments, grade levels, and even schools to ensure coherence.
    - This process includes vertical alignment meetings, curriculum mapping, and cross-grade discussions.

How do various instructional strategies, such as team or collaborative teaching, positively or negatively impact instruction?

Using various instructional strategies such as co-teaching or collaborative teaching is a bit like cooking a meal with another chef in the kitchen. When done well, both chefs bring their strengths, coordinate their timing, and elevate the final dish together. But if one chef dominates, uses the wrong ingredients, or doesn't communicate, the meal can quickly fall apart. The same applies in classrooms. Collaborative teaching can enhance instruction or create confusion, depending on how it's implemented.

Positively, team teaching allows educators to combine their expertise. One teacher might lead a lesson while the other provides targeted support to struggling students. This allows for more differentiation and personalized learning. For example, in a co-taught 5th-grade classroom, a general education teacher and a special education teacher might run learning stations together. One focuses on reteaching a skill while the other enriches or extends learning. Students also benefit from diverse teaching styles and more individual attention, which can boost engagement and achievement.

Moreover, collaborative teaching models promote professional growth. Teachers learn from each other in real time, share new strategies, and reflect together on what worked or didn't work. It also improves classroom management, as more adults in the room means better supervision and smoother transitions.

However, like any partnership, team teaching can backfire if there's poor communication or limited planning time. If one teacher dominates or both aren't aligned in their approach, students may receive mixed messages or inconsistent instruction. This can lead to confusion and disrupt learning. Just as in a kitchen with clashing chefs, the classroom needs coordination, respect, and shared goals.

In short, collaborative teaching is a powerful strategy when built on mutual trust, joint planning, and a shared instructional vision. With the right ingredients and teamwork, it can transform instruction into something far richer than one teacher could cook up alone.

Instructional strategies like team teaching and collaborative teaching can have both positive and negative impacts on instruction, depending on how they are implemented, the compatibility of teaching styles, and the level of planning and support involved.

Outline

Positive Impacts of Team or Collaborative Teaching

1. **Differentiated Instruction**
   - With two or more teachers, it's easier to group students by need and offer targeted support or enrichment.
   - Teachers can co-plan lessons that include multiple access points and scaffolded activities.
   - *Example:* One teacher leads a mini lesson while another circulates and supports struggling students.

2. **Stronger Classroom Management**

- More adults in the room mean increased supervision, quicker redirection of behavior, and smoother transitions.
- One teacher can manage the flow while the other handles individual needs discreetly.

3. **Increased Student Engagement**

- Students benefit from varied teaching styles and personalities, which can increase interest and motivation.
- Collaborative strategies (e.g., think-pair-share, group investigations) model real-world teamwork and communication.

4. **Professional Growth and Shared Expertise**

- Teachers learn from each other by observing instructional practices in real time.
- Co-teaching can promote a culture of shared leadership and continuous learning.

5. **Improved Support for Special Populations**

- Collaborative teaching is especially effective in inclusive classrooms, where general and special educators work together.
- It ensures individualized supports are embedded into whole-class instruction.

Potential Negative Impacts of Team or Collaborative Teaching

1. **Lack of Planning Time**

- Effective co-teaching requires extensive, regular planning, which can be hard to coordinate.
- Without time to co-plan, instruction may become disjointed or repetitive.

2. **Unequal Participation**

- If one teacher dominates, it may feel more like one teaching, one assisting, rather than true collaboration.
- This undermines the value of the strategy and may lead to teacher resentment or confusion among students.

3. **Mismatch in Teaching Styles**

- Differences in instructional philosophies, classroom management, or communication styles can cause conflict or inconsistency.
- Students may become confused or disengaged if the teachers are not aligned.

4. **Student Confusion About Authority**

- If roles and expectations aren't clear, students may test boundaries or struggle with conflicting directions.
- Clear communication and role clarity are essential.

5. **Inconsistent Implementation**
   - Without training and administrative support, collaborative teaching may be used inconsistently or ineffectively.
   - Teachers may feel unprepared or unsupported, which impacts instructional quality.

Essential Questions 7

What steps may need to be taken to ensure that the curriculum and instruction are aligned to student assessment and content standards?

Aligning curriculum, instruction, and assessment to academic standards is like building a house: the standards are the blueprint, the curriculum is the foundation, instruction is the construction process, and assessments are the final inspection. If one part is uncoordinated, the structure becomes unstable. Just as no builder would lay bricks without first reviewing the blueprint, educators must begin by unpacking the standards, breaking them down into clear, student-friendly learning targets. This step reveals exactly what skills are needed and at what depth. For example, a standard that says "explain the relationship between two fractions" requires more than simple computation. It asks students to compare, analyze, and reason.

Once the blueprint is clear, the next step is mapping the standards to the curriculum. This is like organizing construction materials and scheduling the phases of a building. Schools must ensure that all standards are not only covered but taught with the right depth and rigor throughout the school year. Tools like pacing guides and unit plans help sequence the learning logically, ensuring that no standard is rushed or overlooked.

Next, we need to ensure that the assessments match the standards. The final inspections must reflect what was planned and built. This means reviewing every quiz, test, and performance task to confirm how it measures what the standards require. If a standard calls for critical thinking but the test only checks recall, it's like inspecting a house's exterior but ignoring the plumbing. Assessment blueprints and question-to-standard alignment can prevent these mismatches and ensure that students are being tested fairly and accurately.

But even the best assessments won't help if the instruction doesn't match the demands of the standards and assessments. Teachers need professional development to design lessons that mirror the complexity of what students will be asked to do. For instance, if students are expected to write persuasive essays on standardized tests, instruction must include modeling, scaffolding, and opportunities to practice those skills, not just vocabulary drills or short answers.

To check whether everything is aligned, educators must analyze student data benchmark scores, classroom performance, and state assessments act as feedback from the final product. If students are struggling, it's important to ask: Is the issue with how we taught the material, how we assessed it, or how it was written in the curriculum? Student performance data helps identify those gaps so that instruction can be adjusted in real time.

This work is most powerful when done in Professional Learning Communities (PLCs), the collaborative teams of teachers and leaders who reflect on practice together. In PLCs, educators unpack standards, create assessments, analyze student work, and make sure everyone is moving in the same direction. It's like having multiple contractors checking the blueprints together to ensure each room of the house meets code.

Throughout the school year, schools must monitor and adjust regularly just like builders double-check measurements and make last-minute changes to improve the building. Walkthroughs, lesson plan reviews, and feedback help ensure everything stays aligned. Adjustments might include shifting a unit, revising an activity, or slowing the pace to meet students' needs.

Lastly, no construction project is successful without teamwork. All stakeholders, teachers, coaches, administrators, and assessment teams must be involved in curriculum alignment. This ensures consistency, builds buy-in, and addresses the needs of all learners, including English Language Learners (ELLs), students with disabilities, and gifted students.

In short, aligning curriculum, instruction, and assessment to standards ensures that students are not just being taught, but being taught the right things in the right way. Like a well-constructed house built from a solid blueprint, this alignment supports long-term success, equity, and measurable academic growth.

Ensuring that curriculum and instruction are aligned to student assessment and content standards is essential for improving student achievement, closing equity gaps, and meeting accountability measures. Misalignment can result in ineffective instruction and inaccurate measures of student learning.

<u>Outline</u>

1. **Unpack the Standards**
   - Break down state or national content standards (e.g., NJSLS, Common Core) into clear learning targets and skills.
   - Identify the cognitive demand (e.g., recall, analysis, synthesis) and specific language used in each standard.
   - *Example:* "Explain the relationship between two fractions" involves both comparison and reasoning, not just computation.

2. **Map Standards to Curriculum**
   - Conduct a curriculum mapping process to ensure every standard is:
     - Appropriately addressed
     - Taught at the correct depth and rigor
     - Covered within the school year
   - Use pacing guides and unit plans to sequence instruction logically and efficiently.

3. **Align Assessments with Standards**
   - Review all formative and summative assessments to ensure they measure what the standards require.
   - Use assessment blueprints that link each question or task to a specific standard.

- Revise assessments that are misaligned (e.g., low-level recall questions for a standard that requires analysis).

4. **Ensure Instructional Practices Match Assessment Demands**
   - Provide PD to help teachers design lessons that mirror the format and rigor of both standards and assessments (e.g., multi-step problems, writing with evidence, inquiry tasks).
   - Encourage use of modeling, scaffolding, and academic discourse to build students' readiness.

5. **Use Student Data to Check for Alignment**
   - Analyze results from benchmark tests, classroom assessments, and state exams to identify gaps.
   - *Ask*: Are students struggling because of the instruction, the curriculum, or the assessment format?
   - Use this data to make targeted instructional adjustments.

6. **Collaborate in Professional Learning Communities (PLCs)**
   - Use PLC time to:
     - Unpack standards together
     - Create common assessments
     - Analyze student work and reflect on instructional alignment
   - Promote horizontal and vertical articulation to ensure consistency across grades and subjects.

7. **Monitor and Adjust Continuously**
   - Conduct regular instructional walkthroughs and lesson plan reviews to ensure alignment in real time.
   - Provide feedback that is specific to standards-based teaching practices.
   - Adjust curriculum pacing or instructional strategies as needed based on student performance and feedback.

8. **Involve All Stakeholders in the Alignment Process**
   - Engage teachers in curriculum revision teams to build buy-in and ensure practical application.
   - Including input from coaches, administrators, and assessment coordinators for coherence.
   - Ensure that special populations (ELLs, SWDs, gifted) are considered in both instruction and assessment.

What trends in student achievement data might indicate that there are problems in curriculum alignment?

Recognizing curriculum misalignment through student achievement data is a lot like trying to bake a cake using the wrong recipe. The ingredients might look fine, and the oven might be working, but if the recipe doesn't match what the final cake is supposed to be, the results will fall flat, literally. In education, the recipe is the curriculum, and the final product is student success as measured by assessments. When the curriculum doesn't align with the content standards or the format of assessments, student performance suffers, even if everything "seems" to be going well day-to-day.

One clear sign of this misalignment is when students are earning good grades in class but perform poorly on standardized tests. This is like baking a cake that looks perfect on the outside but tastes horrible. Students may be doing well on teacher-made tests that don't reflect the depth or complexity of state standards. The real test, standardized assessments, reveals that what they've been practicing hasn't prepared them for the actual expectations.

Another clue comes when entire classes or grade levels consistently struggle in the same subject area as fractions, scientific writing, or text-based analysis. That's like following a recipe that forgets to include a key ingredient, such as baking powder. No matter how closely students follow instructions, their learning doesn't "rise" to meet expectations. This kind of trend suggests those standards may be underrepresented or poorly scaffolded in the curriculum.

Similarly, if one grade consistently scores much higher or lower than others, it may indicate a breakdown in vertical alignment. That's like one layer of a multi-tier cake being too thin or too thick. It throws off the whole structure. When curriculum pacing or focus shifts too drastically between grades, students may either repeat material or miss essential learning altogether, affecting long-term progress.

Another frequent issue is when students do well on basic, recall-level tasks but struggle when faced with questions that demand deeper thinking or application. That's like using sugar and flour but forgetting the eggs. You'll get something that resembles a cake, but it won't hold together. If instruction doesn't mirror the cognitive demand of the standards, students won't be able to perform well on higher-order tasks like problem-solving or written analysis.

Equity gaps can also reveal misalignment. If English Language Learners or students with disabilities perform far below their peers, it may indicate that the curriculum isn't inclusive or accessible. It's like using a recipe that assumes everyone has the same kitchen tools some students are trying to whip cream without a mixer. Without proper scaffolds and support, certain groups fall behind not because they can't learn, but because the instruction wasn't designed for their needs.

Lastly, inconsistent test results between teachers teaching the same content often means the curriculum isn't being implemented uniformly. That's like two bakers making the same cake, but one is using a box mix and the other is baking from scratch. Of course the outcomes won't match. When different teachers interpret standards differently or skip essential lessons, students receive uneven preparation.

In the end, student achievement data tells the story of how well the instructional "recipe" is working. When results are flat, inconsistent, or show signs of missing key ingredients, it's time to revise the curriculum, adjust instruction, and make sure the recipe truly matches the cake we expect to see at the end.

Trends in student achievement data can serve as powerful indicators of curriculum misalignment especially when student performance does not reflect the intended learning outcomes outlined in state or district standards. When the curriculum is not properly aligned, it becomes harder for students to meet expectations, and achievement data will reflect that disconnect.

Outline

1. **High Classroom Grades but Low Standardized Test Scores**
    - What it suggests: Students may be succeeding on teacher-created assessments that don't reflect the rigor or format of state standards.
    - Implication: Curriculum and classroom instruction may not be fully aligned to the depth or complexity required by the standards.

2. **Consistent Underperformance in Specific Content Areas or Standards**
    - What it suggests: If large groups of students are consistently struggling with the same standard or domain (e.g., fractions, writing with evidence), it may indicate those areas are underemphasized or poorly addressed in the curriculum.
    - Implication: Curriculum maps or instructional materials may not cover the standard effectively—or may skip essential scaffolding.

3. **Large Gaps Between Grade Levels**
    - What it suggests: If one grade level consistently performs significantly lower or higher than others, it could reflect a curriculum misalignment, pacing issue, or vertical gap.
    - Implication: There may be a disconnect in how standards are taught across grade levels, leading to either redundancy or gaps in learning progression.

4. **Strong Performance on Low-Level Tasks, Weak Performance on Higher-Order Thinking**
    - What it suggests: Students may be exposed primarily to recall-based instruction, even though standards and assessments require application, reasoning, and synthesis.
    - Implication: Curriculum and instruction may not be aligned to the cognitive demand of the standards.

5. **Significant Performance Gaps Across Subgroups**
    - What it suggests: If subgroups (e.g., ELLs, students with disabilities, or economically disadvantaged students) perform significantly lower, it could indicate a lack of inclusive instructional strategies or scaffolds in the curriculum.
    - Implication: The curriculum may not be differentiated or accessible, creating equity gaps.

6. **Inconsistent Assessment Results Across Classrooms or Teachers**
    - What it suggests: Wide variations in student outcomes for the same grade level or subject may point to an inconsistently implemented curriculum.

- Implication: Teachers may be using different materials or pacing, leading to misalignment in what students are taught and assessed on.

7. **Low Growth Percentiles Despite High Proficiency**
   - What it suggests: Students are proficient but not showing expected yearly growth.
   - Implication: The curriculum may lack rigor, or may not provide enough challenge or progression, especially for advanced learners.

Essential Questions 9 Instructional Leadership

What role do formal and informal assessments play in evaluating the effectiveness of a school's instruction and programs?

Evaluating a school's instruction using only one kind of assessment is like trying to judge a restaurant by only looking at the menu. You might get an idea of what's offered, but you'll miss the flavors, the service, and the overall experience. That's why both formal and informal assessments are essential in painting a full picture of instructional effectiveness. Formal assessments like state tests, benchmarks, and end-of-course exams are structured, standardized, and allow schools to compare student performance across classrooms, schools, and districts. They answer big-picture questions: Are students meeting grade-level expectations? Are there gaps among subgroups? These assessments help schools set goals, evaluate programs, and stay accountable to state and federal standards.

But formal data alone can miss the day-to-day reality of teaching and learning. That's where informal assessments such as exit tickets, classroom discussions, quick writes, and student reflections come in. They're like taste tests during the meal, allowing teachers to adjust the seasoning as they go. Informal assessments provide immediate feedback, helping educators catch misconceptions early, adjust instruction in real time, and engage students more meaningfully. Together, formal and informal assessments offer a balanced approach: formal data shows where the school stands, while informal data reveals how students are learning along the way. When schools combine both, they're not just checking off standards. They're building responsive, effective instruction that adapts to student needs and leads to deeper learning.

Formal and informal assessments play a crucial role in evaluating the effectiveness of a school's instruction and programs because they provide evidence of student learning, instructional quality, and program impact. Each type of assessment offers unique insights, and when used together, they give school leaders and teachers a more comprehensive picture of what's working and what needs improvement.

<u>Outline</u>

Role of Formal Assessments

Formal assessments are standardized, structured, and often used for summative evaluation.

- State and district assessments (e.g., NJSLA, MCAS, I-Ready, MAP)
- Benchmark exams

- Common summative assessments
- End-of-course/final exams

Their Role in Evaluating Instruction/Programs:

1. **Measure Mastery of Standards**
    - Show whether students meet grade-level expectations.
    - Help evaluate curriculum alignment and rigor.

2. **Identify Schoolwide Strengths and Gaps**
    - Highlight patterns in performance across grade levels, subgroups, or subjects.
    - Inform decisions about PD, resource allocation, and intervention programs.

3. **Support Accountability and Goal Setting**
    - Provide quantitative data for setting goals, reporting to stakeholders, and evaluating program impact over time.

4. **Drive Data-Informed Decision Making**
    - Used by leadership teams to evaluate instructional effectiveness and prioritize areas for improvement.

Role of Informal Assessments

Informal assessments are flexible, ongoing, and embedded in daily instruction.

Examples:

- Exit tickets
- Class discussions
- Observations
- Student journals or reflections
- Running records and anecdotal notes
- Self-assessments and peer assessments

Their Role in Evaluating Instruction/Programs:

1. **Provide Real-Time Feedback**
    - Allow teachers to adjust instruction immediately based on student understanding.
    - Identify misconceptions before they become learning gaps.

2. **Reveal Instructional Effectiveness at the Classroom Level**
    - Inform whether students are engaging with content, making progress, and applying skills.
    - Highlight which strategies, groupings, or materials are most effective.

3. **Promote Student Ownership and Voice**
    - Encourage students to reflect on their learning, which builds metacognition.
    - Give teachers a window into students' thinking and learning preferences.

4. **Complement Formal Data**
   - Fill in gaps between formal testing windows.
   - Help triangulate data for a fuller picture of student growth and program impact.

Essential Questions 10 — Instructional Leadership

What are the strengths and limitations of authentic assessment? Standardized testing?

Imagine trying to evaluate a garden's health by only measuring the height of the plants once a year. That's what relying solely on standardized tests in schools can feel like. To truly understand what's thriving and what needs attention, you'd also need to check the soil, observe how plants respond to sunlight and water daily, and watch for signs of stress. In education, that deeper, more contextual understanding comes through authentic assessment.

Standardized testing is like the official measuring tape of the garden. These assessments, including state exams, district benchmarks, and common end-of-course tests, are standardized and intended to evaluate whether students are achieving grade-level standards. They help identify system-wide trends, highlight achievement gaps across subgroups, and inform decisions about funding, curriculum alignment, and accountability.

However, just as a gardener can't wait months to notice that a plant lacks water or nutrients, educators can't wait for yearly test scores to understand how students are progressing. This is where authentic assessment plays a vital role. Authentic assessments involve real-world tasks that require students to apply their knowledge and skills in meaningful ways, such as writing a persuasive letter, conducting a science experiment, or solving a real-life math problem. These assessments reflect deeper understanding, critical thinking, and problem-solving skills.

Authentic assessment allows teachers to observe learning as it happens and make real-time instructional adjustments. It also gives students the chance to reflect, revise, and demonstrate growth over time. While these assessments may not be easily standardized or scored on a scale, they provide rich insight into how well students can transfer their learning beyond the classroom.

When schools blend authentic assessments with standardized testing, they create a more complete picture of student learning. For instance, a school may implement a new writing curriculum and see modest gains in test scores. However, through authentic writing portfolios, student-teacher conferences, and peer review sessions, teachers may observe increased creativity, clarity, and stamina in students' writing indicators that signal long-term growth.

In short, standardized assessments provide a high-level snapshot like a drone image of the entire garden while authentic assessments offer a close-up walk among the plants, allowing educators to respond to the learning environment with care and immediacy.

Outline

Authentic assessments: evaluate students' ability to apply knowledge and skills to real-world tasks. *Examples* include projects, presentations, portfolios, experiments, essays, and performances.

Strengths

1. **Real World Relevance**
   - Mirrors tasks students may encounter in college, careers, or life (e.g., problem-solving, critical thinking, collaboration).

2. **Deepens Learning**
   - Encourages higher-order thinking, creativity, and student ownership.
   - Promotes application over memorization.
   - Allows for multiple modalities (writing, speaking, designing, performing), which can support ELLs and students with special needs.

3. **Provides Insight into Process and Progress**
   - Teachers can evaluate students' methods for approaching and solving problems, rather than focusing solely on the final answer.
   - Encourages Metacognition and Reflection
   - Students regularly assess their own work and reflect on their learning, which supports self-monitoring and independent learning skills.

Limitations

1. **Time-Consuming**
   - Planning, conducting, and scoring authentic assessments take more time than traditional tests.
2. **Subjectivity in Scoring**
   - Requires clear rubrics and training to ensure reliable, consistent grading across students and teachers.
3. **Limited Comparability Across Classrooms or Schools**
   - Results are less standardized, making them difficult to use for high-level comparisons or accountability.
4. **May Lack Breadth of Content Coverage**

   - A single performance task may go deep but not cover as many standards as a broader assessment.

Standardized Testing
Standardized tests are uniform assessments administered and scored in a consistent manner. Examples include state tests (e.g., NJSLA, MCAS), SATs, or district-wide benchmarks.

Strengths

1. **Reliable and Consistent**
   - Provides objective data that can be compared across students, schools, and districts.

2. **Covers a Wide Range of Content**

- Efficiently assesses knowledge across multiple standards in a single session

3. **Supports Accountability and Equity Monitoring**
    - Helps identify achievement gaps across subgroups and drives funding, support, and policy decisions.

4. **Useful for Large-Scale Trends and Goal Setting**
    - Essential for tracking school or district performance over time.

Limitations

1. **Narrow Focus on Measurable Outcomes**
    - Often emphasizes recall and low-level skills, missing deeper understanding, creativity, and real-world application.

2. **Test Anxiety and Pressure**
    - It can cause stress for students and teachers, especially in high-stakes environments.

3. **Cultural and Linguistic Bias**
    - Questions may disadvantage students from diverse backgrounds or those learning English.

4. **Limits Curriculum and Instruction ("Teaching to the Test")**
    - May narrow instruction to test-related content, reducing depth, engagement, and enrichment opportunities.

What methods can a school leader use to support teachers in the development of assessments that provide meaningful feedback about student progress?

Supporting teachers in developing meaningful assessments is a bit like coaching a sports team, you don't just hand players the rules and expect them to win. You watch them practice, help them reflect, adjust strategies, and give feedback that helps them improve over time. In the same way, a school leader plays a vital role in helping teachers create assessments that do more than measure learning. They guide it. One of the most important ways to do this is by offering professional development focused on high-quality assessment design. That might mean showing teachers how to turn a multiple-choice test into a performance task, use rubrics for consistency, or create culturally responsive assessments that speak to all learners.

School leaders can also strengthen assessment practice by creating regular time for collaborative planning, such as PLCs or grade-level meetings, where teachers co-create assessments, analyze student work, and ensure they are aligned to the standards. These sessions foster shared understanding and allow teams to fine-tune their expectations. Beyond planning, strong leaders model how to use data to drive instruction like reviewing assessment results to reteach concepts, adjust grouping, or provide enrichment. They also coach teachers by reviewing assessments and offering feedback on how well those tools reflect learning goals and support instructional decisions.

Promoting formative assessments like exit tickets, quick writes, and think-pair-share activities, gives teachers real-time insight into student thinking, while also keeping the pressure low for students. Leaders should encourage strategies that let students take ownership of their learning too, such as self-assessments, portfolios, or peer feedback, where students learn to reflect and grow from their own performance.

To ensure assessments measure what truly matters, leaders can guide teachers in using tools like backward design or assessment blueprints starting with the standards and designing tasks that match the learning goals in both depth and complexity. Finally, just like a good coach celebrates growth, school leaders should recognize and uplift strong assessment practices in faculty meetings, newsletters, or informal shout-outs. This reinforces a school culture where assessment isn't about collecting grades it's about supporting growth. When done right, assessment becomes an engine for learning, not just a snapshot of performance.

A school leader plays a critical role in helping teachers develop high-quality assessments that provide meaningful feedback about student progress. This involves fostering a culture of collaborative planning, instructional clarity, and data literacy.

<u>Outline</u>

1. Facilitate Professional Learning on Assessment Design
    - Provide PD focused on:
        - Formative vs. summative assessments
        - Creating aligned and rigorous questions

    - Developing rubrics and scoring guides
- Include topics such as feedback strategies, depth of knowledge (DOK), and culturally responsive assessment practices.
- *Example:* Host a workshop on how to turn a multiple-choice quiz into a standard-aligned performance task.

2. **Encourage Collaborative Planning and Calibration**
    - Structure regular PLC or grade-level team meetings for teachers to:
        - Co-create assessments aligned to standards and learning targets
        - Review and revise assessment questions
        - Analyze student work together for consistency and rigor
        - Use protocols such as the "tuning protocol" or "looking at student work" to promote reflection.

3. **Model Use of Data-Driven Instruction**
    - Support teachers in analyzing assessment results and using them to:
        - Adjust instruction
        - Reteach key concepts
        - Group students for intervention or enrichment
    - Use data chats, dashboards, and student progress monitoring tools to make assessment data actionable.

4. **Provide Feedback and Coaching**
    - Review teacher-created assessments as part of coaching cycles or lesson plan reviews.
    - Offer constructive, standards-based feedback that promotes:
        - Clarity of learning objectives
        - Alignment between instruction, assessment, and outcomes
        - Use of assessments to drive formative checkpoints, not just grades

5. **Encourage Formative Assessment Practices**
    - Promote ongoing, low stakes checks for understanding such as:
        - Exit tickets
        - Think-pair-share responses

Brief writing sessions or short meetings

- Help teachers understand how these tools inform the next steps and build a culture of continuous feedback.

6. **Promote Student-Involved Assessment**
    - Support strategies that give students ownership over their progress:
        - Self-assessments and goal setting
        - Peer feedback with rubrics
        - Portfolios and reflection journals

          Example: Guide teachers to include reflection prompts like "What strategy helped you most during this task?"

7. **Ensure Assessment Alignment with Standards and Instruction**

- Use tools like backward design or assessment blueprints to help teachers start with the standard and build assessments that truly measure what students are expected to learn.
- Support the alignment of:
    - Curriculum
    - Instruction
    - Assessment
    - Feedback

8. **Celebrate Effective Assessment Practices**

- Highlight examples of strong assessments and meaningful student feedback during:
    - Faculty meetings
    - Walkthrough feedback
    - Newsletters or shout-outs

How does high-stakes testing influence a school's curriculum and instructional practice?

Preparing students under high-stakes testing can feel a lot like teaching someone to drive by only focusing on passing the written exam. Sure, the test covers essential rules and road signs, but it doesn't teach you how to merge onto a highway, handle unexpected detours, or drive in heavy rain. Similarly, when schools prioritize standardized test performance above all else, instruction can become narrowly focused on memorizing facts, practicing test formats, and drilling isolated skills.

This might help students "pass the test," but it doesn't necessarily prepare them for deeper thinking, problem-solving, or real-world application. While high-stakes tests can promote accountability, align instruction to standards, and highlight achievement gaps, they can also lead to a narrowing of the curriculum, especially in non-tested subjects like the arts or social studies. Teachers may feel pressure to "teach to the test," sacrificing creative, student-centered approaches in favor of scripted lessons and practice tests.

The stress placed on both students and educators can be overwhelming, especially when test outcomes are tied to evaluations, funding, or public rankings. In some cases, schools may even focus most intensely on students just below proficiency levels, those likely to boost the school's performance ratings while overlooking others who also need support. To prevent these side effects, effective school leaders treat test data as one part of a larger instructional picture. They protect time for rich, balanced learning, support teachers with strong assessment literacy, and ensure that instruction prepares students not just for a test but for the road ahead.

High-stakes testing has a significant influence on a school's curriculum and instructional practices both positively and negatively. Because these tests often impact school ratings, funding, and accountability, they can shape what is taught, how it is taught, and how instructional time is used.

<u>Outline</u>

Positive Influences

1. **Promotes Standards Alignment**
   - High-stakes tests are based on state or national standards, which encourages schools to align curriculum and instruction accordingly.
   - Teachers become more intentional in backward planning, ensuring their lessons target tested skills and knowledge.
   - *Example:* Teachers prioritize standards-based objectives in lesson planning to ensure coverage of key content areas.

2. **Encourages Data-Driven Instruction**
   - Results from high-stakes tests provide data that schools can use to:
     - Identify achievement gaps
     - Group students for intervention/enrichment
     - Adjust instructional strategies

- Data teams and PLCs often use test results to drive curriculum refinement and lesson design.

3. **Raises Accountability**
   - Testing promotes a focus on results and outcomes, helping schools monitor progress across subgroups.
   - Encourages schools to evaluate the effectiveness of programs, teachers, and resources.

4. **Improves Focus on Core Academic Skills**
   - Emphasizes critical areas like reading comprehension, writing with evidence, mathematical reasoning, and problem-solving.

Negative Influences

1. **Narrowing of Curriculum**
   - Subjects not tested (e.g., social studies, art, music, physical education) may be marginalized or eliminated.
   - Curriculum may focus heavily on tested content, limiting exposure to a well-rounded education.

2. **Teaching to the Test**
   - Instruction may shift from deep learning to test prep, emphasizing rote skills and test strategies over conceptual understanding.
   - Lessons may mimic test formats instead of promoting real-world application or critical thinking.

3. **Reduced Instructional Creativity**
   - Pressure to improve scores can discourage teachers from using innovative, student-centered strategies like project-based learning, interdisciplinary units, or inquiry.

4. **Increased Student and Teacher Stress**
   - The high stakes tied to performance (e.g., grade promotion, teacher evaluation, school ratings) can cause anxiety and burnout.
   - May result in less risk-taking and exploration in instruction.

5. **Overemphasis on Certain Students**
   - Struggling or "bubble" students (just below proficiency) may receive disproportionate attention, while high-achievers or lower-performers receive less support.
   - This undermines equity and whole-child development.

Balanced Leadership Response

Effective school leaders mitigate the negative effects of high stakes testing by:

- Using test data as one of many tools, not the sole driver of instruction
- Protecting non-tested subjects and promoting whole-child development
- Supporting assessment literacy so teachers understand what the test measures and what it doesn't measure
- Encouraging standards-based, not test-based instruction

How can a school leader make data and other information on school effectiveness understandable to parents and the community?

Explaining school data to families is a lot like giving someone directions in an unfamiliar town. If you simply say, "Head north on Route 47 for 2.6 miles, then turn left at Junction 12," most people will feel lost. But if you say, "Drive past the grocery store, turn left at the library, and your destination is just after the park," the path becomes clear and familiar. In the same way, school leaders must guide families through academic data using relatable reference points, clear visuals, and straightforward language, rather than dense spreadsheets or educational jargon. This approach ensures that families feel included, informed, and empowered to support student learning.

Visuals like pie charts, bar graphs, and infographics help translate abstract numbers into something parents can quickly see and understand. But data alone isn't enough context is key. Families want clear explanations of the numbers and guidance on how to support their child. That's why effective communication includes not only what the data reveals, but also how the school is responding and how parents can partner in the solution. For example: "We noticed a drop in reading scores among our English learners. In response, we're offering targeted small-group instruction and additional bilingual support. At home, you can help by reading with your child in your home language for 15 minutes each night.

In short, data is most powerful when it becomes a conversation, not a report. By using clear language, visual aids, relatable examples, and actionable steps just like giving someone a map with helpful landmarks, school leaders empower families to engage, understand, and walk alongside the school on the journey toward student success.

A school leader can make data and information on school effectiveness understandable to parents and the community by focusing on clarity, relevance, and accessibility. Most families and community members aren't data experts so it's essential to communicate in ways that are clear, visual, meaningful, and actionable.

<u>**Outline**</u>

1. **Simplify the Language**
    - Avoid educational jargon and technical terms.
    - Use plain language and relatable examples.
    - Avoid language like "Our SGP increased in ELA by 12 points."
      "On average, our students made more progress in reading this year than they did last year."

2. **Use Visuals and Infographics**
    - Translate complex data into graphs, charts, and visuals that are easy to read.
    - Include legends, short explanations, and icons for quick understanding.
    - *Example*: Use a pie chart to show the percentage of students meeting or exceeding reading standards instead of a dense table of scores.

3. **Focus on What Matters to Families**
    - Highlight data that connects to student learning, safety, behavior, and engagement.

- Show how the school addresses concerns and celebrating progress.
- *Example:* "We reduced chronic absenteeism by 10%, which means more students are showing up ready to learn."

4. **Provide Context and Comparison**
   - Help families interpret numbers by comparing them to:
     - District or state averages
     - Past school performance
     - Target goals
     - *Example*: "Last year, 60% of our students met math standards. This year, we've grown to 72%, which puts us above the state average."

5. **Host Data Nights and Interactive Sessions**
   - Organize family-friendly events like "State of the School" nights or "Understanding Your Child's Progress" workshops.
   - Use visuals, storytelling, and Q&A time to build understanding.

6. **Use Multilingual and Culturally Responsive Communication**
   - Translate reports, presentations, and materials into the home languages of your community.
   - Use culturally familiar analogies or examples to make information more relatable.

7. **Incorporate Student and Teacher Voices**
   - Share stories, examples of student work, or video testimonials alongside data.
   - This helps families connect numbers to real experiences and outcomes.
   - *Example: Show how a new writing initiative helped students, then share writing samples from before and after.*

8. **Send Home Short, Consistent Updates**
   - Use newsletters, social media, or flyers to share small data bites over time (e.g., monthly attendance trends, reading progress updates).
   - Keep the format consistent and easy to scan.

9. **Make It Actionable**
   - Tell parents what they can do to help.
   - Include tips, questions to ask teachers, or community resources.

What types and sources of classroom data can be used to evaluate student improvement?

Evaluating student improvement using only one piece of classroom data is like proposing to a stranger after just one brief conversation. You wouldn't make such an important decision without getting to know the person learning their values, seeing how they react in different situations, and spending time together over weeks or months. In the same way, teachers can't truly understand student growth by relying on a single test or assignment. They need to build a relationship with the data.

Daily formative assessments like exit tickets, class discussions, and journal entries offer ongoing insights into how students are thinking and progressing, just like regular conversations help reveal someone's character over time. Summative assessments, such as unit tests or final projects, are more like important milestones meeting the family or attending an event together that confirm the bigger picture of the relationship.

Student work samples and observations provide texture and nuance, helping teachers see not just what students know, but how they apply and express it. Progress monitoring tools help track change over time especially for those who may be growing slowly but steadily, just like noticing someone's growth in patience or communication in a relationship. And when students set goals or reflect on their learning, it's like hearing someone's hopes for the future offering powerful clues about their investment and direction.

In short, just as you wouldn't commit to marriage based on a single impression, teachers need multiple, varied data points to evaluate student improvement accurately and fairly. It's about seeing the whole story, not just a snapshot.

To evaluate student improvement, educators must collect and analyze multiple types and sources of classroom data. These data points help measure both academic growth and skill development over time, giving a well-rounded picture of how students are progressing.

Outline

1. **Formative Assessment Data**

Purpose: Monitor ongoing progress and guide instruction in real time.

Sources:

- Exit tickets
- Do Now's / Bell ringers
- Quick quizzes or checks for understanding
- Whiteboard responses, polls (e.g., Kahoot, Nearpod)
- Think-pair-share observations

How it helps:

- Shows whether students are grasping content during instruction, and highlights when reteaching is needed. Tracks small, incremental learning gains.

2. **Summative Assessment Data**
Purpose: Measure mastery of learning at the end of a unit or period.
Sources:

- End-of-unit or chapter tests
- District-created benchmarks
- Midterms and finals
- Performance tasks scored with rubrics

3. **Student Work Samples**
Purpose: Provide insight into the depth of thinking and application.
Sources:

- Writing assignments
- Math journals and notebooks
- Science lab reports or projects
- Artifacts from portfolios
- Helps evaluate critical thinking, problem solving, and application of knowledge not just correctness. Work overtime can show improvement in complexity, accuracy, and expression.

4. **Rubrics and Checklists**
Purpose: Track skill development over time using consistent criteria.
Sources:

- Writing rubrics
- Speaking and listening performance checklists
- Project-based learning rubrics
- Reading fluency or comprehension scoring guides
- Allows for objective measurement of growth in areas like writing structure, oral communication, collaboration, or inquiry.

5. **Observational Data**
Purpose: Document behavior, participation, and skill application in real-time.
Sources:

- Anecdotal records
- Learning walks and observations
- Conference notes from small groups or 1:1 session
- Running records (especially for literacy)
- Captures qualitative indicators of growth such as increased independence, confidence, or use of academic language.

6. **Student Self-Assessment and Reflection**
Purpose: Involve students in evaluating their own learning progress.
Sources:

- Goal-setting sheets
- Learning logs or journals
- "Glow and grow" reflections
- Rating scales or progress trackers

- Builds metacognitive awareness, promotes self-regulation, and shows growth in student ownership of learning.

7. **Peer Assessment**
Purpose: Offer alternative feedback and support collaborative learning.
Sources:

- Peer review protocols
- Group discussion scoring
- Partner feedback forms
- Provides additional perspectives on student improvement, especially in communication, collaboration, and clarity of ideas.

8. **Digital Learning Data**
Purpose: Track skill mastery and engagement through adaptive platforms.
Sources:

- I-Ready, Khan Academy, IXL, Nearpod, Google Classroom
- LMS usage reports
- Clickstream or task completion data

Essential Questions 15 — Instructional Leadership

What types and sources of data can be used to monitor and evaluate instructional strategies?

Evaluating student improvement is a lot like watching someone learn to play an instrument. You wouldn't judge their talent based on a single performance; instead, you'd observe how they practice each day, how well they remember past lessons, how they respond to feedback, and how confidently they tackle new challenges. Similarly, in the classroom, teachers must gather multiple types of data to truly understand student growth. Formative assessments like exit tickets, warm-up problems, and quick polls capture what students can do in the moment, tapping into their short-term memory. This is valuable for gauging immediate understanding, but it doesn't always reflect deep learning. On the other hand, summative assessments like end-of-unit tests, projects, or essays rely more heavily on long-term memory, showing what knowledge and skills students have internalized over time.

Student work samples, journals, and portfolios act like practice recordings, showing how understanding develops and improves with repetition. Observational notes reveal habits, misconceptions, or breakthroughs that formal assessments may miss. Meanwhile, student reflections and self-assessments offer a window into metacognition on how students perceive their own learning process and memory strategies.

By combining short-term snapshots with long-term evidence, teachers can distinguish between what students temporarily recall and what they truly retain. In this way, data becomes more than a score. It becomes a narrative of growth, just like the evolving sound of a musician mastering their craft.

To monitor and evaluate instructional strategies, school leaders and teachers must collect and analyze a range of data types from various sources. These data help determine whether instructional approaches are improving student learning, engagement, and equity and guide decisions about continuing, refining, or replacing strategies.

Outline

1. **Student Achievement Data**
Purpose: Measures academic outcomes linked to instructional practices.
Sources:

- State assessments (e.g., NJSLA, STAAR)
- District benchmarks or interim assessments
- Unit tests and end-of-course exams
- Standardized growth assessments (e.g., MAP, I-Ready)
- It tells whether instruction is leading to mastery of standard and if the growth trends are tied to instructional shifts or identify equity gaps

2. **Formative Assessment Data**
Purpose: Provides real-time feedback on student understanding during instruction.
Sources:

- Exit tickets
- Quizzes
- Whiteboard checks, digital polls (e.g., Nearpod, Kahoot)
- Classwork and in-the-moment questioning
- It tells whether students are learning and what is being taught
- It tells Immediate effectiveness of a specific instructional move (e.g., modeling, scaffolding)

3. **Classroom Observation Data**
Purpose: Captures teacher implementation and student response to strategies.
Sources:

- Instructional walkthroughs
- Formal evaluations using rubrics (e.g., Danielson Framework)
- Coaching cycles with feedback logs
- Peer observations
- It tells whether strategies are being used with fidelity and quality
- Teacher-student interaction patterns, pacing, questioning, engagement

4. **Student Work Samples**
Purpose: Reflects the depth and quality of learning tasks and student thinking.
Sources:

- Writing samples, math journals, science labs, project-based artifacts
- Annotated rubrics or performance task scoring guides
- It tells if instruction is fostering critical thinking, creativity, and problem-solving
- It tells whether students can apply learning beyond rote memorization

5. **Student Engagement and Behavior Data**
Purpose: Tracks how students respond to instructional methods.
Sources:

- On-task behavior observations
- Participation tracking
- Behavior referrals
- Classroom engagement surveys
- It tells If a strategy increases or decreases student engagement and motivation
- Early signs of misalignment between instruction and student needs

6. **Student and Family Feedback**
Purpose: Offers insight into how instruction is perceived and experienced.
Sources:

- Student surveys (e.g., Panorama, Google Forms)
- Focus groups or student panels
- Parent feedback on homework, communication, and progress
- Tells whether strategies support clarity, access, and engagement from the learner's perspective

7. Teacher Self-Assessment and Reflection
Purpose: Encourages reflective practice and personal evaluation.
Sources:

- Teacher reflection logs
- Post-lesson analysis or video reflections
- Goal setting aligned to instructional strategies
- It tells Teachers' own insights into what's working and what's not
- Help triangulate data from external sources

8. **PLC and Data Team Analysis**
Purpose: Promotes collective evaluation of strategies across classrooms.
Sources:

- Collaborative review of common assessments
- Student work protocols
- Shared lesson studies
- It tells which instructional strategies are effective schoolwide or grade-level wide
- Opportunities to scale or revise approaches

How and when should parents and other stakeholders be informed about the results of tests or other data collected within the school and district?

Sharing student test results and academic data with families is a lot like how banks keep customers informed about their finances. Think about it: you wouldn't want your bank to only send you a balance update once a year. Without regular statements or alerts, you could miss signs of fraud, rack up overdraft fees, or go over budget problems that could have been avoided with timely information. In the same way, when schools delay or limit communication about student progress, families are left in the dark, unable to offer support or intervene before academic struggles grow into larger setbacks.

To prevent this, schools should provide updates not just at the end of a marking period or after state testing, but throughout the year in ways that are clear, consistent, and meaningful. Informal updates like progress reports, weekly folders, parent-teacher check-ins, and classroom apps help keep parents aware of how their child is doing day to day. Formal data, such as benchmarks or standardized test results, should be shared with explanations that make the information easy to understand and relevant. For instance, when sending home I-Ready reading scores, a school might include a growth chart and tips for practicing reading strategies at home.

When families receive regular, easy-to-follow academic updates, much like how banks keep customers posted on account activity they're empowered to take action, ask questions, and partner with the school in real time. In short, timely communication builds trust, prevents larger issues, and helps ensure every child stays on a path toward academic success.

Parents and stakeholders should be informed about test results and other school or district data in a way that is timely, clear, respectful, and action oriented. Sharing data is not just a compliance step, it's an opportunity to build trust, transparency, and collaboration around student achievement and school improvement.

Outline

How Should Parents and Stakeholders Be Informed?

1. **Use Clear, Accessible Language**
   - Avoid jargon (e.g., SGP, Lexile bands) and explain data in plain terms.
   - Include visual aids like graphs, color-coded charts, and short definitions to support understanding.
   - *Example:* "Your child met the grade-level reading benchmark and showed 20% growth since the fall."

2. **Provide Individualized Reports for Families**
   - Share student-specific reports for state, benchmark, and classroom assessments.
   - Include:
     - The student's score
     - How it compares to grade-level expectations
     - Strengths and areas for growth
     - Suggested next steps or resources for support

    - All of which should be shared at report card conferences, parent-teacher nights, or mailed home with guidance notes.

3. **Hold Schoolwide Data Meetings or Family Nights**
    - Host events like:
        - "Understanding the Scores" workshops
        - "Data and Donuts" sessions
        - State of the School" presentations
        - These help parents interpret schoolwide trends and understand what the school is doing in response.

4. **Use Digital Tools for Ongoing Updates**
    - Share class-level or schoolwide data trends through:
        - Email newsletters
        - Parent portals (e.g., PowerSchool, ClassDojo, Schoology)
        - School websites or apps
        - *Example:* Monthly "data snapshots" showing trends in attendance, math progress, or reading growth.

5. **Offer Multilingual and Culturally Inclusive Communication**
    - Translate all materials into the home languages spoken in the community.
    - Use culturally familiar formats (e.g., videos, infographics, Q&A documents).

6. **Explain the Purpose of the Assessments**
    - Help families understand why the data was collected:
        - Measuring growth
        - To plan instruction
        - To identify student needs
        - Not simply to rank or label

When Should Data Be Shared?

7. **Immediately After Major Assessments**
    - State or district assessments: Within 30–60 days after results are released.
    - Progress reports/benchmarks: At the end of each assessment window (e.g., fall, winter, spring).
    - Include a follow-up opportunity for parents to ask questions or meet with staff.

8. **During Key School Events**
    - Parent-teacher conferences: Review individual progress, assessments, and goals.
    - Back-to-School or Curriculum Nights: Preview how assessments align with instruction.
    - School improvement meetings or Board presentations: Share schoolwide trends and goals.
    - Proactively and Consistently
    - This fosters transparency and prevents surprises at the end of the year.

What are some sources of teacher evaluation data and information (other than direct classroom observation)?

Evaluating a teacher's effectiveness without multiple data sources is like trying to judge a book by glancing at one page. You might catch a glimpse of the story, but you'll miss the plot, the development, and the impact. In the real world, we wouldn't evaluate an employee's performance in any profession by watching them for 30 minutes once or twice a year. Imagine trying to assess a personal trainer based only on how they give warm-up instructions, without checking client progress, workout plans, or client feedback. In education, the same logic applies.

Beyond classroom observations, meaningful evaluation should include student achievement data, which shows whether students are progressing academically over time. For example, if a teacher's students consistently improve in writing or math benchmarks, that reflects effective instruction. Student work samples like essays, science projects, or math journals offer a window into how deeply students are thinking and applying what they learn. Lesson plans and unit designs also provide valuable insight into how teachers structure learning, differentiate instruction, and align to standards.

Surveys from students help capture how supported, safe, and engaged they feel just as customer reviews give insight into a service or product. Similarly, feedback from parents reveals how well teachers communicate, support home learning, and build family partnerships. Evidence of professional growth, such as participating in training, mentoring colleagues, or leading initiatives, shows leadership and collaboration beyond the classroom.

In short, just as a complete medical diagnosis includes lab results, patient history, and specialist input not just a five-minute exam. Teacher evaluation must combine various forms of evidence to reflect the full scope of their work. This richer, more accurate portrait supports not only fair assessment but also meaningful professional growth.

While direct classroom observation is a core component of teacher evaluation, effective and well-rounded evaluation systems include multiple sources of data to provide a more comprehensive and fairer picture of teacher effectiveness.

Outline

1. **Student Achievement and Growth Data**
   - Standardized test scores (e.g., NJSLA, MAP, I-Ready)
   - Student growth percentiles (SGP) or value-added models (VAM)
   - Common formative and summative assessments
   - Pre- and post-assessment comparisons
   - Shows the impact of instruction on student learning over time.

2. **Student Work Samples**

- Artifacts such as essays, projects, math journals, lab reports
- Annotated with standards and learning objectives
- Often analyzed during PLCs or instructional rounds
- Reflects the level of rigor, alignment to standards, and depth of student thinking fostered by instruction.

3. Student Surveys

- Age-appropriate surveys (e.g., Panorama, Tripod)
- Focus on classroom environment, engagement, clarity, and relationships
- Gives voice to students and captures their perceptions of instructional effectiveness and emotional support.

4. **Parent or Family Feedback**

- Surveys or feedback forms about communication, responsiveness, and classroom climate
- Participation in parent-teacher conferences, outreach logs, or digital communications (ClassDojo, Remind, etc.)
- Reflects the teacher's ability to build partnerships with families.

5. **Lesson and Unit Plans**

- Evidence of standards alignment, differentiation, pacing, and assessments
- Can be reviewed for quality, coherence, and instructional intent
- Shows a teacher's planning and instructional decision-making process.

6. Assessment Tools and Student Data Use

- Quality of teacher-created assessments (e.g., rubrics, performance tasks)
- Evidence of formative assessment use and data-driven instruction
- Data binders or student progress tracking logs
  Demonstrates how teachers monitor learning and adjust instruction.

7. **Professional Responsibilities and Contributions**

- Attendance and participation in:
  - PLCs, PD, coaching sessions
  - School committees, extracurriculars, or leadership roles
- Evidence of professional growth goals and reflections
- Evaluates professionalism, leadership, and collaboration (Danielson Domain 4).

8. **Portfolios or Teacher Artifacts**

- Compiled evidence including lesson plans, student work, feedback samples, reflections, and PD certificates
- Used in evaluation conferences or portfolio-based review systems
- Provides structured, self-curated evidence of instructional practice and growth.

9. **Peer Collaboration and Feedback**

- Peer observations or co-teaching reflections
- Notes from lesson study or instructional rounds
- Promotes collegial feedback and shared learning across teams.

How can a school leader encourage staff to be creative risk takers while ensuring they follow the adopted course of study?

A teacher can apply creative risk-taking in a real-life classroom context by reimagining how students interact with the curriculum while still meeting required standards. For instance, a middle school social studies teacher, instead of assigning a traditional essay on the American Revolution, decides to let students create a mock podcast series, where they take on the roles of historical figures such as George Washington, King George III, or Deborah Sampson. Each student records a scripted segment reflecting their character's perspective on major events, ensuring they include key facts and vocabulary aligned to the state standards.

While this approach departs from the typical assignment format, it still covers the necessary learning outcomes, understanding causes of the war, key events, and differing viewpoints. The teacher is taking a creative risk by stepping away from a predictable model and trusting students with a new form of expression. However, by using a rubric tied directly to the learning objectives, the teacher ensures accountability and alignment with the adopted course of study. A school leader who supports this type of innovation reinforces that creativity and curriculum compliance are not mutually exclusive but can coexist when planning is thoughtful and standards are clear.

Outline

1. Clearly Communicate Curriculum Expectations and Non-Negotiables

- Set a strong foundation by defining what must be taught and what flexibility exists.
- *Example:* The principal provides pacing guides and identifies priority standards, while allowing room for instructional innovation.

2. Promote a Culture of Innovation Within Boundaries

- Reinforce that creativity is encouraged if it aligns with learning goals.
- *Example:* Teachers are invited to design project-based learning units that address standards in novel ways.

3. Celebrate and Share Examples of Aligned Creative Teaching

- Highlight successful practices that honor both rigor and innovation.
- *Example:* A teacher who integrates art and science to teach ecosystems is featured in the staff newsletter.

4. Provide Collaborative Planning Time

- Allow teachers to co-create lessons that are both standard-aligned and engaging.
- *Example:* During PLCs, teachers brainstorm creative strategies (e.g., simulations, debates, flipped lessons) to meet objectives.

5. Offer Professional Development on Instructional Creativity

- Support teachers in designing lessons that spark curiosity while meeting curriculum goals.

- *Example:* A workshop on "Design Thinking in the Standards-Based Classroom" helps teachers innovate within structured frameworks.

6. Encourage Risk-Taking Through Trust and Support

- Foster psychological safety by assuring staff that thoughtful risks are valued, even if outcomes are imperfect.
- *Example:* The principal observes a new instructional method and offers constructive feedback rather than punitive criticism.

7. Use Data to Reflect on and Refine Creative Approaches

- Evaluate whether innovative strategies improve student engagement and mastery.
- *Example:* After a project-based unit, the team reviews student work and assessment data to adjust and scale what worked.

8. Align Creative Efforts with School-Wide Goals and Vision

- Ensure that all instructional risk-taking contributes to the broader mission of the school.
- *Example:* Teachers create interdisciplinary units that support the school's vision of global citizenship and collaboration.

Instructional Leadership Quiz

1. **A principal notices that students in multiple classrooms are struggling with reading comprehension on both formative and summative assessments. What is the principal's best first step to improve instructional effectiveness?**
   A. Assign teachers to a district-provided online literacy course
   B. Review student work and assessment data with teachers to identify gaps
   C. Replace current instructional materials with a scripted reading program
   D. Schedule daily walkthroughs focused solely on classroom behavior

2. **During an observation, the principal notices a teacher is delivering a lesson with limited student engagement. What is the most effective way to support this teacher's growth?**
   A. Record the lesson and send feedback via email
   B. Provide a generic list of engagement strategies
   C. Conduct a post-observation conference with specific examples and questions
   D. Note it in the teacher's summative evaluation without follow-up

3. **A school's PLC meetings have become unproductive, with little focus on student data. What should the principal do to reestablish purpose?**
   A. Cancel the PLCs and replace them with faculty meetings
   B. Assign PLC leads to report minutes only to administration
   C. Provide protocols for data analysis and model an effective meeting
   D. Rotate PLC facilitators weekly to build shared leadership

4. **To evaluate the effectiveness of a school's math curriculum, which combination of data sources would provide the most accurate insight?**
   A. Teacher evaluations and lesson plans
   B. Student attendance records and behavioral logs
   C. Formative assessments, summative assessments, and student work samples
   D. Parent satisfaction surveys and enrollment trends

5. **A new teacher is struggling with classroom management, impacting instructional delivery. What is the most supportive leadership action?**
   A. Assign the teacher to observe a peer with strong management skills
   B. Extend the teacher's probationary period
   C. Focus walkthroughs only on academic instruction
   D. Increase the teacher's class size to improve confidence

6. **After reviewing disaggregated assessment data, the leadership team identifies achievement gaps among ELL students. What should be the next step?**
   A. Send home translated versions of student report cards
   B. Provide teachers with strategies for scaffolding instruction
   C. Hold a school-wide assembly addressing diversity
   D. Lower grading expectations for ELL students

7. **How can a principal most effectively ensure that classroom assessments are aligned with state standards?**
   A. Require weekly assessment submissions
   B. Review a sample of assessments during PLCs and provide feedback
   C. Have the district created all assessments
   D. Let teachers decide their own alignment methods

8. A principal wants to promote reflective practice among teachers. What leadership strategy is most effective?

A. Provide teachers with standardized lesson plans
B. Require teachers to submit reflection journals monthly
C. Facilitate peer observation cycles with collaborative debriefs
D. Post instructional videos of "model teachers" for silent viewing

9. When analyzing a teacher's effectiveness, which combination of evidence is most comprehensive?

A. Student test scores, peer reviews, and instructional artifacts
B. Daily attendance records and school newsletters
C. Teacher credentials and seniority
D. Parent complaints and formal observations only

10. What is the primary purpose of using walk-through observations in instructional leadership?

A. To evaluate teachers for their annual review
B. To identify patterns in instructional delivery for coaching and support
C. To gather data for board presentations
D. To record how often teachers use technology

11. A walkthrough reveals that learning objectives are not clearly posted or referenced in lessons. What is the most appropriate action?

A. Send an email to all staff reminding them to post objectives
B. Conduct a mini training on the use of learning targets and revisit in follow-up observations
C. Ignore it, as experienced teachers already know the goals
D. Include objectives only in formal evaluations

12. The district is requiring more integration of technology in instruction, but some teachers are hesitant. What should the principal do?

A. Mandate daily use of a specific platform
B. Offer differentiated PD and allow teachers to pilot strategies in their own classrooms
C. Evaluate teachers more frequently until compliance is met
D. Purchase expensive new devices to motivate staff

13. A teacher receives high marks on formal observations but has poor student growth results. What is the leader's best next step?

A. Revisit classroom practices with a focus on student learning outcomes
B. Disregard the student data due to the teacher's strong instructional rating
C. Increase classroom walkthroughs in other teachers' rooms
D. Move the teacher to a different grade level

14. **The school improvement plan includes a goal to increase writing proficiency. Which action best supports that goal?**

A. Require weekly writing homework across all subjects
B. Host a parent workshop on grammar rules
C. Provide cross-curricular PD on writing strategies and monitor student samples
D. Eliminate multiple-choice assessments from ELA classes

15. Some staff feel overwhelmed by new instructional initiatives. How should the school leader respond?

A. Pause all new initiatives indefinitely
B. Engage staff in prioritizing and streamlining initiatives that align with school goals
C. Increase after-school training hours to improve readiness
D. Ask staff to ignore what they find most difficult

16. **After reviewing student work, the leadership team identifies a gap in higher-order thinking. What should be the next step?**

A. Replace the current curriculum
B. Train teachers on Depth of Knowledge (DOK) levels and question design
C. Focus on classroom management instead
D. Reduce assessment frequency

17. **The principal wants to build the teacher's capacity for data-driven instruction. What's the most effective approach?**

A. Require teachers to submit weekly data reports
B. Provide collaborative data sessions with guided protocols and coaching
C. Assign one teacher to analyze data for the grade level
D. Focus on test prep strategies instead of data analysis

18. Student engagement has declined, especially in core classes. What strategy is most effective for addressing this trend?

A. Mandate participation grades in all subjects
B. Ask teachers to include games and music daily
C. Encourage instructional planning that includes choice, relevance, and active learning
D. Focus only on behavior management strategies

19. The instructional leadership team wants to improve lesson rigor. What is the most effective first step?

A. Revisit standards and increase alignment during PLC meetings
B. Provide teachers with more worksheets
C. Limit project-based learning to test-prep months
D. Ask teachers to assign longer homework

20. A teacher frequently uses group work, but students are off-task and unproductive. What is the best coaching response?

A. Advise the teacher to stop using group work
B. Offer a model lesson on managing group roles and accountability
C. Require the teacher to assign individual work only
D. Ignore the issue since collaboration is encouraged

Answer Key Strategic Leadership #1-10

Question Number	1	2	3	4	5	6	7	8	9	10
Correct Solution	B	C	C	C	A	B	B	C	A	B

Answer Key Strategic Leadership #11-20

Question Number	11	12	13	14	15	16	17	18	19	20
Correct Solution	B	B	A	C	B	B	B	C	A	B

Domain III:
Climate & Cultural Leadership

This domain focuses on the principal's role in cultivating a safe, inclusive, and supportive environment where all members of the school community feel valued. Climate and culture leadership involves fostering positive relationships, promoting equity and respect, and establishing systems that support both academic and social-emotional growth. By prioritizing a welcoming and caring culture, principals build trust, strengthen engagement, and create the conditions where students and staff can flourish together.

Climate & Cultural Leadership

Real-Life Scenario #A: Community of care and support for teachers of care and support for teachers (PSEL Standard 7)

At Brookside Hills Middle School, Principal Dr. Liana Chen noticed growing signs of staff burnout following the first semester. Several teachers had taken personal days due to stress. Collaboration among grade-level teams was inconsistent, and teacher morale was visibly low. During faculty meetings, participation was minimal, and informal feedback suggested that teachers felt overwhelmed, undervalued, and disconnected from the school's instructional mission.

Rather than immediately implementing new initiatives, Dr. Chen began by creating space for honest dialogue. She hosted a "Staff Voice Circle", an open forum where teachers could anonymously share their concerns, ideas, and needs. She followed this with small group listening sessions, ensuring that every department felt seen and heard. Teachers expressed a strong desire for more meaningful collaboration, professional autonomy, and a better balance between work demands and personal well-being.

In response, Dr. Chen partnered with the school's leadership team to implement a comprehensive Community of Care and Professional Growth Plan, which focused on both emotional support and instructional improvement.

Dr. Chen launched monthly "Teaching Lab Dialogues," where faculty could voluntarily discuss instructional beliefs, challenges, and ideas without judgment. Topics ranged from grading equity to culturally responsive teaching. She introduced a "Try It and Tweak It" cycle, where teachers could pilot innovative strategies such as flexible grouping or inquiry-based learning without fear of penalty. Teachers shared reflections during professional learning community (PLC) meetings and received peer support.

Dr. Chen restructured the master schedule to embed weekly common planning periods and provided stipends for cross-grade PLC leads. She also ensured that instructional coaches were accessible during those sessions to guide lesson planning and data discussions. Teachers were invited to lead mini workshops during PD days and co-design campus improvement goals. Several volunteers were to mentor new staff, design school-wide SEL activities, and serve on the school climate committee.

Dr. Chen collaborated with the counselor and union rep to create a Wellness Corner in the staff lounge, featuring mindfulness resources and relaxation activities. She also launched "No-Meeting Wednesdays" and a quarterly "Early Dismissal for Staff Planning" initiative. Instead of punitive measures, Dr. Chen focused on solution-oriented coaching, using classroom visits to affirm strengths and offering timely, personalized support. Expectations remained high, but teachers felt they were growing with leadership, not under pressure.

Dr. Chen led by example, leaving the building at a healthy hour, respecting staff lunch breaks, and being transparent about the importance of mental wellness for herself and others.

By spring, the school's staff climate survey reflected a 42% increase in positive responses regarding collaboration and support. Teachers began volunteering to share best practices during faculty meetings, and lesson quality improved as seen in walkthrough trends. Staff absences declined, and a greater sense of community and shared ownership emerged evidence that Dr. Chen's leadership had cultivated a safe, caring, and professionally empowering school culture.

Climate & Cultural Leadership

Real-Life Scenario #B: Equity and cultural responsiveness (PSEL Standard 3)

When Principal Mr. Jordan Ellis reviewed the midyear academic performance and discipline data at Valley Crest Middle School, he noticed troubling trends. While the overall proficiency rate in English Language Arts had risen by 8%, a deeper look revealed that Black and Latino students, English language learners (ELLs), and students with IEPs were still performing significantly below grade level. Moreover, a disaggregated analysis of discipline referrals showed that students of color and multilingual learners were receiving a disproportionate number of suspensions and detentions for subjective infractions like "defiance" or "disrespect."

Determined to address these inequities, Mr. Ellis committed to a schoolwide initiative focused on equity, cultural responsiveness, and dismantling institutional bias. Mr. Ellis led his leadership team through an equity audit, examining access to honors classes, teacher assignments, enrichment programs, and intervention services. The audit revealed that students from marginalized groups were underrepresented in advanced courses and lacked consistent access to certified, experienced teachers.

He implemented a data-driven placement system for academic programming and redistributed resources to ensure that all students had equitable access to high-quality instruction and enrichment.
Mr. Ellis facilitated a professional development series on restorative practices, implicit bias, and culturally responsive behavior management. He required the use of a restorative referral form, which guided teachers through reflection questions before submitting discipline referrals.

The school reduced out-of-school suspensions by 45% within one semester and increased the use of student conferences, restorative circles, and peer mediation for non-violent infractions.
Through PLCs and instructional coaching, teachers redesigned units to include multicultural texts, community voices, and student-chosen inquiry projects. Classroom libraries were diversified, and teachers learned to incorporate students' home languages and cultural contexts into lessons.

ELL students and students from non-dominant cultural backgrounds began to see themselves reflected in the curriculum, increasing both engagement and achievement. Mr. Ellis formed a Student Equity Council made up of diverse student leaders who met monthly to discuss school climate, curriculum, and student well-being. He also launched a Cultural Advisory Board including parents, bilingual aides, and local community leaders. Family engagement events were redesigned to reflect the cultural traditions of the community, with interpretation services, cultural celebrations, and flexible meeting times that acknowledged working families.

Mr. Ellis led the faculty in examining policies, traditions, and assumptions that contributed to deficit-based thinking such as rigid grading practices, limited family outreach, and tracking systems. Teachers were expected to create culturally responsive action plans as part of their professional growth goals.
Teachers reported stronger relationships with students from marginalized backgrounds, and the school climate survey reflected increased feelings of belonging among all student groups. Mr. Ellis made it clear that equity was not about lowering standards but ensuring everyone had the tools to succeed. He worked with instructional coaches to create differentiated support for students while maintaining rigorous expectations.

Students who had previously been tracked into remedial courses began to thrive in co-taught, standards-aligned classrooms with embedded support. By the end of the year, achievement gaps narrowed across all subgroups, and student engagement rose schoolwide. Parent participation in school events nearly doubled, and a renewed sense of shared purpose took hold. Mr. Ellis's leadership demonstrated that equity is not a one-time initiative, but an ongoing commitment embedded in every decision, policy, and interaction.

Climate & Cultural Leadership

Real-Life Scenario #C: Community of care and support for students (PSEL Standard 5)

When students returned from winter break at Ridgeway High School, Principal Mrs. Johnson noticed a troubling shift in school climate. Referral rates had increased, several students had experienced anxiety-related absences, and teachers expressed concern that many students were disengaged, withdrawn, or acting out. A review of mid-year data confirmed the concerns: behavioral incidents had risen by 35%, attendance rates had dropped particularly among economically disadvantaged students and several students with IEPs and 504 plans were struggling to meet progress goals.

Rather than treating these issues in isolation, Mrs. Johnson led her staff to examine how the school could holistically support students' academic, social, emotional, and physical needs. She launched a comprehensive "Culture of Connection" initiative to build a stronger, more inclusive, and supportive environment for all students.
Mrs. Johnson collaborated with the school counselor and school resource officer to update the school's safety plan and implemented monthly peer mediation and conflict resolution workshops led by trained students and staff. She expanded access to the district crisis counseling team and ensured that social workers conduct regular check-ins with students referred for support. A school-wide Positive Behavior Interventions and Supports (PBIS) framework was adopted, reinforcing kindness, accountability, and safety with student recognition and classroom incentives.

To ensure students felt seen and supported, Mrs. Johnson established a "Check-In & Connect" mentor program, where every staff member was paired with 2–3 students to meet with weekly. Teachers also received training on trauma-informed practices and anti-bullying awareness protocols, ensuring that all students felt protected and respected. An anonymous student voice survey revealed an increase in students reporting that they felt safe and connected to at least one adult in the building.

The leadership team created a Student Support Hub, integrating services like tutoring, counseling, health referrals, hygiene supplies, and weekend food kits. Mrs. Johnson worked with local nonprofits to offer vision screenings, dental checkups, and back-to-school supply drives for low-income families.

The school developed a "Student Success Tracker" to monitor attendance, grades, and behavior flags across support teams allowing for early intervention. To deepen relationships and student voice, Mrs. Johnson supported the creation of student-led clubs, increased morning circle time in classrooms, and launched a monthly "Student Voice Town Hall", where students proposed ideas for improving school culture.

The Student Council helped plan events like "Culture Celebration Week" and a "Random Acts of Kindness" challenge, creating stronger peer bonds and school pride.

Mrs. Johnson emphasized the connection between student engagement and behavior. She encouraged project-based learning, student goal-setting conferences, and leadership roles in school events, ensuring that students were active contributors of their school experience. Behavioral referrals declined by 28% over the next two months, and attendance among targeted students improved significantly.

By the end of the school year, Ridgeway Intermediate had made significant strides in creating a safe, caring, and inclusive environment. Student voice increased, staff-student relationships improved, and academic outcomes rose especially among previously disengaged students. Mrs. Johnson's leadership demonstrated that academic growth thrives in an environment where every student feels valued, supported, and connected.

Essential Questions #1 Climate & Culture Leadership

How can the professional culture and climate of a school impact school and student success?

The professional culture and climate of a school have a powerful influence on both school effectiveness and student success because they shape the environment in which teachers work, and students learn. A positive professional culture is one where collaboration, trust, shared responsibility, and continuous learning are valued. When teachers feel respected, supported, and empowered, they are more motivated to innovate, reflect on their practice, and stay committed to student growth.

For example, in a school where teachers regularly meet in professional learning communities (PLCs) to analyze student data, share strategies, and support one another, the instruction tends to be more responsive and consistent across classrooms. This leads to higher levels of student engagement and achievement. Conversely, in a school where teachers feel isolated, undervalued, or fearful of taking risks, instructional quality may suffer, and students can sense that disconnect.

Additionally, a healthy professional climate encourages emotional well-being and stability, which directly affects how teachers interact with students. A teacher who feels burnt out and unsupported may unintentionally show frustration in class, while one who feels encouraged and heard is more likely to create a positive, safe learning space. In short, a strong professional culture supports the adults in the building so they can do their best work and that directly benefits students.

Outline

1. Foster Culture of Collaboration and Shared Leadership

- A positive professional climate encourages teamwork, trust, and open dialogue.
- *Example:* Grade-level teams meet weekly to co-plan lessons and review student data, leading to more consistent instruction and improved student outcomes.

2. Support Teacher Morale and Retention

- A healthy professional culture reduces burnout and increases job satisfaction.
- *Example:* A school with strong mentorship and recognition programs retains teachers longer, helping students benefit from experienced, committed educators.

3. Model and Maintain High Expectations for All

- A shared belief in student potential leads to instructional consistency and excellence.
- *Example:* Teachers collaborate to uphold rigorous expectations, resulting in higher levels of academic engagement and performance.

4. Encourage Risk-Taking and Innovation

- A safe, supportive culture gives staff the freedom to try new instructional practices.
- *Example:* Teachers pilot new assessment tools with administrative support, which improve student feedback and engagement.

5. Build Trust Between Staff and Leadership

- Transparency and follow-through from leadership strengthens morale and collaboration.
- *Example:* The principal includes teachers in decision-making processes, creating a sense of shared ownership and mutual respect.

6. Influence on Student Behavior and Relationships

- A strong adult culture shapes how students interact and engage.
- *Example:* When staff model respect and empathy, students mirror those behaviors in peer relationships and classroom conduct.

7. Promote Continuous Professional Growth

- A culture that values learning supports both staff development and student success.
- *Example:* Job-embedded PD aligned to school goals becomes a norm, leading to improved instructional strategies and academic gains.

Essential Questions #2 Climate & Cultural Leadership

Why is taking risks important for improving teaching and learning?

Taking risks is important for improving teaching and learning because it encourages innovation, growth, and responsiveness to students' evolving needs. When educators are willing to try new strategies whether it's using unfamiliar technology, differentiating instruction in new ways, or incorporating student voice into lessons they open the door to discovering more effective practices. These risks may not always yield immediate success, but they often lead to valuable insights, reflection, and long-term improvement.

For example, a teacher who takes the risk of replacing traditional lectures with project-based learning might initially face uncertainty or pushbacks. However, that change could lead to greater student engagement, deeper understanding, and collaboration skills that traditional methods didn't foster. In the same way, when school leaders create a safe environment where teachers feel supported to take instructional risks without fear of judgment or punishment, it builds a culture of learning and professional growth.

Ultimately, taking risks moves education forward. It breaks the cycle of "what we've always done" and replaces it with practices that are more inclusive, student-centered, and effective. Without risk, there is no meaningful change.

Outline

1. Encourages Innovation in Instruction

- Taking risks allows teachers to try new strategies, tools, and approaches that may better meet student needs.
- *Example:* A teacher experiments with project-based learning, resulting in increased student engagement and deeper understanding of real-world applications.

2. Promotes Reflective Practice and Growth

- Risk-taking fosters professional self-reflection by allowing educators to learn from both successes and failures.
- *Example:* After implementing a new discussion format that flopped, a teacher revises her approach and improves student participation the next time.

3. Models a Growth Mindset for Students

- When teachers take risks, they model perseverance, flexibility, and continuous learning.
- *Example:* A teacher openly shares with students that they're trying a new method and welcomes feedback, showing students that learning is a lifelong process.

4. Drives Differentiation and Responsiveness

- Trying new methods helps educators meet the diverse needs of learners, especially struggling students.
- *Example:* A teacher adopts voice-recorded feedback for MLL students and sees improvements in comprehension and writing revision.

5. Builds a Culture of Trust and Collaboration

- A risk-taking mindset encourages shared learning among staff and invites collective problem-solving.
- *Example:* A grade-level team decides to co-develop interdisciplinary units, despite initial uncertainty, and finds success through collaboration.

6. Leads to Lasting Instructional Improvement

- Innovations that begin as risks can evolve into best practices that benefit students schoolwide.
- *Example:* A teacher introduces student-led conferences; after success in her class, the model is adopted schoolwide to increase family engagement and student ownership.

What strategies can a school leader use to build or repair staff morale?

A school leader can build or repair staff morale by creating a culture of trust, support, and appreciation. One of the most effective strategies is to actively listen to teachers by providing safe opportunities for feedback through surveys, listening sessions, or informal conversations. When staff feel heard, they're more likely to engage and trust leadership. Additionally, recognizing and celebrating staff efforts both publicly and privately helps teachers feel valued and motivated. Simple acts like shout-outs during faculty meetings or personalized thank-you notes after walkthroughs can have a powerful impact.

School leaders should also ensure teachers have the tools, time, and support they need to do their jobs well. This might include reducing unnecessary paperwork, protecting planning time, or providing instructional coaching. Equally important is promoting work-life balance by avoiding excessive meetings and respecting teachers' personal time. By implementing "no-meeting" days or providing time during PD sessions for grading or collaboration.

Transparency and follow-through also matter; when school leaders keep staff informed and act on concerns, they strengthen trust. Finally, building morale isn't just about reducing stress. It's also about fostering joy and connection. Organizing team-building events, celebrating milestones, and creating moments of levity can renew a sense of community. When staff feel supported, respected, and connected, morale improves and so does the school's ability to meet the needs of its students.

Outline

1. Foster Open and Transparent Communication

- Trust is rebuilt when leaders communicate honestly and regularly with staff.
- *Example:* The principal holds weekly check-ins and sends out transparent updates about decisions, timelines, and expectations.

2. Recognize and Celebrate Staff Contributions

- Public and private recognition shows that leadership values effort and impact.
- *Example:* Monthly "Staff Shout-Outs" highlight teacher accomplishments in newsletters and meetings.

3. Involve Staff in Decision-Making

- Empowering teachers with a voice boosts ownership and reduces resentment.
- *Example:* The principal forms teacher advisory teams to give input on school schedules, policies, and PD planning.

4. Provide Opportunities for Professional Growth

- Offering relevant, choice-based learning shows investment in staff success.
- *Example:* Teachers choose from a menu of PD workshops that align with their interests and classroom needs.

5. Offer Flexibility and Support When Possible

- Small acts of flexibility can reduce burnout and boost morale.
- *Example:* The leader creates a rotating coverage schedule to allow teachers planning time or a mental health break.

6. Address Conflict and Toxicity Directly

- Ignoring negative behaviors harms morale; leaders must address it constructively.
- *Example:* The principal meets privately with staff involved in ongoing conflict and facilitates solution-focused mediation.

7. Build Community Through Team-Building Activities

- Positive shared experiences strengthen relationships and trust.
- *Example:* Staff participate in a "Wellness Wednesday" challenge or a collaborative team-building event during in-service days.

8. Model Positivity and Presence

- A leader's tone and presence set the emotional tone for the building.
- *Example:* The principal makes a point to visit classrooms, greet staff by name, and maintain an approachable demeanor even during high-stress periods.

Essential Questions #4 Climate & Cultural Leadership

How can a school leader foster a school environment that supports a rigorous curriculum and high student expectations?

A school leader can foster an environment that supports a rigorous curriculum and high student expectations by setting a clear vision for academic excellence and ensuring that all staff understand and commit to that vision. This begins with aligning curriculum, instruction, and assessment to rigorous state standards and ensuring that teaching practices challenge students to think critically, solve problems, and apply knowledge in meaningful ways.

The leader should provide ongoing professional development that helps teachers implement high-impact instructional strategies and differentiate instruction without lowering expectations. It is also essential to create a culture where every student is believed capable of success, regardless of background or ability. This means using data to identify and close achievement gaps, promoting equity in access to advanced coursework, and celebrating growth not just proficiency.

The principal should model high expectations by consistently reinforcing the importance of quality instruction and academic integrity during classroom walkthroughs, coaching sessions, and faculty meetings. In addition, fostering strong student-teacher relationships helps build a learning environment where students feel safe to take academic risks and persist through challenges. Finally, involving families and the broader school community in promoting academic goals reinforces a shared commitment to excellence. Through these combined efforts, the leader helps create a school culture where rigor is the norm and student success is a collective responsibility.

Outline

1. Establish a Clear Vision for Academic Excellence

- A strong vision communicates the belief that all students can achieve at high levels.
- *Example:* The principal shares a schoolwide motto: "Every student, every day, without exception," and ties all instructional goals to that message.

2. Align Curriculum to Standards and Rigor

- Ensure the curriculum is standards-based and reflects appropriate cognitive demand.
- *Example:* The leadership team leads teachers through curriculum audits to align tasks with state standards and rigor levels.

3. Provide High-Quality Professional Development

- Equip teachers with strategies to challenge students and differentiate instruction.
- *Example:* Teachers participate in PD on Depth of Knowledge (DOK) questioning and scaffolding strategies for diverse learners.

4. Monitor Instruction and Provide Feedback

- Frequent classroom walkthroughs help ensure instructional consistency and rigor.
- *Example:* The principal uses a walkthrough tool to check for evidence of critical thinking tasks and provides timely, actionable feedback.

5. Use Data to Inform and Adjust Instruction

- Data-driven decisions support targeted interventions and enrichment.
- *Example:* Teachers use common assessments to identify students who need reteaching or extension activities.

6. Celebrate Academic Growth and Effort

- Recognizing achievement motivates students to meet and exceed expectations.
- *Example:* The school holds quarterly academic award ceremonies and spotlights student growth—not just final outcomes.

7. Set High Expectations Through Consistent Messaging and Modeling

- Leaders set the tone by reinforcing high standards for all stakeholders.
- *Example:* The principal shares examples of rigorous student work in faculty meetings and newsletters to elevate instructional expectations.

8. Create Systems of Support for Struggling Learners

- Rigor is accessible when students receive the support they need to succeed.
- *Example:* The school implements tiered interventions, tutoring, and academic mentoring to ensure no student falls through the cracks.

What plans and strategies can be implemented to ensure equitable treatment of students and/or staff?

To ensure equitable treatment of students and staff, school leaders must implement intentional plans and strategies that address both systemic barriers and daily practices. First, leaders should begin with a comprehensive equity audit to analyze data on student achievement, discipline, teacher placement, and access to programs. This helps identify patterns of disparity among subgroups, such as students of color, English language learners, students with disabilities, or economically disadvantaged populations. Once gaps are identified, the leader can work with staff to develop an Equity Action Plan with measurable goals, timelines, and accountability structures.

Key strategies include providing ongoing professional development focused on cultural responsiveness, implicit bias, and inclusive practices so that staff can reflect on their own mindsets and instructional decisions. Leaders should also review and revise discipline policies to ensure they are restorative rather than punitive and that they are applied fairly across student groups. Creating student support systems such as mentoring, peer mediation, and multilingual counseling helps address individual needs and build a more inclusive climate.

For staff, equitable treatment means ensuring fair workload distribution, equal access to leadership opportunities, and transparent evaluation processes. Leaders should also cultivate a culture of open communication and psychological safety, where staff and students feel empowered to report concerns without fear of retaliation. Most importantly, equity work must be ongoing, not a one-time training or policy change, but a daily commitment to treating everyone with fairness, dignity, and respect.

Outline

1. Conduct Equity Audits to Identify Gaps
- Assess disparities in discipline, achievement, hiring, and access to resources.
- *Example:* The school reviews data disaggregated by race, gender, language status, and disability to uncover patterns of inequity.

2. Develop and Enforce Clear Equity-Focused Policies
- Policies should explicitly protect and support all groups and guide consistent, fair practices.
- *Example:* The school implements a restorative discipline policy that replaces punitive suspensions with conflict resolution practices.

3. Provide Equity-Centered Professional Development
- Ongoing training helps staff recognize bias and implement inclusive practices.
- *Example:* Teachers participate in sessions on anti-bias education, trauma-informed teaching, and inclusive curriculum design.

4. Ensure Diverse Representation in Staffing and Leadership

- Representation matters for students and improves cultural responsiveness in the school community.
- *Example:* Hiring committees are trained to avoid bias and prioritize qualified candidates from diverse backgrounds.

5. Promote Student Voice and Choice

- Students thrive when their identities, cultures, and perspectives are honored.
- *Example:* A student equity council meets monthly to advise school leadership and propose inclusive initiatives.

6. Provide Targeted Academic and Social Supports

- Equitable treatment includes differentiated support to ensure all students succeed.
- *Example:* Multilingual learners receive small group instruction, while students with IEPs are given access to co-teaching and accommodations.

7. Create Safe, Inclusive School Environments

- Equity requires spaces where every student and staff member feel valued and respected.
- *Example:* The school designates gender-neutral restrooms, adopts anti-discrimination language in the handbook, and trains staff in inclusive classroom practices.

8. Engage Families and Communities as Equity Partners

- Inclusive family engagement helps ensure that policies reflect the values of the community.
- *Example:* The principal hosts multilingual family nights and surveys families about school culture and inclusion efforts.

What steps can a school leader take to change negative assumptions that affect teaching and learning?

To change negative assumptions that affect teaching and learning, a school leader must take intentional steps to shift mindsets, build awareness, and create a culture rooted in high expectations and equity. The first step is to identify the presence of deficit thinking such as beliefs that certain students "can't learn" because of their background, language, behavior, or home life through observation, dialogue, and data analysis. Once these patterns are recognized, the leader should create safe spaces for staff to reflect on their beliefs and biases, such as during professional learning communities, book studies, or equity-focused workshops.

Next, the leader must model asset-based thinking, consistently reinforcing the idea that every student brings strengths, experiences, and potential to the classroom. This includes highlighting success stories, elevating student voice, and sharing evidence of growth and resilience across diverse groups of learners. Additionally, leaders can facilitate collaborative data analysis, helping teachers look beyond surface-level assumptions and instead use evidence to inform instructional decisions.

Another critical step is to align policies and practices with high expectations, ensuring that curriculum, grading, interventions, and discipline systems do not unintentionally reinforce bias or lower the bar for certain students. Finally, school leaders should recognize and celebrate inclusive teaching practices, promote teacher collaboration, and create conditions for continuous reflection and improvement. By shifting the culture from judgment to curiosity, and from blame to belief, school leaders can transform harmful assumptions into a collective commitment to equity and excellence.

<u>Outline</u>

1. Acknowledge and Surface Harmful Beliefs

- Leaders must recognize that negative assumptions exist and create space to name them.
- *Example:* The principal facilitates staff discussions around common phrases like "these kids can't handle rigorous work" to raise awareness and disrupt deficit thinking.

2. Use Data to Challenge Misconceptions

- Share student performance, growth, and engagement data to replace bias with evidence.
- *Example:* The school highlights year-over-year progress for English learners and students with IEPs to reframe perceptions of their capabilities.

3. Model Asset-Based Language and Behavior

- Leaders set the tone by consistently focusing on strengths, potential, and possibilities.
- *Example:* The principal reframes concerns in meetings by asking, "What strengths does this student bring, and how can we build on them?"

4. Provide Professional Development on Bias and Equity

- Ongoing training helps staff confront unconscious bias and adopt inclusive mindsets.
- *Example:* Teachers attend a series on culturally responsive teaching and reflect on how personal beliefs may impact expectations.

5. Showcase Student Success Stories

- Highlighting examples of excellence helps shift the collective mindset.
- *Example:* The school newsletter features student achievements from diverse backgrounds to reinforce a belief in every child's potential.

6. Engage Students and Families as Experts

- Listening to those directly impacted builds empathy and changes perspective.
- *Example:* Students share their learning journeys in town halls, while families provide input on how the school can better support their children.

7. Examine and Change Systems That Reinforce Bias

- Structural changes are often required to support belief changes.
- *Example:* The school eliminates tracked classes and creates inclusive grouping practices to ensure equal access to rigorous instruction.

8. Celebrate a Culture of High Expectations

- Cultivating a school culture grounded in high standards reinforces the idea that all students can succeed.
- *Example:* Every classroom displays affirmations like "We believe in your greatness" and celebrates effort alongside achievement.

.

How do collaborative structures help promote shared responsibility and accountability?

Collaborative structures help promote shared responsibility and accountability by creating systems in which educators work together toward common goals, rather than in isolation. When teachers and staff regularly meet in professional learning communities (PLCs), grade-level teams, or vertical content groups, they engage in joint planning, data analysis, and reflective discussions that deepen their ownership of both student outcomes and instructional practices. These structures encourage transparency, as teachers share successes, challenges, and strategies, which fosters a culture of mutual support and constructive feedback.

Through collaboration, educators begin to see student achievement as a collective responsibility, not just the result of one classroom, but of coordinated efforts across the school. For example, if formative data shows that students across multiple classes are struggling with inference in reading, the team can co-develop targeted strategies, monitor progress, and adjust instruction together. This shared problem-solving approach not only leads to better results, but also builds accountability, because every team member has a clear role in achieving the goal.

School leaders reinforce this by setting clear expectations, providing time and structures for collaboration, and recognizing team contributions. Through this approach, collaborative frameworks shift school culture from individual autonomy to a climate characterized by shared commitment, professional interdependence, and collective responsibility for student achievement.

<u>Outline</u>

Encourage Collective Ownership of Student Success

- When teams work together, student outcomes become a shared priority not an individual burden.
- *Example:* Grade-level PLCs analyze data together, identifying students who need support and co-developing interventions.

2. Foster a Culture of Transparency and Reflection

- Collaboration invites open discussion about strengths, challenges, and next steps.
- *Example:* During data team meetings, teachers share classroom results and discuss instructional adjustments in a nonjudgmental setting.

3. Align Instructional Practices and Expectations

- Collaborative structures help standardize high-quality teaching practices across classrooms.
- *Example:* Departments co-plan units to ensure consistency in rigor, pacing, and assessment, supporting equity in instruction.

4. Provide Built-In Accountability Through Peer Support

- Teams help hold one another accountable for commitments and progress.
- *Example:* Instructional teams set shared goals and check in weekly to review progress, creating a natural structure for accountability.

5. Strengthen Professional Learning Through Shared Expertise

- Teachers learn from one another, promoting ongoing professional growth.
- *Example:* A literacy coach leads a lesson study cycle, where teachers observe peers and reflect together to improve practice.

6. Promote Trust and Team Cohesion

- Regular collaboration builds relationships, reduces isolation, and supports a unified school culture.
- *Example:* Cross-grade teams meet monthly to align priorities and celebrate progress, fostering a sense of community.

7. Empower Staff to Influence School Improvement

- Shared structures give staff voice and leadership roles in driving schoolwide change.
- *Example:* A school improvement committee includes teachers from each department who co-create and monitor action plans.

Essential Questions #8 Climate & Cultural Leadership

What are some practices to ensure that student misconduct is addressed in a fair manner?

To ensure that student misconduct is addressed in a fair and equitable manner, school leaders must implement practices that are consistent, transparent, and culturally responsive, while also focusing on restorative approaches that promote student growth and accountability.

First, it is essential to have a clearly defined and well-communicated code of conduct that outlines expectations and consequences. This ensures that all students, families, and staff understand the behavioral guidelines and that rules are applied consistently. However, fairness also requires recognizing that a one-size-fits-all approach may not address the root causes of behavior. Therefore, leaders should train staff in restorative practices, such as peer mediation, restorative circles, and conflict resolution strategies that give students a voice, promote accountability, and repair harm rather than simply punishing infractions.

Another important practice is to analyze disaggregated discipline data regularly to identify patterns of disproportionality such as overrepresentation of students of color or students with disabilities in suspensions or referrals and take corrective action. Leaders should also ensure that discipline decisions are based on clear evidence, follow due process, and consider contextual factors, such as trauma, mental health, or cultural misunderstandings. Collaborating with counselors, social workers, and families helps provide support systems that address the underlying needs behind misconduct.

<u>Outline</u>

1. Establish Clear, Consistent Expectations and Consequences

- A shared behavior framework ensures that all students understand the rules and potential consequences.
- *Example:* The school uses a consistent behavior matrix posted in all classrooms outlining what respect, responsibility, and safety look like.

2. Use Restorative Practices to Promote Accountability and Repair

- Restorative approaches allow students to take ownership and rebuild relationships.
- *Example:* After a conflict, students participate in a restorative circle to discuss the harm caused and agree on steps to make things right.

3. Ensure Consequences Are Proportionate and Educational

- Discipline should be corrective, not punitive, and tailored to the behavior and context.
- *Example:* A student caught cheating completes a reflection activity and participates in a lesson on academic integrity.

4. Avoid Disproportionate Discipline Through Data Monitoring

- Regularly review disciplined data for patterns by race, gender, language status, or disability.
- *Example:* The leadership team notices a trend of higher suspensions among MLL students and revises protocols to reduce bias.

5. Involve Multiple Perspectives Before Making Disciplinary Decisions

- Gathering full context helps ensure fairness in consequences.
- *Example:* Before assigning a suspension, the principal meets with the student, teacher, and parent to hear each side and explore alternatives.

6. Train Staff on Implicit Bias and Culturally Responsive Discipline

- Professional development equips staff to respond fairly and equitably to misconduct.
- *Example:* Teachers engage in training on de-escalation and cultural awareness to reduce unnecessary referrals.

7. Communicate Discipline Policies Transparently with Families

- Clear, accessible communication builds trust and accountability.
- *Example:* The school handbook is available in multiple languages and reviewed at family orientations.

8. Provide Support Systems for Students with Repeated Infractions

- Chronic behavior issues should trigger intervention, not exclusion.
- *Example:* A student with ongoing disruptions is connected to a behavior intervention plan and a mentor check-in program.

What are culturally relevant curriculum and instructional strategies?

Culturally relevant curriculum and instructional strategies are teaching approaches that affirm students' cultural backgrounds, languages, identities, and lived experiences as assets, not barriers to learning. These practices help students see themselves reflected in what they learn, feel valued in the classroom, and stay engaged in meaningful ways.

A culturally relevant curriculum includes materials, topics, and examples that represent a wide range of cultures, histories, and perspectives, especially those that are traditionally underrepresented. For example, instead of only teaching classic literature from one cultural lens, a culturally relevant curriculum might include novels, articles, and primary sources from diverse authors that connect to students' backgrounds and real-world experiences.

Culturally relevant instructional strategies involve how the material is taught. This includes using student-centered learning, incorporating collaborative group work, encouraging student voice and choice, and connecting academic content to students' communities and current events. For instance, a math teacher might relate proportional reasoning to local shopping or family budgeting, while a science teacher might highlight contributions of scientists from various cultures.

At the core, culturally relevant teaching promotes academic rigor, cultural competence, and critical consciousness. It not only helps students succeed academically but also encourages them to think critically about the world around them and their role within it. When students feel their identities are respected and represented, they are more likely to engage deeply and take ownership of their learning.

Outline

1. Center on Students' Cultural Backgrounds in the Curriculum

- Instruction reflects students' identities, languages, and lived experiences.
- *Example:* A history teacher includes primary sources from multiple cultural perspectives when teaching about American revolutions.

2. Use Instructional Materials That Reflect Student Diversity

- Texts, media, and examples should affirm students' cultures and challenge stereotypes.
- *Example:* An elementary classroom library includes books with characters from various racial, linguistic, and family backgrounds.

3. Make Learning Socially and Politically Conscious

- Lessons connect content to real-world issues that matter in students' communities.
- *Example:* In a writing unit, students research and write persuasive letters on local topics such as food insecurity or environmental justice.

4. Foster a Classroom Culture of Respect and Inclusion

- The environment promotes student voice, identity, and collaboration.
- *Example:* Teachers establish discussion norms that honor multiple perspectives and encourage students to share personal connections.

5. **Incorporate Students' Language and Communication Styles**
   - Teachers value and incorporate multilingualism, dialects, and nontraditional forms of expression.
   - *Example:* A teacher allows bilingual students to draft essays in their home language before translating them into English.

6. **Use Differentiated and Student-Centered Instruction**
   - Lessons are tailored to meet diverse learning needs, strengths, and preferences.
   - *Example:* A math teacher uses flexible grouping and culturally relevant real-life problems to engage students in meaningful learning.

7. **Build Relationships and Know Your Students**
   - Culturally relevant teaching starts with understanding students as individuals.
   - *Example:* A teacher incorporates students' family traditions and interests into project-based learning opportunities.

8. **Challenge Biases and Promote Critical Thinking**
   - Instruction helps students analyze systems of power and advocate for equity.
   - *Example:* A middle school class studies bias in media coverage and creates public service announcements to counter misinformation.

Essential Questions #10 Climate & Cultural Leadership

How can a school leader ensure that students have equitable access to effective teachers and learning opportunities?

A school leader can ensure that students have equitable access to effective teachers and learning opportunities by taking intentional, data-informed actions that address both staffing practices and instructional systems.

First, leaders must examine teacher placement across grade levels and student subgroups to avoid patterns where the most experienced or highly effective teachers are concentrated in advanced classes or less diverse classrooms. By strategically assigning strong teachers to support struggling students such as inclusive classrooms, ESL programs, or entry-level courses, leaders help close opportunity gaps. Additionally, leaders should ensure that all teachers have access to ongoing professional development focused on culturally responsive teaching, differentiation, and high-impact strategies so that instruction is strong across the board.

Second, school leaders need to review student access to rigorous courses and enrichment opportunities. This includes identifying and addressing barriers to honors, gifted, or STEM programs for students from underrepresented groups. Leaders can develop more inclusive criteria for advanced coursework, offer bridge or support programs, and closely monitor enrollment trends by race, language status, and special education needs.

Third, ensuring equitable access also involves providing support tailored to student needs, such as academic interventions, co-curricular activities, mentoring programs, and language services. Leaders should regularly review data such as test scores, attendance, and classroom engagement to identify gaps and respond proactively with additional resources.

Finally, equity must be embedded in the school's culture and expectations. Leaders should communicate a belief in every student's potential, foster high expectations for all learners, and create an environment where every student, regardless of background, has the tools and opportunities to succeed. By doing so, school leaders make equity not just a policy but a daily, lived practice.

Outline

1. Use Data to Identify and Address Inequities in Teacher Assignment

- Ensure that all students, especially those in historically underserved groups, have access to skilled and experienced teachers.
- *Example:* The principal reviews student demographics by classroom and ensures that students with the greatest academic needs are not disproportionately assigned to novice teachers.

2. Support and Develop All Teachers to Be Effective

- Ongoing coaching and PD help ensure that every classroom provides high-quality instruction.
- *Example:* Instructional coaches provide targeted support to teachers based on student data and walkthrough observations.

3. Equitable Scheduling Practices

- Scheduling decisions must avoid tracking and ensure that students have equal access to advanced coursework and interventions.
- *Example:* The school redesigns the master schedule so that multilingual learners can access core classes and electives without being pulled out during instruction.

4. Diversify and Strengthen the Teacher Workforce

- Hiring practices should prioritize cultural responsiveness and representation.
- *Example:* The school recruits teachers from diverse backgrounds and screens candidates for commitment to equity and inclusive instruction.

5. Expand Access to Enrichment and Advanced Programs

- Remove barriers to gifted, honors, and extracurricular opportunities.
- *Example:* The principal revises the gifted eligibility criteria to include multiple measures, such as portfolios and teacher recommendations.

6. Provide Targeted Academic and Social-Emotional Supports

- Equity requires differentiated support to ensure all students can thrive.
- *Example:* The school offers tutoring, mentoring, and SEL groups for students who are at risk of falling behind.

7. Engage Families and Communities in Access Planning

- Family input helps leaders understand barriers and co-create solutions.
- *Example:* A multilingual parent advisory group provides feedback on access to services and suggests improvements to outreach efforts.

8. Monitor and Adjust Equity Goals Regularly

- Continual review ensures accountability and improvement.
- *Example:* The leadership team tracks student participation in AP courses, intervention programs, and teacher access, and uses the data to refine staffing and resource allocation.

What are strategies that can be used to alter institutional biases?

To alter institutional biases, school leaders must take intentional and strategic action to transform systems, policies, and mindsets that contribute to inequity. One of the first steps is conducting an equity audit to examine data such as student achievement, discipline, access to advanced courses, and teacher assignments, disaggregated by race, language, gender, ability, and socioeconomic status. This helps identify patterns of exclusion or underrepresentation.

Leaders should then review and revise school policies such as grading, discipline, and placement criteria to ensure they are fair and inclusive. For example, replacing zero-tolerance discipline policies with restorative practices can reduce the disproportionate suspension of students of color. Providing ongoing professional development on implicit bias, cultural responsiveness, and equity literacy is also critical, allowing staff to reflect on their beliefs and instructional choices.

Additionally, leaders should work to diversify curriculum and teaching practices, ensuring students see themselves and their cultures reflected in the learning environment. Including student and family voice especially from marginalized communities in decision-making processes reinforces inclusivity and shared ownership of change. Setting equity goals with clear outcomes and accountability structures ensures that progress is monitored and sustained. Most importantly, school leaders must model equity-focused leadership by challenging deficit thinking, communicating high expectations for all students, and fostering a culture where every individual is valued. These strategies, when combined, help shift institutional norms and promote lasting change that benefits the entire school community.

<u>**Outline**</u>

1. Conduct an Equity Audit to Reveal Systemic Patterns

- Use data to uncover disparities in access, outcomes, discipline, and representation.
- *Example:* A school reviews student achievement, referral rates, and course enrollment by race, language status, and IEP status to identify disproportionality.

2. Review and Revise Policies and Procedures Through an Equity Lens

- Institutional bias often hides in outdated or one-size-fits-all policies.
- *Example:* The school revises its dress code and discipline policies to eliminate language that disproportionately impacts specific student groups.

3. Provide Ongoing Anti-Bias and Equity Training for All Staff

- Shifting mindsets requires deep and continuous professional learning.
- *Example:* Staff engage in workshops on implicit bias, structural racism, and culturally responsive practices throughout the year.

4. Diversify Curriculum, Instruction, and Materials

- Ensure that what students learn reflects multiple perspectives and identities.
- *Example:* Teachers audit classroom texts to include diverse authors, cultures, and voices, especially in core subjects like ELA and social studies.

5. Increase Diversity in Hiring and Leadership Roles

- Representation challenges institutional bias and supports inclusive decision-making.
- *Example:* The school broadens its recruitment network to attract qualified candidates from underrepresented communities.

6. Include Student and Family Voices in School Decision-Making

- Inclusion shifts power and reveals how policies affect people directly.
- *Example:* The principal creates equity focus groups made up of students and families to review school policies and practices.

7. Use Disaggregated Data to Drive Continuous Improvement

- Equity-focused data analysis helps track progress and maintain accountability.
- *Example:* The leadership team tracks the impact of new policies on student groups and adjusts based on ongoing feedback and outcomes.

8. Encourage Reflective Leadership and Courageous Conversations

- Leaders must be willing to question traditions and practices that no longer serve all students.
- *Example:* The principal models vulnerability by sharing how their own assumptions have changed and invites staff into open dialogue about equity.

Essential Questions #12 Climate & Cultural

How can an instructional leader act with cultural competence and responsiveness?

An instructional leader can act with cultural competence and responsiveness by intentionally recognizing, respecting, and leveraging the diverse backgrounds, identities, and experiences of students, staff, and families in all aspects of school leadership. This begins with cultivating an awareness of one's own biases and being open to learning about the cultures and communities represented within the school. A culturally competent leader actively listens to different perspectives, creates space for dialogue, and ensures that students' languages, histories, and traditions are reflected in the curriculum, school events, and daily interactions.

In practice, this may involve supporting teachers in designing culturally relevant instruction, selecting inclusive materials, and incorporating student voice into lesson planning. It also includes addressing inequities such as disproportionate discipline or limited access to advanced coursework by regularly analyzing disaggregated data and taking steps to remove barriers that prevent full participation. A culturally responsive leader builds trusting relationships with families by offering translation services, flexible meeting times, and opportunities for shared decision-making.

Moreover, they engage staff in ongoing professional development on equity, implicit bias, and inclusive practices, promoting a school climate where every student feels seen, valued, and empowered. By embedding cultural responsiveness into leadership decisions, instructional practices, and community partnerships, the leader creates an environment where academic excellence and belonging go hand in hand.

Outline

1. Build Deep Understanding of the School Community's Cultures

- Leaders must actively learn about the backgrounds, values, and experiences of the students and families they serve.
- *Example:* The principal attends community events, visits local cultural centers, and surveys families about their traditions and communication preferences.

2. Promote Inclusive and Culturally Relevant Curriculum

- Ensure instructional materials reflect and affirm students' identities.
- *Example:* The leader works with department heads to diversify literature selections and include multiple perspectives in history instruction.

3. Provide Professional Development on Cultural Competence

- Equip teachers with tools to recognize bias, build inclusive classrooms, and teach with cultural awareness.
- *Example:* Staff engage in equity-focused PD, including training on implicit bias, trauma-informed practices, and multilingual learner support.

4. Model Respectful and Inclusive Communication

- Language matters leaders must demonstrate inclusive, bias-free interactions.
- *Example:* The principal consistently uses students' preferred names and pronouns and ensures that translated communication is available for families.

5. Support Culturally Responsive Pedagogy in Classrooms

- Instruction should connect to students' cultural knowledge and life experiences.
- *Example:* The instructional leader observes and coach teachers on practices such as using real-world examples from students' communities or allowing multiple modes of expression.

6. Create Equitable Access to High-Quality Instruction and Resources

- Responsiveness includes addressing systemic inequities in opportunity.
- *Example:* The leader ensures all students, regardless of language ability or background, have access to advanced coursework and well-trained teachers.

7. Engage Families as Partners in Learning

- Family involvement should honor and reflect cultural values and practices.
- *Example:* The school hosts multilingual family nights and invites community leaders to share insights on how best to support students at home and in school.

8. Continuously Reflect on Leadership Practices and Bias

- Culturally competent leaders engage in ongoing self-reflection and adjust their approach as needed.
- *Example:* The principal journals after difficult decisions, seeks feedback from diverse staff members, and reviews data with an equity lens.

What are strategies for building a safe, caring, and healthy school environment that meets the needs of students?

To build a safe, caring, and healthy school environment that meets the academic, social, emotional, and physical needs of students, school leaders must implement strategies that are proactive, inclusive, and student-centered. One key approach is to establish a clear, schoolwide vision that prioritizes student well-being and safety, supported by consistent routines, expectations, and relationship-building practices. Leaders can implement positive behavior support (PBIS), peer mediation programs, and restorative practices to promote a respectful and accountable school climate. Additionally, ensuring access to counseling, mental health services, and crisis intervention is essential for supporting students dealing with trauma, anxiety, or other emotional challenges.

A safe school also addresses physical needs by coordinating with local agencies to provide services such as vision screenings, dental care, hygiene kits, and weekend food bags, especially for economically disadvantaged students. Social-emotional learning (SEL) programs should be embedded in daily instruction to teach students self-awareness, empathy, conflict resolution, and responsible decision-making. Leaders can further promote a caring culture by ensuring that each student is known and connected to at least one trusted adult, such as through advisory periods or mentorship programs. Engaging families and community partners in supporting student development and providing inclusive extracurricular activities helps ensure that every student feels welcomed and valued. By prioritizing safety, trust, and access to resources, school leaders create an environment where students can thrive both personally and academically.

Outline

1. Establish Clear Expectations for Behavior and Relationships

- A consistent, positive behavior framework promotes respect and safety.
- *Example:* The school implements a schoolwide PBIS system that reinforces kindness, responsibility, and safe choices through posters, lessons, and rewards.

2. Implement Social-Emotional Learning (SEL) Programs

- SEL helps students build skills for managing emotions, relationships, and decision-making.
- *Example:* Students participate in daily SEL lessons and morning meetings that focus on empathy, self-regulation, and conflict resolution.

3. Provide Access to Mental Health and Counseling Services

- Support systems are essential for students' emotional well-being.
- *Example:* The school hires a full-time counselor and partners with a local agency to provide therapy sessions on campus.

4. Foster Strong Relationships Between Staff and Students

- Students thrive when they feel seen, known, and supported by caring adults.
- *Example:* Teachers conduct student interest surveys and hold weekly check-ins with students who need extra emotional support.

5. Promote Health and Wellness Through Schoolwide Initiatives

- Physical well-being impacts learning, focus, and behavior.
- *Example:* The school provides healthy meal options, builds movement breaks into the day, and teaches health education across grade levels.

6. Create Safe, Inclusive Physical and Emotional Spaces

- Students must feel physically and emotionally secure to engage in learning.
- *Example:* The school includes sensory spaces, calm-down corners, and anti-bullying procedures that empower students to report concerns safely.

7. Engage Families as Partners in Safety and Wellness

- Family collaboration supports consistency between home and school.
- *Example:* The school offers parenting workshops on digital safety, stress management, and behavior strategies.

8. Use Trauma-Informed Practices

- Acknowledge and respond to the impact of trauma on student behavior and learning.
- *Example:* Teachers use calm, predictable routines and restorative language to de-escalate conflicts rather than relying solely on punishment.

Essential Questions #14 Climate & Cultural

What resources are available to meet the range of learning needs of students and promote student engagement?

To meet the diverse learning needs of students and promote engagement, schools can utilize a variety of resources and support systems that address academic, social-emotional, and physical development. One essential resource is differentiated instructional materials, such as leveled texts, graphic organizers, and adaptive technology tools that allow students to access content at their readiness level. Intervention programs such as reading and math support, small group instruction, and individualized tutoring, help close learning gaps and ensure struggling students receive targeted help.

Technology also plays a key role, with tools like learning management systems, interactive apps, and virtual simulations promoting personalized and engaging learning experiences. Additionally, schools can use formative assessment platforms to monitor student progress and adjust instruction in real time. For students with specific needs, IEPs and 504 plans ensure accommodations and modifications are in place, while English learners benefit from language support services, such as ESL instruction or bilingual aides.

Beyond academics, schools should also provide counseling services, SEL programs, and mentoring to support emotional well-being and student motivation. Enrichment programs like STEM clubs, arts, sports, and leadership opportunities increase engagement by connecting learning to students' interests and strengths. Finally, collaboration with community agencies can extend access to resources such as healthcare, mental health services, and after-school programs. By combining instructional tools, targeted support, and enrichment opportunities, school leaders can create an environment where every student is engaged and empowered to succeed.

Outline

. Differentiated Instructional Materials

- Resources that support multiple learning levels, modalities, and interests.
- *Example:* Leveled readers, choice boards, and adaptive digital learning platforms like I-Ready or Newsela that adjust to student ability.

2. Specialized Support Staff and Services

- Personnel who address academic, linguistic, and social-emotional needs.
- *Example:* Interventionists, ESL teachers, special education staff, paraprofessionals, and school counselors.

3. Technology Tools for Personalization and Accessibility

- Digital platforms that promote engagement, scaffold instruction, and provide accommodation.
- *Example:* Tools like Google Read & Write, Flipgrid, and Khan Academy support accessibility and personalized learning paths.

4. Universal Design for Learning (UDL) Frameworks

- A proactive planning approach that builds in multiple means of representation, action, and expression.
- *Example:* A science lesson includes video, hands-on experiments, and a written lab report or verbal explanation option.

5. Social-Emotional Learning (SEL) Curricula

- Programs that support emotional intelligence, behavior regulation, and peer collaboration.
- *Example:* Programs like Second Step or RULER help students build self-awareness and interpersonal skills, improving focus and classroom behavior.

6. Culturally Relevant and Responsive Materials

- Instructional resources that reflect students' cultural identities and experiences.
- *Example:* Teachers use books, case studies, and historical perspectives that include diverse voices and narratives.

7. Academic Enrichment and Acceleration Programs

- Opportunities for advanced learners to be challenged beyond grade-level expectations.
- *Example:* STEM clubs, robotics competitions, AP courses, and dual enrollment options provide challenge and extend learning.

8. Family and Community Engagement Resources

- Tools that involve families as partners and tap into community expertise.
- *Example:* Bilingual communication apps, parent resource centers, and guest speakers from local organizations enhance relevance and connection.

9. Professional Development for Teachers

- Ongoing training ensures staff are equipped to meet diverse needs.
- *Example:* Workshops on trauma-informed practices, differentiated instruction, and strategies for engaging reluctant learners.

Climate & Cultural Leadership Quiz

1. **A new assistant principal observes that discipline referrals disproportionately involve male students of color. What is the most appropriate next step for the principal?**
   A. Remind teachers to enforce rules equally
   B. Conduct equity-focused classroom walkthroughs and review referral data trends with staff
   C. Refer all disciplinary decisions to the assistant principal
   D. Develop a zero-tolerance policy for misbehavior

2. **During a faculty meeting, a teacher voices concerns that staff morale is low and communication from administration feels unclear. What should the principal do first?**
   A. Ask the teacher to address the issue in writing
   B. Defend current communication methods
   C. Invite staff input through a climate survey and small group discussions
   D. Ignore the comment to maintain authority

3. **A school has recently experienced a spike in absenteeism. Which of the following actions should the principal take first to address school culture?**
   A. Implement detention for all unexcused absences
   B. Host a schoolwide assembly on attendance expectations
   C. Analyze absenteeism data to identify patterns and collaborate with staff to address root causes
   D. Ask teachers to call families each morning

4. **Several students report feeling unsafe in the hallways during class transitions. What should the principal do first?**
   A. Suspend students who cause hallway disruptions
   B. Increase security presence
   C. Shorten passing periods
   D. Assign additional staff to hallway duty and collect feedback from Students

5. **The school climate survey reveals that students feel their voices are not heard. Which of the following would be the most effective leadership response?**
   A. Ignore the survey and focus on academic priorities
   B. Start a student advisory council and integrate student feedback into decision-making
   C. Schedule a one-time student town hall
   D. Create stricter rules to reduce student complaints

6. **A teacher frequently uses sarcasm and negative language with students. Multiple parents and students have raised concerns. What is the best leadership response?**
   A. Document concerns and hold a private coaching conversation with the teacher
   B. Reassign the teacher to a different grade level
   C. Publicly confront the teacher during a staff meeting
   D. Ignore the complaints unless student performance drops

7. **The principal wants to improve the culture of learning and student motivation. Which strategy is most likely to foster a schoolwide culture of achievement?**
   A. Give weekly rewards to the highest-performing students only
   B. Display only honor roll students on bulletin boards
   C. Set high expectations for all students and recognize diverse types of achievement
   D. Tell teachers to "motivate" students more

8. **The principal learns that a group of staff members regularly exclude a new teacher from informal planning sessions. What is the most appropriate leadership action?**
   A. Do nothing, since planning is not required to be collaborative
   B. Meet with the staff and reinforce expectations for inclusive professional behavior
   C. Ask the new teacher to form their own planning group
   D. Reassign the new teacher to a different department

9. **After implementing a new restorative discipline program, teachers report confusion about the process. What should the principal do next?**
   A. Discontinue the program immediately
   B. Ask students to explain the process during class meetings
   C. Tell teachers to figure it out independently
   D. Offer follow-up professional development and clarify expectations

10. A parent complains that their child was bullied, and no one followed up. What is the best first step the principal should take?

A. Apologize and document the complaint

B. Investigate the situation immediately and review the school's bullying prevention protocols

C. Send the family the school handbook

D. Tell the parents to talk to the guidance counselor

11. A principal notices that some students feel disconnected and are not participating in school activities. What is the most appropriate first step to improve school climate?

A. Increase academic expectations in all subject areas

B. Create a student advisory council to elevate student voice

C. Send home behavior contracts for students not involved

D. Restrict extracurricular access to students with good grades only

12. A school leader wants to build a culture of trust and collaboration among staff. Which strategy is most effective?

A. Schedule more mandatory staff meetings to ensure alignment

B. Allow teachers to work independently without oversight

C. Create shared leadership opportunities and promote transparent communication

D. Focus only on formal evaluations to monitor performance

13. During a climate survey, students report feeling unsafe during unstructured times (e.g., hallway transitions). What should the leader do first?

A. Reduce the number of class transitions in the schedule

B. Add more visible adult supervision and review behavioral expectations

C. Install new lockers and signage throughout the school

D. Eliminate hallway transitions altogether

14. A teacher consistently uses sarcastic language that students say makes them uncomfortable. What is the principal's best response?

A. Do nothing, as the teacher is well-liked by parents

B. Publicly confront the teacher during a staff meeting

C. Meet privately, provide coaching on professional tone, and monitor improvement

D. Transfer the teacher to a different grade level

15. Staff feedback indicates inconsistent enforcement of school rules across classrooms. What action best supports a positive school culture?

A. Co-create consistent expectations with staff and provide PD on implementation

B. Encourage teachers to handle discipline as they see fit

C. Eliminate the rules that are difficult to enforce

D. Delegate rule enforcement to student leaders

16. A school has recently experienced community tension around issues of equity and inclusion. What should the school leader do to foster a safe and inclusive environment?

A. Avoid the topic to prevent further conflict

B. Invite community voices to a listening session and reaffirm the school's equity commitment

C. Post a general statement on the website but take no further action

D. Cancel future events that may trigger controversial conversations

17. New students often report difficulty adjusting to the school's culture. What is the best leadership action?

A. Require teachers to assign extra homework to new students

B. Place new students only in classes with the most experienced teachers

C. Encourage new students to participate in activities without support

D. Develop a peer mentorship program and orientation that emphasizes belonging

18. A school's mission promotes respect and inclusion, but the principal observes frequent hallway teasing and exclusion among students. What is the most effective next step?

A. Increase punitive consequences for negative behavior

B. Ignore minor behaviors that don't involve physical aggression

C. Launch a student-led initiative to promote kindness and peer respect

D. Require all students to sign a code of conduct agreement

19. How can a principal best recognize and celebrate staff efforts to build a positive school culture?

A. Privately thank staff but avoid public recognition to prevent jealousy

B. Host quarterly shout-outs during staff meetings tied to school values

C. Limit recognition to the most senior staff members

D. Leave recognition to the district's formal award process

20. The school climate survey reveals that students from marginalized groups feel less connected to adults in the building. What should the principal prioritize?

A. Reassign these students to new classrooms

B. Create intentional relationship-building opportunities between staff and students

C. Offer incentives for students who participate in activities

D. Focus on raising test scores before addressing relationships

Answer Key Climate & Cultural Leadership #1-10

Question Number	1	2	3	4	5	6	7	8	9	10
Correct Solution	B	C	C	D	B	A	C	B	D	B

Answer Key Climate & Cultural Leadership

Question Number	11	12	13	14	15	16	17	18	19	20
Correct Solution	B	C	B	C	A	B	D	C	B	B

Domain IV: Ethical Leadership

This domain focuses on the principal's role in modeling integrity, fairness, and professional norms in every aspect of school leadership. Ethical leadership involves making decisions that prioritize students' best interests, promoting equity and justice, and upholding transparency and accountability in all actions. By leading with honesty and consistency, principals build trust, strengthen credibility, and create a culture where ethical behavior guides both teaching and learning.

Ethical Leadership

Real-Life Scenario A: Ethical and legal behavior

At Elmwood Middle School, Principal Dr. Tanya Wallace was conducting a routine review of grading data when she noticed a concerning pattern: in several senior English classes, students with excessive absences had received high final grades with little supporting evidence in the gradebook. Upon further investigation, Dr. Wallace discovered that one veteran teacher, Mr. Raines, had been giving passing grades to students who had not submitted the required work, to keep them on track to graduate.

Although Mr. Raines believed he was acting in the students' best interest, his actions violated the school's grading policy, undermined academic integrity, and created inequity among students who had completed the work. Dr. Wallace understood the seriousness of the situation and took immediate, ethically sound action. She scheduled a private meeting with Mr. Raines to share the data, discuss her concerns, and review the district's grading guidelines. Mr. Raines admitted to the practice and explained that he felt pressure from families and counselors to "do whatever it takes" to help students graduate.

Dr. Wallace responded with firm yet fair leadership. While acknowledging Mr. Raines' desire to support students, she emphasized that such support must operate within ethical and legal boundaries. Granting unearned grades, she explained, not only undermines the efforts of students who complete their work but also fails to adequately prepare others for the demands of postsecondary education. She reminded Mr. Raines of the school's mission to promote equity, integrity, and accountability for all learners. As a corrective measure, she required him to complete a professional ethics refresher course and to revise his gradebook to reflect accurate student performance, offering students appropriate opportunities to complete missing work and legitimately improve their grades.

In addition to addressing the individual incident, Dr. Wallace took broader action to improve transparency and accountability among the staff. She clearly communicated the rationale behind her decisions in follow-up conversations with her leadership team and during a staff-wide professional development session, reinforcing the direct connection between grading integrity and student achievement.

To prevent similar issues in the future, she led a collaborative discussion focused on the dangers of deficit thinking and the importance of maintaining high expectations for all students, regardless of background or circumstance. She also facilitated a comprehensive review of the school's grading policies, clarified professional expectations, and promoted a shared understanding of ethical instructional practices. To ensure ongoing consistency, Dr. Wallace implemented a quarterly grade audit system to identify discrepancies early and uphold professional standards.

By acting decisively and modeling ethical leadership, Dr. Wallace not only addressed misconduct but also upheld fairness, protected student interests, and strengthened a culture of trust, integrity, and academic excellence.

Ethical Leadership

Real-Life Scenario B: Ethical values and beliefs (PSEL Standard 2)

At Northview Middle School, Principal Ms. Delaney Moore had just completed her third year as building leader. Though academic scores were improving and behavior incidents had declined, an anonymous staff climate survey revealed a lingering concern: some faculty felt there was a lack of transparency in hiring decisions, and certain student groups particularly English language learners and students with disabilities did not feel fully included in school activities or advanced academic programming.

Rather than becoming defensive, Ms. Moore viewed this as an opportunity for self-reflection and growth. She took time to review past decisions related to hiring, course enrollment trends, and student access to extracurriculars. What she found validated the concerns: most internal promotions had gone to the same small group of staff, and data showed that multilingual learners were underrepresented in enrichment and honors programs.

Recognizing the need to realign her leadership with the school's mission of equity and inclusion, Ms. Moore set two personal leadership goals: (1) increase equitable access to opportunities for both students and staff, and (2) model ethical, transparent decision-making in all school operations.

She began by revamping the staff hiring and promotion process, ensuring that postings were widely advertised and that a diverse interview panel was included in all candidate reviews. For students, she led the creation of a student access audit team composed of counselors, teachers, and family liaisons to examine enrollment in advanced courses, club participation, and student leadership roles. The team developed new, inclusive criteria for advanced placement and proactively reached out to underrepresented students.

In every staff meeting and leadership team conversation, Ms. Moore intentionally reinforced the importance of fairness, inclusion, and moral responsibility. She also facilitated reflection sessions for staff, encouraging teachers to examine their own assumptions about student ability and access. Her vulnerability in sharing her own growth and missteps created space for others to reflect as well.

Over time, the culture at Northview began to shift. Student enrollment in honors programs became more diverse, and staff reported increased confidence in the fairness of hiring and promotion processes. Through ethical self-reflection, equitable policy review, and moral leadership, Ms. Moore not only addressed institutional barriers but also strengthened trust, integrity, and shared responsibility across the school community.

Ethical Leadership

Real-Life Scenario # 3 B: Ethical values and beliefs (PSEL Standard 2)

At Westbrook High School, Principal Mr. Adrian Cole received a phone call from the district's athletic director notifying him that the starting quarterback on the varsity football team, Devin, had a failing grade in Algebra II but was still listed as eligible to play in Friday's playoff game. Upon checking the student information system, Mr. Cole discovered that the teacher had recently updated Devin's grade from a 58 to a 72 without any documented makeup work or reassessment submitted.

The situation presented a dilemma. The team's success had brought positive attention to the school, and several staff and parents were pressuring Mr. Cole to "let it go" in the interest of school spirit and community support. However, Mr. Cole recognized that allowing an unearned grade change to stand would be a violation of district grading policy, compromise academic integrity, and send the wrong message about the school's values.

Mr. Cole began by reviewing the district's athletic eligibility policy and confirmed that student-athletes must meet academic performance standards based on verified grades, not informal agreements. He then met privately with the Algebra II teacher, who admitted to inflating Devin's grade because of pressure from the coach and concern about "ruining the kid's future." Mr. Cole acknowledged the teacher's intent to help, but emphasized the importance of ethical grading practices, fairness to all students, and professional responsibility.

Mr. Cole required the teacher to revise the grade based on actual student performance and worked with the school counselor to offer Devin targeted academic support. He informed the coach and athletic director that Devin would be ineligible for the upcoming game and transparently communicated the reasoning with Devin's family. Although disappointed, they appreciated the school's willingness to support Devin academically rather than simply removing him from the team.

To prevent future conflicts, Mr. Cole initiated schoolwide training on academic integrity, grade transparency, and eligibility procedures, ensuring that all staff understood the importance of maintaining clear documentation and upholding ethical standards. He also created a process for peer review of grade changes that require administrative approval, adding a layer of oversight and consistency.

Though the football team lost the playoff game without its starting quarterback, the school community began to shift its focus from winning at all costs to upholding academic integrity and equity. Staff reported a renewed confidence in the fairness of grading policies, and students saw that ethical decisions are more important than temporary success. Mr. Cole's leadership demonstrated that ethical norms must guide every decision even in high-pressure situations solidifying a culture of trust, professionalism, and accountability at Westbrook High School.

In What Ways Do Current Laws, Regulations, Policies, and Procedures Impact Meeting Various Student Needs?

At Westbridge Middle School, a diverse urban public school, Principal Dr. Martinez began her first year by identifying a troubling trend: students with IEPs and English Language Learners (ELLs) were significantly underperforming in science and social studies, despite strong classroom behavior and participation. Concerns from families particularly Spanish-speaking parents were also increasing. Complaints centered on unfair grading, lack of communication, and confusion about accommodations.

To understand the root causes, Dr. Martinez led a comprehensive review of IEP implementation fidelity, 504 accommodation logs, and ELL student performance data. Her findings revealed that several teachers were unaware of the accommodation required under students' IEPs or 504 Plans. ELLs were being assessed using grade-level English assessments without linguistic scaffolds, violating their right to equitable access under ESSA. Additionally, FERPA violations were discovered that teachers had shared confidential information about students' disabilities during grade-level meetings.

Because disability status and IEP/504 information are part of a student's protected educational record, sharing that information with staff who do not have a legitimate educational interest is considered unauthorized disclosure. Grade-level meetings often include staff members who may not serve or interact with a particular student and therefore do not have a legal need to know. This lapse in confidentiality highlighted an urgent need for corrective leadership action.
Dr. Martinez began by delivering mandatory professional development sessions led by the district's special education and ELL compliance officers. These trainings clarified the distinctions between IEP services and 504 accommodations, reinforced FERPA protocols regarding confidentiality, and included Title IX training
with an emphasis on gender identity and harassment prevention.

She then collaborated with instruction coaches and department heads to revise common assessments, ensuring they included simplified language, visual supports, and bilingual glossaries for ELLs. She ensured that 504 and IEP testing accommodations such as extended time and small-group settings were consistently applied across classrooms. In addition, Dr. Martinez implemented co-teaching models in science and social studies to foster inclusive instruction.
To rebuild family trust, the school launched a monthly bilingual parent forum, with live translation provided for Spanish and Haitian-Creole-speaking families. Dr. Martinez ensured that all progress reports and IEP/504 documents were translated and sent home in families' preferred languages. She also introduced a FERPA-compliant consent form for all interpreters working with parents. These efforts led to a 40% increase in IEP meeting participation, signaling a renewed sense of trust and inclusion.

To sustain progress, Dr. Martinez established an Equity and Access Team composed of teachers, parents, and support staff. The team meets every six weeks to:

- Review student achievement data by subgroup
- Track teacher compliance logs related to accommodation delivery
- Conduct surveys with families and students about inclusion, classroom support, and access to services

As a result of Dr. Martinez's leadership, the school saw significant gains within six months:

- Science proficiency rates improved by 18%
- Students with IEPs had 25% fewer missing assignments

- Discipline referrals for students with disabilities dropped by 30%

Dr. Martinez's work at Westbridge Middle School serves as a powerful example of how school leaders must use laws not merely for compliance, but as tools for equity. By understanding and applying federal mandates such as IDEA, Section 504, ADA, ESSA, FERPA, and Title IX, she created systems that honored student rights, improved academic outcomes, and restored family engagement. This legally aligned, student-centered approach reflects the core of 21st-century instructional leadership.

Key Federal Laws and Definitions

1. **IDEA** – Ensures FAPE for students with disabilities via IEPs
2. **Section 504** – Accommodations for students with physical or mental impairments
3. **ADA** – Ensures equal access and facilities for students with disabilities
4. **Title IX** – Protects against sex-based discrimination
5. **ESSA** – Focuses on equitable achievement and accountability
6. **FERPA** – Safeguards student records and privacy

Outline

1. Ensure Equal Access to Education Through Federal Laws

- Laws protect students from discrimination and ensure access to a free, appropriate public education (FAPE).
- *Example:* The Individuals with Disabilities Education Act (IDEA) requires schools to provide IEP services tailored to students with disabilities.

2. Guide Services for English Language Learners (ELLs)

- Policies ensure multilingual learners receive equitable instruction and language support.
- *Example:* Under Title III of ESSA, schools must provide language development programs and monitor student progress in English acquisition.

3. Promote Equity Through Civil Rights Protections

- Regulations such as Title VI and Title IX prohibit discrimination based on race, color, national origin, or sex.
- *Example:* A school investigates reports of harassment and adjusts policies to ensure a safe, inclusive learning environment for all students.

4. Shape Discipline Policies to Protect Student Rights

- Laws require fair, non-discriminatory disciplinary procedures.
- *Example:* Students must be afforded due process before suspension, and schools must monitor for disparities in discipline practices.

5. Influence Data Use and Student Privacy Protections

- Regulations like FERPA safeguard student information and limit data sharing.
- *Example:* Schools must obtain parental consent before sharing identifiable academic or behavioral data with third parties.
-

6. Require Accommodations for Health and Access Needs

- Section 504 ensures students with medical or physical condition receive the necessary accommodation.
- *Example:* A student with diabetes is given access to snacks and nurse visits during class to manage their condition safely.

7. Shape Funding and Resource Allocation

- Funding laws impact what supports can be offered to students in high-need communities.
- *Example:* Title, I funding is used to provide additional intervention staff and instructional materials in schools with high poverty rates.

8. Inform Crisis Response and Safety Procedures

- School safety and emergency policies must align with local and federal regulations.
- *Example:* Mandated drills, threat assessments, and protocols are required to ensure physical safety for all students and staff.

9. Establish Protocols for Inclusive Enrollment and Participation

- Policies must ensure students are not excluded from programs due to disability, language, or socioeconomic status.
- *Example:* A school must allow a student with a mobility impairment to fully participate in field trips and extracurricular activities with proper support.

What are the laws and regulations regarding privacy and confidentiality of information?

Every school collects and stores information about students like grades, attendance, health records, behavior, and even family details. But this information isn't just casual data; it's protected by law.

Just like a doctor can't tell someone else about your medical history, teachers, principals, and school staff are legally responsible for keeping student information private. There are laws that clearly define who can see this information, how it can be shared, and when parents and students must give permission.

Imagine your personal diary private, sensitive, and meant for your eyes only. What if someone read it aloud to your class without asking you first? That would be a huge invasion of privacy.

Student records are like diaries. They include sensitive information, and only certain people (like parents, the students, or necessary school staff) are allowed to see them. Laws make sure that these "diaries" are not shared with people who shouldn't have access.

FERPA (Family Educational Rights and Privacy Act): gives parents (and students 18 and older the right to access and control education records. Schools cannot share personally identifiable information (like grades or addresses) without written permission unless in certain legal or safety situations.

IDEA (Individuals with Disabilities Education Act): requires confidentiality of records for students with disabilities and Protection of sensitive data like IEPs and evaluation results. These can only be shared with professionals who serve the student.

HIPAA (Health Insurance Portability and Accountability Act): usually doesn't apply in schools, but if a school runs a health clinic, this law protects students' medical records. In most cases, school health records are protected by FERPA instead.

PPRA (Protection of Pupil Rights Amendment): Requires parental consent before students participate in federally funded surveys about sensitive topics (like religion, family life, or mental health).

Many states have their own laws for student data protection, especially around mental health, counseling records, and child abuse reports.

Outline

1. Family Educational Rights and Privacy Act (FERPA)

- Federal law that protects the privacy of student education records.
- *Example:* Schools must obtain written parental consent before releasing a student's academic records to third parties, except under specific legal exceptions (e.g., to other school officials with a legitimate educational interest).

2. Individuals with Disabilities Education Act (IDEA)

- Protects the confidentiality of information in Individualized Education Programs (IEPs) and related services.
- *Example:* A teacher may access a student's IEP only if they are directly involved in implementing or supporting the student's services.

3. Section 504 of the Rehabilitation Act

- Requires schools to protect the privacy of students receiving accommodation under a 504 Plan.
- *Example:* A student's medical or psychological diagnosis should not be discussed publicly or shared beyond the staff who need to know.

4. Health Insurance Portability and Accountability Act (HIPAA) *(in specific school-based settings)*

- Applies primarily to health care providers but may intersect with school services like counseling or school-based clinics.
- *Example:* A school nurse working in partnership with a health agency must follow HIPAA when handling medical records that aren't part of the student's education file.

5. Protection of Pupil Rights Amendment (PPRA)

- Governs the administration of surveys, evaluations, or instructional materials funded by the U.S. Department of Education.
- *Example:* Parents must be notified and given the opportunity to opt their child out of surveys that collect sensitive information, such as political beliefs or family income.

6. State-Specific Privacy Laws and Policies

- Many states have additional laws that further define or restrict how student data can be shared or stored.
- *Example:* Some states prohibit schools from using biometric data or restrict third-party vendor access to student information without strict agreements.

7. Confidentiality in Counseling and Mental Health Services

- School counselors are bound by ethical standards and laws to keep student disclosures private, with exceptions for safety concerns.
- *Example:* A counselor may not share a student's personal issue with teachers unless the student consents unless there is a risk of harm to self or others.

8. Technology and Digital Data Security

- Schools must secure student data in digital platforms to comply with FERPA and state data protection rules.
- *Example:* Districts must ensure that online learning platforms meet privacy requirements and do not misuse student information.

9. Staff Responsibilities and Training

- School employees are legally responsible for protecting student confidentiality.
- *Example:* Staff receive annual training on FERPA and sign confidentiality agreements when handling student records.

What Types of Situations Often Involve Issues of Ethics and Integrity?

Being a school leader isn't just about rules and policies, it's also about doing the right thing, even when it's hard. Ethics and integrity show up in the everyday decisions that school leaders and educators make, especially when there's pressure, conflict, or ambiguity.

Imagine you're driving and the light turns yellow. You have a choice: stop or speed through. The rules don't always tell you what to do. You must decide based on judgment, safety, and the right thing to do.

School leaders face "yellow light" situations all the time where rules may be vague or pressures are high, but a decision must still be made with integrity.

School leaders frequently encounter ethical dilemmas that require balancing competing values and responsibilities. One such tension is confidentiality vs. transparency. For example, when a parent inquiry about another student's behavior following a serious incident, the principal may know important details but is legally bound by FERPA and can only discuss the parent's own child not another student's disciplinary action or personal information. Another common challenge is equity vs. equality.

While some educators believe in treating all students the same, effective leaders understand that equity means meeting each student's unique needs, which may require additional support for those facing trauma, learning disabilities, or language barriers. Leaders also face loyalty vs. accountability, especially when a well-liked teacher repeatedly arrives late or uses inappropriate language. In such cases, principals must uphold professional standards, even if it risks straining staff relationships. Similarly, in the dilemma of pressure vs. honesty, leaders may be urged to alter test results to improve school performance.

However, maintaining honesty protects the integrity of the school and the trust of students and families. Lastly, when personal beliefs conflict with professional responsibility, such as a teacher refusing to use a student's preferred pronouns, the ethical course is clear: protecting student dignity and fostering inclusion must come first. These scenarios illustrate that ethical leadership is not about avoiding conflict, it's about consistently choosing.

Outline

1. Confidentiality and Student Privacy

- Protecting sensitive student information is a core ethical responsibility.
- *Example:* A staff member is asked by a parent about another student's disciplinary record. Ethical leaders maintain confidentiality and do not share private details.

2. Fairness in Grading and Assessment

- Educators must ensure grades reflect true student performance without favoritism or manipulation.
- *Example:* A coach pressures a teacher to adjust grades for athletes to maintain eligibility, and an ethical teacher refuses and follows grading policy.

3. Equitable Discipline and Student Treatment

- Students must be treated consistently regardless of race, gender, disability, or background.
- *Example:* A principal notices disproportionate suspensions for multilingual learners and reviews discipline practices to ensure equity.

4. Conflicts of Interest and Favoritism

- Decisions should be made in the best interest of students, not based on personal relationships or gain.
- *Example:* A staff member applies for a leadership role; the principal recuses themselves from the decision-making process due to a close personal connection.

5. Misuse of School Resources or Time

- Ethical conduct includes responsible use of school funds, materials, and time.
- *Example:* A teacher consistently leaves early without approval; an ethical leader addresses the issue to protect team morale and fairness.

6. Honesty in Reporting Data and Information

- Integrity requires that school leaders report accurate academic, financial, and behavioral data.
- *Example:* A testing coordinator is asked to alter student responses to improve school ratings. An ethical response would be to report and reject the request.

7. Hiring and Evaluation Practices

- Hiring and promotion decisions must be based on merit and transparency.
- *Example:* A principal ensures that interview questions are standardized, and candidate scoring is documented objectively

8. Relationships with Students and Staff

- Boundaries must be maintained to protect professionalism and student welfare.
- *Example:* A teacher builds strong rapport with students but avoids oversharing personal details or engaging in social media communication outside school.

9. Responding to Ethical Dilemmas

- Leaders must use policies, codes of conduct, and personal integrity to make difficult decisions.
- *Example:* A teacher discovers a colleague is mistreating students. An ethical leader addresses the concern through proper reporting channels.

What steps, strategies, and procedures can a school leader take to protect the privacy and confidentiality of students and staff?"

In schools, privacy isn't just a policy, it's a promise. Students and staff trust school leaders with sensitive information every day, from medical records to behavioral incidents. Protecting that trust means safeguarding their confidentiality, following the law, and creating clear systems for managing personal information.

Whether it's a counselor's notes, a disciplinary record, or an IEP, the wrong disclosure could damage reputations, harm student safety, or even break the law. Privacy protection isn't just a moral responsibility, it's a legal one.

Think of confidential information as documents in a locked filing cabinet. Only certain staff have the key. Sharing student or staff data without proper permission is like handing out copies of those files to strangers, it's a violation of trust and law.

A teacher overhears a conversation in the main office where someone mentions a student's medical condition aloud. A parent who was waiting nearby heard this. Later, the parent files a complaint.

When addressing an ethics violation in a school setting, leaders must follow a structured approach to ensure legal compliance and maintain a culture of integrity. First, it is essential to understand the laws that govern ethical conduct in education, such as FERPA, Title IX, and state-specific codes of ethics. Next, school leaders should create clear policies outlining acceptable behavior, confidentiality protocols, and consequences for violations.

These policies must be supported by regular training for all staff, ensuring that every employee understands their legal and ethical responsibilities. To protect sensitive information, leaders must also limit access to student records and confidential data only to individuals with a legitimate educational need. Additionally, schools should have systems in place to monitor compliance and swiftly address any violations, including documentation and appropriate disciplinary actions. Most importantly, leaders must always model confidentiality and ethical conduct, setting the tone for a professional and legally sound school environment.

Outline

1. Understand and Comply with Federal and State Privacy Laws

- School leaders must be well-versed in FERPA, IDEA, HIPAA (where applicable), and state-specific regulations.
- *Example:* The principal ensures that student education records are only shared with individuals who have a legitimate educational interest under FERPA guidelines.

2. Train Staff Regularly on Confidentiality Protocols

- Ongoing professional development is essential for maintaining compliance and awareness.
- *Example:* All staff complete annual training on data privacy, secure communications, and proper handling of sensitive information.

3. Limit Access to Confidential Information

- Access should be role-specific and based on the principle of "need to know."
- *Example:* Only staff directly supporting a student with an IEP are granted access to their records and service plans.

4. Secure Physical and Digital Records Appropriately

- Protect records using locked storage for physical files and encrypted systems for digital data.
- *Example:* Student files are kept in locked cabinets, and password-protected student information systems are regularly updated for security.

5. Monitor and Audit Data Practices

- Regular reviews help identify risks and reinforce secure data handling.
- *Example:* The IT department conducts quarterly audits of digital access logs and reports any anomalies to school leadership.

6. Establish Clear Communication Protocols

- Confidential conversations and emails should follow secure and approved channels.
- *Example:* Staff are instructed to never discuss student behavior or academic issues in public areas or via unencrypted email.

7. Handle Parent and Community Inquiries with Caution

- Leaders must protect student and staff information even when facing pressure or curiosity.
- *Example:* When a parent asks about another student's discipline, the principal explains that they cannot share information about other individuals.

8. Protect Staff Information with Equal Care

- Personnel records, evaluations, and personal information must remain confidential.
- *Example:* Staff discipline or health issues are handled privately and shared only with authorized personnel.

9. Establish and Enforce a Clear School Confidentiality Policy

- A written policy clarifies expectations and consequences for violations.
- *Example:* The staff handbook includes a confidentiality agreement signed annually by all employees.

10. Respond Promptly to Privacy Breaches

- Quick action mitigates damage and upholds institutional accountability.
- *Example:* When a staff member mistakenly shares a student's medical condition, the leader documents the incident, informs affected parties, and retrains the staff involved.

Essential Questions #5 Ethical Leadership

What federal laws protect the rights of students? Staff members?

At Harmony Middle School, a parent contacted Principal Mrs. Smith to report that her child, who has a diagnosed learning disability, was not receiving the accommodation outlined in his IEP (Individualized Education Program). The student had missed multiple extended time opportunities and was penalized for incomplete work that should have been modified.

Mrs. Smith immediately recognized this as a violation of the Individuals with Disabilities Education Act (IDEA) and Section 504 of the Rehabilitation Act of 1973, both of which ensure that students with disabilities receive appropriate support and are not discriminated against due to their disability. She met with the IEP team, including the parent, special education teacher, and general education staff, to review the plan, provide corrective action, and retrain all staff on compliance procedures. The students' support was restored, and regular progress monitoring was implemented to ensure future adherence.

Meanwhile, during the same semester, a staff member Mr. Jameson, a teacher who identifies as Muslim expressed concern after overhearing a colleague make discriminatory remarks related to his religion in the staff lounge. Mrs. Smith took the complaint seriously, recognizing that the behavior could violate Title VII of the Civil Rights Act of 1964, which protects employees from workplace discrimination based on religion, race, national origin, and more. She conducted a confidential investigation in coordination with HR, addressed the incident through formal documentation, and facilitated cultural sensitivity training for the entire staff. Mr. Jameson was assured of his rights, and follow-up steps were taken to foster a respectful, inclusive environment.

Federal Laws:

1. **IDEA (Individuals with Disabilities Education Act)** – Ensures that students with disabilities receive special education services and accommodations.
2. **Section 504 of the Rehabilitation Act** – Prevents discrimination and provides accommodations for students with disabilities in any school receiving federal funds.
3. **Title VII of the Civil Rights Act of 1964** – Prohibits workplace discrimination on the basis of race, color, religion, sex, or national origin.
4. **Title IX of the Education Amendments of 1972** – Prohibits discrimination based on sex in any federally funded education program or activity.

Mrs. Smith's actions demonstrated a strong understanding of federal protection. Her timely response not only resolved both incidents fairly but also reinforced a culture of legal compliance, student-centered leadership, and equity for all staff and students at Harmony Middle School.

Outline

1. Family Educational Rights and Privacy Act (FERPA)

- Protects the privacy of student education records and grants parents the right to review and request corrections.
- *Example:* Schools must obtain written permission before releasing a student's records, except in certain legal cases.

2. Individuals with Disabilities Education Act (IDEA)

- Ensures that students with disabilities receive a Free Appropriate Public Education (FAPE) in the least restrictive environment.
- *Example:* Students with IEPs must be provided with services tailored to their unique needs.

3. Section 504 of the Rehabilitation Act of 1973

- Prohibits discrimination against individuals with disabilities in any program receiving federal funds.
- *Example:* Students with medical conditions may receive accommodation through a 504 Plan.

4. Title VI of the Civil Rights Act of 1964

- Prohibits discrimination based on race, color, or national origin in federally funded programs.
- *Example:* Schools cannot exclude students from programs or activities based on race or language background.

5. Title IX of the Education Amendments of 1972

- Prohibits sex-based discrimination in educational programs or activities receiving federal financial assistance.
- *Example:* Schools must respond to and prevent sexual harassment and ensure equal opportunities in athletics.

6. McKinney-Vento Homeless Assistance Act

- Protects the educational rights of children and youth experiencing homelessness.
- *Example:* Students have the right to enroll immediately and attend their school of origin, even without typical documentation.

7. Protection of Pupil Rights Amendment (PPRA)

- Governs the administration of surveys and collection of information from students.
- *Example:* Parents must be informed and have the right to opt their child out of surveys involving sensitive topics.

II. Federal Laws Protecting the Rights of School Staff

1. Title VII of the Civil Rights Act of 1964

- Prohibits employment discrimination based on race, color, religion, sex, or national origin.
- *Example:* A teacher cannot be denied a promotion due to their religion or ethnicity.

2. Americans with Disabilities Act (ADA)

- Prohibits discrimination against individuals with disabilities in all areas of public life, including employment.
- *Example:* A staff member with a disability is entitled to reasonable accommodation to perform their job duties.

3. Age Discrimination in Employment Act (ADEA)

- Protects employees and job applicants aged 40 and older from discrimination based on age.
- *Example:* A school cannot refuse to hire a qualified older candidate solely due to their age

4. Equal Pay Act of 1963

- Requires that men and women receive equal pay for equal work in the same establishment.
- *Example:* A female and male teacher performing the same duties must be compensated equally.

5. Title IX (also applies to staff)

- Prohibits sex-based discrimination in employment within educational institutions.
- *Example:* Staff have the right to report sexual harassment or discrimination and expect timely action from the school.

6. Fair Labor Standards Act (FLSA)

- Sets minimum wage, overtime pay, recordkeeping, and youth employment standards.
- *Example:* A non-exempt school employee must be paid overtime for hours worked beyond 40 in a workweek.

Essential Questions #6 Ethical Leadership

What Are the Key Elements in a Transparent Decision-Making Process?

Imagine a school as a glass house. Everyone inside can see what is happening, and those outside can look in as well. A transparent decision-making process works the same way. Decisions are not made in secret, but in clear view, with stakeholder input, fairness, and clear explanations.

In contrast, schools that make decisions "behind closed doors" often exclude stakeholder voices. This leads to confusion, mistrust, and resistance. Transparency, on the other hand, fosters shared ownership, improves communication, and strengthens school culture.

At Riverbend High School, Principal Lewis needed to revise the bell schedule to make time for academic interventions. In the past, leadership had made schedule changes with little teacher or parent input, which led to widespread dissatisfaction.

This time, Principal Lewis applied a transparent decision-making process:

- **Step 1: She formed a task force** that included teachers, students, support staff, and parents.
- **Step 2: The team reviewed data** on student needs, transitions, and staff workload.
- **Step 3: Multiple schedule drafts** were shared schoolwide with feedback forms.
- **Step 4: She held forums** and meetings to explain trade-offs and answer questions.
- **Step 5: The final decision was shared**, along with the rationale and timeline for review.

Outline

1. Clear Communication of Purpose and Goals

- Stakeholders should understand why the decision is being made and what it aims to achieve.
- *Example:* A principal introduces a new scheduling change by explaining the goals which was designed to improve instructional time and reduce transitions.

2. Inclusive Stakeholder Involvement

- Gathering input from those affected ensures multiple perspectives are considered.
- *Example:* Teachers, parents, and students are surveyed before implementing a new grading policy.

3. Open Sharing of Data and Rationale

- Data, research, and other evidence used to guide the decision should be accessible and clearly explained.
- *Example:* The leadership team presents academic data, and equity reports to justify changes to course placement procedures.

4. Defined Roles and Decision-Making Authority

- Everyone involved should understand who makes the final decision and how input is weighed.
- *Example:* A principal clarifies that while the school improvement team offers recommendations, the administrative team makes the final call.

5. Opportunities for Feedback and Dialogue

- Stakeholders should have opportunities to ask questions, express concerns, and offer input throughout the process.
- *Example:* After a policy is proposed, a town hall meeting is held to gather additional feedback and make revisions.

6. Consistent and Timely Updates

- Keeping stakeholders informed builds credibility and reduces misinformation.
- *Example:* The school sends regular email updates outlining where the decision stands and what comes next.

7. Documentation and Transparency of Outcomes

- The final decision, rationale, and next steps should be shared in writing.
- *Example:* The school posts the approved new attendance policy and an FAQ document on the website for reference.

8. Reflection and Review of Impact

- Transparent leaders revisit decisions to evaluate effectiveness and make adjustments if necessary.
- *Example:* Three months after a bell schedule change, the principal collects feedback and reviews data to assess whether the goal was met.

Essential Questions #7 Ethical Leadership

How Can Schools and School Leaders Function as Instruments of Social Justice?

During a middle school lunch period, a student reported hearing a racial slur directed at them in the cafeteria. Instead of treating the incident as an isolated behavior issue, the principal recognized it as part of a broader equity challenge. The school convened restorative conversations, engaged families, and partnered with the equity team to educate students about racism, respect, and inclusivity.

By addressing the issue directly and transparently, the leader showed that the school does not tolerate discrimination and that every student deserves dignity and safety. Beyond discipline, the response included revisiting schoolwide expectations, integrating culturally responsive curriculum, and ensuring professional development on equity and bias for staff.

Schools become instruments of social justice when leaders:

- Acknowledge harm and respond to incidents with fairness and care.
- Educate students and staff about equity, diversity, and inclusion.
- Model ethical courage by addressing racism openly rather than avoiding it.
- Build systems that promote belonging and respect for all.

Outline

1. Promote Equity in Access, Opportunity, and Outcomes

- Ensure all students regardless of background receive the support they need to succeed.
- *Example:* The school eliminates tracked classes and offers all students access to advanced coursework with embedded support.

2. Address and Disrupt Institutional Bias

- Leaders challenge policies and practices that perpetuate inequality.
- *Example:* The principal leads a review of disciplinary data and revises procedures to address racial disproportionality in suspensions.

3. Implement Culturally Responsive Teaching Practices

- Schools affirm and reflect the cultural identities of all students in instruction and curriculum.
- *Example:* Teachers incorporate diverse voices, histories, and perspectives into core subjects to broaden student understanding and belonging.

4. Amplify Student and Family Voice

- Social justice leadership includes shared decision-making and elevating marginalized voices.
- *Example:* The school creates student-led forums and multilingual family advisory councils to inform school improvement efforts.

5. Advocate for Policy Changes That Support Equity

- School leaders speak out and act on behalf of underrepresented or underserved students.
- *Example:* Principal partners with local leaders to advocate for broadband access in low-income communities to close the digital divide.

6. Provide Professional Development in Anti-Bias and Inclusive Practices

- Teachers and staff must be equipped to recognize and dismantle personal and systemic bias.
- *Example:* Staff participate in ongoing PD on equity, restorative practices, and culturally sustaining pedagogy.

7. Create a Safe, Inclusive, and Identity-Affirming School Environment

- Every student should feel respected, valued, and emotionally safe.
- *Example:* The school adopts inclusive language in its handbook, creates gender-neutral restrooms, and displays visual affirmations of diversity throughout the building.

8. Engage in Self-Reflection and Ethical Leadership

- Social justice leaders continually reflect on their own biases, decisions, and impact.
- *Example:* The principal regularly journals, seeks mentorship, and encourages open dialogue about equity challenges with staff.

Essential Questions #8 Ethical Leadership

What Criteria Should Be Considered in Developing a Plan for Professional Development?

Think of professional development (PD) as a treatment plan created by a skilled doctor. A good doctor wouldn't prescribe medication without first examining the patient, reviewing test results, and considering lifestyle and medical history. In the same way, effective PD is not one-size-fits-all, it must be based on real data, aligned to the school's goals, and responsive to teacher needs.

Just like a health plan aims to strengthen the body, a PD plan must be designed to strengthen teacher capacity, improve instruction, and ultimately improve student learning outcomes.

Principal Smith noticed that while teachers attended multiple PD sessions throughout the year, student outcomes remained stagnant particularly in reading and math. A staff survey revealed that many found the sessions irrelevant and disconnected from daily classroom realities.

To address this, Principal Smith began by:

- Analyzing student achievement and walkthrough data
- Surveying teachers about their strengths and areas for growth
- Identifying school-wide goals (e.g., improving questioning techniques, supporting English learners)
- Job-embedded coaching
- Collaborative planning time
- Choice-based PD pathways aligned to grade levels and subject areas.
- Follow-up opportunities to apply, reflect, and refine practices.

By midyear, teachers reported feeling more confident and supported. Classroom walkthroughs showed more active engagement, and student performance began to climb. Smith's approach showed that PD is most effective when it's intentional, data-informed, and personalized, not just scheduled.

Outline

1. Alignment with School Vision, Mission, and Strategic Goals

- PD should support the overall direction and improvement priorities of the school or district.
- *Example:* If the school's goal is to improve literacy outcomes, PD should focus on effective reading instruction and intervention strategies.

2. Needs Assessment Based on Data

- Use student achievement, teacher evaluation, and climate survey data to identify staff development needs.
- *Example:* After analyzing math benchmark scores, leadership identifies a need for PD in conceptual math instruction and student questioning techniques.

3. Relevance to Teacher Roles and Classroom Practice

- PD should be meaningful, grade-level appropriate, and directly tied to instructional responsibilities.
- *Example:* Early childhood teachers receive PD on play-based learning, while high school teachers focus on strategies for academic discourse.

4. Opportunities for Job-Embedded Learning

- The most effective PD is ongoing, collaborative, and connected to teachers' daily work.
- *Example:* Teachers participate in professional learning communities (PLCs), engage in peer observations, and receive coaching cycles throughout the year.

5. Inclusion of Differentiated and Personalized Learning Options

- Just as students learn in different ways, teachers benefit from PD that reflects their experience levels and growth goals.
- *Example:* Novice teachers receive support on classroom management, while veteran teachers select from workshops on leadership or technology integration.

6. Use of Evidence-Based Practices and Expert Facilitators

- PD should be grounded in research and led by credible educators with experience and content expertise.
- *Example:* A literacy consultant models small group guided reading techniques using current best practices.

7. Built-In Time for Reflection and Application

- Teachers need time to process new learning and apply strategies with feedback.
- *Example:* After a session on student engagement, teachers try a new technique, then reflect in PLCs and share results.

8. Clear Outcomes and Measurable Impact

- PD should have defined goals and evaluation criteria to measure effectiveness.
- *Example:* A PD series on formative assessment includes pre- and post-surveys and classroom walkthroughs to monitor implementation.

9. Sustainability and Follow-Up Support

- One-time workshops are less effective without ongoing reinforcement.
- *Example:* After trauma-informed training, counselors and coaches provide monthly check-ins to support implementation.

10. Inclusive and Collaborative Planning Process

- Involve teachers and staff in developing PD plans to ensure buy-in and relevance.
- *Example:* A teacher leadership team helps select PD topics based on staff feedback and instructional trends.

Essential Questions #9 — Ethical Leadership

What steps should be taken to ensure that others are acting ethically?

Think of a school as a garden. For a garden to thrive, every plant must be properly nurtured. But one unhealthy plant can spread disease to others. A good gardener doesn't just water their favorite flowers. They monitor the entire garden, prune when necessary, and ensure every plant receives sunlight and support.

In this analogy the principal is the gardener. The teachers and staff are the plants. The school's ethics and integrity are the soil. Policies and training are the watering schedule and nutrients. Monitoring and accountability systems are the fencing and pest checks.

To ensure ethical behavior, school leaders must prepare the soil, guide growth, support weak stems, and remove harmful practices not to punish, but to protect the health of the whole garden.

At Bridgeview High School, Principal Clark received a complaint from a staff member who believed a colleague was inflating grades to avoid parent conflict. There was no clear evidence, just suspicion. Principal Clark didn't jump to conclusions. Instead, she:

1. Reviewed the school's ethics policies with all staff.
2. Hosted a workshop on academic integrity.
3. Revisited the grading policy with the leadership team.
4. Created a non-punitive way for teachers to discuss ethical gray areas.
5. Observed that after support and clarity, teachers made more consistent grading decisions and staff trust began to rebuild.

Her leadership ensured everyone was reminded of their ethical responsibilities, given tools, and held accountable through a fair, respectful process.

1. Establish and Communicate a Clear Code of Ethics

- Provide explicit expectations for professional conduct aligned with district, state, and organizational standards.
- *Example:* Staff receive a written code of ethics during onboarding and review it annually during mandatory training.

2. Model Ethical Behavior as a Leader

- Leaders must demonstrate honesty, fairness, and professionalism in daily actions and decisions.
- *Example:* A principal admits a scheduling error to staff and explains the correction process, modeling transparency and accountability.

3. Provide Ongoing Ethics Training and Reflection Opportunities

- Regular professional development reinforces ethical awareness and application.

- *Example:* Staff attend sessions on confidentiality, equity in discipline, and digital responsibility, followed by group discussion.

4. Create a Safe and Transparent Reporting System

- Employees should know how to report unethical behavior without fear of retaliation.
- *Example:* The district offers an anonymous ethics hotline and protects whistleblowers through clear non-retaliation policies.

5. Monitor Practices and Decision-Making Processes

- Ethical oversight includes reviewing systems, documentation, and professional actions.
- *Example:* A school leader reviews disciplinary referrals and grading trends for equity and fairness across classrooms.

6. Encourage Open Dialogue and Ethical Dilemma Discussions

- Talking about complex situations helps staff make thoughtful, value-driven decisions.
- *Example:* During staff meetings, leaders present real-world ethical dilemmas and facilitate collaborative problem-solving discussions.

7. Address Misconduct Promptly and Fairly

- Ethical leadership includes holding individuals accountable while treating them with dignity.
- *Example:* When a staff member violates policy, the leader investigates, follows due process, and applies appropriate consequences.

8. Recognize and Reinforce Ethical Behavior

- Highlighting integrity promotes a culture of trust and respect.
- *Example:* Staff are acknowledged for making principled choices, such as returning lost items, reporting a concern, or supporting a student in distress.

What are the characteristics of an open and inclusive school community?

Imagine a school as a public library. In a thriving library, every person can find a place to sit, resources that meet their needs, and a welcoming environment where differences are respected. Just as libraries provide books in many languages and formats, inclusive schools ensure that learners of all backgrounds, abilities, and identities have equitable access to learning.

If only certain shelves are stocked or only some visitors are welcomed, the library loses its purpose. An inclusive school, like a well-resourced library, thrives when everyone feels represented, valued, and supported.

At Eastlake Elementary, Principal Jamison realized that while the school celebrated diversity on paper, many students and families still felt left out. English Language Learners weren't participating in after-school programs. Students with disabilities sat apart during assemblies. PTA meetings had very few parents from immigrant communities.

Principal Jamison decided it was time to turn words into action. She launched a schoolwide initiative called "Growing Together," focused on building an inclusive culture through small but powerful changes:

- Multilingual signs were posted in hallways and newsletters were translated.
- Student leadership teams included representatives from every class and learning program.
- A quiet sensory-friendly lunch area was introduced for students with sensory needs.
- Teachers participated in equity learning walks to reflect on classroom inclusiveness.

By year's end, more families attended events, peer friendships had diversified, and students reported feeling "more seen and understood." The school had become not just a place of learning, but a home for everyone.

Outline

1. Welcoming Environment for All Students and Families

- The school culture promotes kindness, acceptance, and belonging from the moment people enter.
- *Example:* Office staff greet visitors warmly, signage is multilingual, and students are welcomed by name each morning.

2. Respect for Diversity in All Forms

- All cultural, linguistic, racial, religious, ability-based, and gender identities are acknowledged and respected.
- *Example:* Classrooms celebrate cultural heritage months, and the curriculum integrates diverse perspectives year-round.

3. Equitable Access to Opportunities and Support

- Every student has access to high-quality instruction, enrichment programs, and support services.
- *Example:* Advanced classes, extracurriculars, and leadership roles are promoted to all students, with scaffolds in place to support participation.

4. Inclusive Curriculum and Instruction

- Lessons reflect students' identities and experiences and encourage critical thinking about equity and justice.
- *Example:* Teachers use books and case studies from varied cultures and communities to ensure representation and relevance.

5. Student Voice and Empowerment

- Students are involved in shaping school policies, programs, and culture.
- *Example:* A student equity council works with administrators to provide input on school improvement initiatives.

6. Family and Community Engagement

- Families are treated as essential partners and welcomed into the life of the school.
- *Example:* Family nights are multilingual and culturally responsive, and events are scheduled flexibly to increase participation.

7. Safe and Supportive Climate

- Bullying, exclusion, and discrimination are actively addressed, and emotional safety is prioritized.
- *Example:* The school uses restorative circles and SEL programs to help students resolve conflict and build positive relationships.

8. Diverse and Representative Staffing

- Hiring practices prioritize building a staff that reflects the student population and brings diverse perspectives.
- *Example:* The school recruits educators from underrepresented backgrounds and provides mentorships for all new staff.

9. High Expectations Paired with Individual Support

- The belief that all students can succeed is paired with responsive, individualized instruction.
- *Example:* Teachers differentiate lessons and provide flexible groupings to ensure each student is challenged and supported.

Essential Questions #11 — Ethical Leadership

Why is it important for a school leader to administer educational policies equitably and legally?

When a new attendance policy was introduced at Lincoln Middle School, the principal noticed that students from certain neighborhoods were being disciplined more harshly for tardiness than others. Some families relied on public transportation that was often late, while others lived within walking distance of the school.

Instead of applying the rule rigidly, the principal reviewed the policy with staff, gathered input from families, and worked with the district to add a grace period and bus passes for students most affected. By applying the policy equitably and in compliance with district and state guidelines, the principal not only upheld the law but also demonstrated fairness. This built trust with families and ensured that all students were held to the same standard while still receiving the support they needed to succeed.

Educational policies must be implemented with both legal precision and equity in mind. A leader who applies rules inconsistently or unfairly undermines student rights, exposes the school to legal risks, and breaks community trust. A leader who leads with both justice and lawfulness helps all students reach their full potential.

Outline

1. Protects the Rights of All Students and Staff

- Equitable and legal administration ensures that everyone is treated fairly and has access to opportunities.
- *Example:* A principal follows IEP guidelines exactly, ensuring that students with disabilities receive their legally mandated services.

2. Builds Trust and Credibility Within the School Community

- Consistent and fair leadership fosters confidence among students, families, and staff.
- *Example:* When handling discipline, the principal applies the same process to all students, reinforcing that no one receives special treatment or bias.

3. Prevents Legal Liability and Ethical Violations

- Noncompliance with laws and policies can lead to lawsuits, audits, or loss of licensure.
- *Example:* A school leader ensures Title IX policies are enforced to address complaints of gender-based discrimination and avoid federal investigation.

4. Promotes Equity and Closes Opportunity Gaps

- Administering policies equitably helps dismantle systemic barriers and creates a more just learning environment.
- *Example:* The principal removes eligibility restrictions for gifted programs that disproportionately exclude multilingual learners and students of color.

5. Ensures Consistent and Transparent Decision-Making

- Fair policy application eliminates favoritism and reduces conflict.
- *Example:* Staff know exactly how performance evaluations are conducted, because procedures are followed and clearly communicated every year.

6. Sets a Positive Example for Ethical Leadership

- Leaders who follow the law and apply policies fairly model professionalism for staff and students.
- *Example:* A principal refuses to alter test scores under pressure, reinforcing academic integrity and accountability.

7. Upholds the Mission and Core Values of the School

- Equity and legality are foundational to creating a school culture rooted in respect, justice, and continuous improvement.
- *Example:* The school's mission states that "all students will thrive," and the principal ensures discipline, hiring, and resource allocation reflect that belief.

Essential Questions #12 Ethical Leadership

How can a school leader refocus attention on the school's vision and goals when controversial issues arise?

At Westview Middle School, the district updated its policy to allow transgender students to use bathrooms and locker rooms that align with their gender identity. While many families supported the decision as a matter of dignity, inclusion, and compliance with civil rights law, others expressed concerns about privacy and safety. The disagreement escalated at board meetings and in community forums, leaving the school divided.

The principal recognized the need to bring the focus back to the school's vision: "Creating a safe and supportive environment where every student feels valued and respected." She reminded staff, families, and students that the school's commitment to safety, equity, and belonging applied to all learners. By facilitating open forums, providing clear information about the legal framework, and emphasizing the school's mission, the leader redirected the conversation away from conflict and toward the shared goal of student well-being.

By grounding the discussion in the school's vision and goals, the leader helped the community move past polarization and refocused on what united them: ensuring every student could learn in a safe and inclusive environment.

Outline

1. Ground All Communication in the School's Mission and Core Values

- Use the shared vision to frame responses and guide decisions during challenging times.
- *Example:* During a debate about book selection, the principal emphasizes the school's commitment to inclusive, high-quality learning for all students.

2. Acknowledge Controversy While Maintaining Focus

- Address concerns respectfully without allowing them to derail instructional priorities.
- *Example:* In response to parent concerns about curriculum, the principal listens, clarifies facts, and reaffirms the school's academic and equity goals.

3. Facilitate Open Dialogue with Civility and Respect

- Provide structured opportunities for stakeholders to voice concerns in constructive ways.
- *Example:* The leader hosts a listening session with clear norms, then follows up with a summary that ties feedback to shared school goals.

4. Use Data and Evidence to Keep the Focus on Student Success

- Facts help shift the conversation from emotion to student outcomes.
- *Example:* When questioned about instructional strategies, the principal shares achievement data showing student growth aligned to the school improvement plan.

5. Involve Staff and Leadership Teams in Re-centering Conversations

- Empower teams to help maintain focus on what matters most.

- *Example:* The school leadership team revisits the vision statement and updates team norms to ensure alignment in all decisions and messaging.

6. Reiterate the Vision Consistently Across All Communication Platforms

- Keep the mission visible in newsletters, meetings, social media, and classroom visits.
- *Example:* Weekly updates include a "Vision in Action" section that highlights how decisions and events connect to the school's core goals.

7. Lead with Transparency and Calm Resolve

- Leadership during controversy requires steadiness and clarity.
- *Example:* The principal explains how decisions are made, who is involved, and how they align with district policy and the school's guiding principles.

8. Maintain Instructional Momentum

- Don't allow distractions to derail teaching and learning.
- *Example:* Professional development and PLC meetings continue to focus on student engagement, formative assessment, and instructional equity even amid external debate.

Essential Questions #13 Ethical Leadership

What resources are available to school leaders for nurturing their professional growth?

Imagine a school leader as a mountain guide leading a team (staff, students, and families) to the summit academic success and school improvement. The trail is steep, and sometimes unexpected obstacles like fog (ethical dilemmas), loose rocks (policy violations), or bad weather (community pressure) get in the way.

One day, the guide (principal) realizes that one experienced hiker (a veteran teacher) is taking a shortcut that seems helpful but endangers the integrity of the journey. Now the guide faces a tough choice: ignore the shortcut because the hiker is popular and has good intentions or address it even though it may cause discomfort.

The guide pauses. Rather than react impulsively, she opens her compass, checks the trail map, and radios other guides for advice. These tools represent her professional resources: mentors, policy documents, legal guidance, and training opportunities. With their help, she reorients her team, corrects the course, and ensures everyone is moving ethically and safely even if it's the harder path.

At Evergreen Elementary School, Principal Mrs. Julia Benton found herself facing a difficult ethical situation. During a teacher observation cycle, she discovered that a well-liked veteran teacher had been giving students exam questions in advance to help them "feel confident" before a district-wide benchmark. While her intent was not malicious, the action directly compromised the validity of the assessment and violated the district's academic integrity policy.

Mrs. Benton was conflicted. She respected the teacher's long-standing contributions to the school and understood her desire to support anxious students. However, as the instructional leader of the building,

Mrs. Benton knew she had to act in accordance with ethical and professional standards even when doing so was uncomfortable.

Unsure how to navigate the situation while maintaining trust and accountability, Mrs. Benton turned to several professional growth resources to support her leadership:

Mrs. Benton reached out to her district-assigned leadership mentor, who had 15 years of experience. Together, they reviewed the district's code of ethics and brainstormed a fair and growth-oriented response that prioritized student integrity while giving the teacher a chance to reflect and improve.

She participated in a virtual leadership forum through her state principal association, where she posed the ethical dilemma (anonymously) and received input from leaders in other districts who had faced similar situations.

Mrs. Benton consulted the district's Employee Code of Conduct and collaborated with the Human Resources department to ensure her next steps complied with school board policy and state education law. Wanting to grow from the experience herself, she completed a self-assessment tool based on the PSEL (Professional Standards for Educational Leaders), reflecting on how her decision-making aligned with Standard 2: Ethics and Professional Norms.
She enrolled in an online ethics in education leadership course offered through a regional university partnership, giving her structured opportunities to sharpen her decision-making and promote a stronger culture of fairness and professionalism.

With guidance and professional learning, Mrs. Benton met with the teacher, addressed the breach in a supportive but clear manner, and arranged for ethics training through the district's PD portal. She also used the situation as a schoolwide teaching moment by leading a staff session on professional responsibility and ethical assessment practices. Her decision-making upheld fairness, maintained trust, and modeled integrity for the entire school. Through self-reflection, consultation, and access to leadership resources, Mrs. Benton grew as an ethical leader and reinforced the school's commitment to doing what is right even when it's hard.

Outline

1. Professional Learning Communities (PLCs) and Leadership Networks

- Collaborating with peers fosters shared learning and continuous improvement.
- *Example:* A principal joins a district-wide leadership PLC to exchange strategies on instructional coaching, equity, and school improvement planning.

2. State and National Leadership Associations

- These organizations offer conferences, certifications, mentorship, and policy updates.
- *Example:* Membership in the **National Association of Secondary School Principals (NASSP)** or **ASCD** provides access to journals, webinars, and leadership toolkits.

3. University and Certification Programs

- Advanced degrees and certificate programs offer formal development in leadership, policy, and instructional supervision.

- *Example:* A school leader enrolls in an Ed.D. program or completes a certification in educational leadership or special education supervision.

4. Coaching and Mentorship Opportunities

- Personalized guidance from experienced leaders can accelerate professional growth.
- *Example:* A new principal is paired with a veteran mentor through a district-led induction program.

5. Online Learning Platforms and Webinars

- Flexible, on-demand resources make it easy to learn new strategies and stay current.
- *Example:* The leader completes a micro-credential course on trauma-informed leadership through **Coursera, Ed Web**, or **Learning Forward**.

6. Professional Reading and Research Journals

- Staying informed about educational trends, research, and best practices enhances decision-making.
- *Example:* A school leader subscribes to **Educational Leadership (EL)** magazine and follows publications from **The Wallace Foundation**.

7. Leadership Retreats, Institutes, and Workshops

- Immersive experiences allow time for reflection, planning, and networking.
- *Example:* The leader attends a summer leadership institute focused on equity-centered school improvement.

8. Feedback from Stakeholders and Self-Reflection Tools

- Growth also comes from within leaders benefit from honest input and structured reflection.
- *Example:* A principal uses 360-degree feedback surveys and a leadership reflection journal to assess strengths and areas for growth.

9. District-Level Leadership Development Programs

- Many districts offer tiered leadership pipelines and succession planning support.
- *Example:* An aspiring leader participates in a district program with coaching, shadowing opportunities, and mock interview practice.

10. Peer Networking and Social Media Learning Communities

- Online platforms allow leaders to connect, share resources, and learn in real time.
- *Example:* A school leader joins a Twitter chat like **#edleadership** or follows thought leaders on LinkedIn for daily insight and innovation.

Essential Questions #14 — Ethical Leadership

What are the benefits of reflective practice?

Being a school leader is like driving a car. The road ahead represents your school's goals and initiatives, but the rearview mirror, your reflection, is just as important. If you never look back, you might miss something crucial: miscommunication, an unintended consequence, or a better path you overlooked.

Principal Mrs. Thomas has just wrapped up a heated staff meeting about upcoming changes to the grading policy. She had introduced a new expectation that all teachers use standards-based grading moving forward. While she believed it would improve equity and clarity for students, several teachers were frustrated and felt blindsided. Some walked out of the meeting without saying a word.

That afternoon, instead of immediately moving on to her next task, Mrs. Thomas paused and reflected. She sat at her desk and asked herself a few key questions:

- How did I communicate the change?
- Did I give teachers a chance to process or ask questions?
- Was I listening, or just directing?

This act of thinking critically about her own actions and their impact is called reflective practice. It's like looking in a rearview mirror not to dwell on the past, but to understand where you've been so you can better navigate what's ahead.

Reflective Practice improves Future Decision-Making. It builds Self-Awareness and foster trust and professional growth: It promotes a culture of learning and aligns actions with values:

Reflective practice is the habit of stepping back to think deeply about one's actions, intentions, and impact. Like a driver checking the rearview mirror, school leaders who reflect regularly are better equipped to lead with wisdom, fairness, and focus. For Mrs. Thomas, a moment of honest reflection turned a tense situation into a learning opportunity for her and the school.

<u>Outline</u>

. Improves Instructional and Leadership Effectiveness

- Reflective practice helps educators assess what is working and what needs to change.
- *Example:* A teacher reflects on a failed group activity and redesigns it for better engagement and clearer instructions.

2. Promotes Continuous Professional Growth

- Self-reflection fosters a mindset of learning and improvement over time.
- *Example:* A principal reviews their response to a conflict and commits to improving active listening skills in future situations.

3. Enhances Decision-Making and Problem-Solving

- Reflection allows individuals to think critically and strategically about choices and their consequences.
- *Example:* After analyzing school-wide assessment data, a leadership team reflects on missed opportunities for early intervention and adjusts the school's RTI process.

4. Builds Self-Awareness and Emotional Intelligence

- Reflecting helps individuals understand how their actions, beliefs, and biases affect others.
- *Example:* A teacher journals about a classroom interaction and realizes a personal bias may have influenced their disciplinary response.

5. Strengthens Student Relationships and Classroom Climate

- Reflective educators are more responsive to students' needs, feelings, and feedback.
- *Example:* A teacher reflects on student disengagement and decides to incorporate more student choice and culturally relevant materials.

6. Supports Goal Setting and Accountability

- Reflection creates clarity around progress and areas needing development.
- *Example:* A school leader uses a reflective journal to track progress toward strategic goals and holds themselves accountable to deadlines and commitments.

7. Encourages Innovation and Risk-Taking

- Reflective practice builds confidence to try new approaches and learn from mistakes.
- *Example:* A teacher reflects on a failed attempt at using flipped instruction and identifies how to revise the approach more effectively next time.

8. Promotes a Culture of Growth Across the School

- When leaders and staff reflect openly, it models a commitment to improvement for the whole community.
- *Example:* A principal hosts "Leadership Reflections" during staff meetings to share lessons learned and invite input on key challenges.

Ethical Leadership Quiz

1. **A parent emails the principal asking why a particular student wasn't punished for a fight that happened during recess. The parent's child was involved and received detention. What is the most appropriate response?**
   A. Share the other student's disciplinary outcome to show fairness
   B. Invite both sets of parents to a mediated conference
   C. Explain that student discipline is confidential and only the parent's own child's consequences can be discussed
   D. Forward the concern to the district without responding

2. **A teacher shares with the principal that they suspect a colleague is inflating grades to keep students eligible for sports. What should the principal do first?**
   A. Ignore it unless a parent files a complaint
   B. Quietly warn the teacher that the practice is unethical
   C. Investigate the claim by reviewing student work, grading practices, and speaking with the teacher involved
   D. Report the colleague directly to the superintendent

3. **A well-liked staff member frequently jokes with students using language that makes some feel uncomfortable. What should the principal do?**
   A. Let it go since the staff member is popular and well-meaning
   B. Encourage students to tell the teacher directly how they feel
   C. Provide private coaching, document the behavior, and reinforce expectations for professional conduct
   D. Mention it casually during a faculty meeting.

4. **A teacher refuses to use a student's preferred name and pronouns, citing personal beliefs. What is the principal's ethical and professional responsibility?**
   A. Allow the teacher to opt out to respect their beliefs
   B. Meet with the teacher to review district policies and reinforce the obligation to honor student identity
   C. Let the counselor handle the issue
   D. Notify parents that the teacher has opted out of using preferred pronouns

5. **The district is under pressure to improve test scores. A staff member suggests revising a few student answers after testing to avoid negative ratings. What should the principal do?**
   A. Report the suggestion to the district ethics office and reaffirm testing integrity to the staff
   B. Do nothing unless it happens again
   C. Warn the staff member privately not to share such ideas
   D. Consider it if it helps protect the school's reputation.

6. **A principal discovers that a teacher is using personal social media to criticize students and staff. What is the most appropriate course of action?**
    A. Block the teacher on all social media platforms
    B. Issue a reminder to all staff about social media etiquette
    C. Meet with the teacher to address the concern, document the discussion, and follow district policy
    D. Ignore it since it's off campus and personal

7. **During hiring, a candidate reveals a disability and requests minor accommodation. A school leader is concerned about how this might affect performance. What should the leader do?**
    A. Disqualify the candidate quietly
    B. Proceed with the interview process and ensure accommodations are considered in accordance with ADA
    C. Ask the candidate to withdraw
    D. Share the concern with the entire interview panel

8. **A teacher approaches the principal about privately tutoring students from her own class after school for a fee. What is the most ethical leadership response?**
    A. Allow it if the families consent
    B. Allow it only if the teacher lowers their classroom workload
    C. Deny the request due to conflict of interest and the potential for favoritism
    D. Suggest the teacher advertise tutoring services to students in other schools

9. **A student confides in a teacher about being bullied but asks them not to tell anyone. The teacher tells the principal. What is the principal's ethical responsibility?**
    A. Respect the student's privacy and do nothing
    B. Discipline the teacher for breaking the student's trust
    C. Follow district procedures to investigate and address the bullying while protecting the student's dignity
    D. Inform the student's parents and suspend the accused student immediately

10. A **parent offers to donate sports equipment in exchange for their child receiving a leadership role on the team. What is the most ethical decision for the principal?**
    A. Accept the donation and assign the role to avoid conflict
    B. Decline the offer and remind the parent that leadership roles are based on merit and fairness
    C. Refer the matter to the athletic coach to decide
    D. Tell the parent to make the donation anonymously

11. **A teacher accidentally shares a student's confidential discipline record during a staff meeting. What is the principal's most ethical response?**
    A. Ignore the incident to protect the teacher's reputation
    B. Publicly correct the teacher in front of the staff
    C. Meet privately with the teacher, review confidentiality laws, and document the conversation
    D. Remove the teacher from future meetings.

12. A school leader discovers that a staff member is using their position to promote a private tutoring business during class time. What is the most appropriate action?

A. Allow it since it supports student learning
B. Ask the teacher to limit promotions to after school hours
C. Remind the teacher of the conflict-of-interest policy and take corrective action
D. Offer to promote the business school-wide to ensure fairness.

13. The principal learns that standardized test answers may have been altered by a staff member. What is the most ethical next step?

A. Report the concern to district administration and begin an internal investigation
B. Confront the staff member in front of students to send a message
C. Wait to see if district officials notice
D. Handle it privately and keep it off the record.

14. During an interview, a candidate discloses a disability and requests an accommodation. What is the ethical response from the hiring team?

A. Disqualify the candidate due to concerns about workload
B. Proceed with the interview and ensure accommodations are made
C. Ask the candidate to explain how their disability affects teaching
D. Notify other interviewers to score the candidate more leniently.

15. A student confides in a counselor about potential abuse at home and asks them not to tell anyone. What is the school's ethical obligation?

A. Keep the information confidential out of respect
B. Notify the parent before taking any action
C. Report the disclosure to the proper child welfare authorities as mandated by law
D. Wait until the student gives permission to report it.

16. A teacher grades student works inconsistently, giving higher scores to students they like. What is the principal's most ethical action?

A. Review the grading practices and provide support to ensure fairness
B. Confront the teacher publicly to correct the behavior
C. Ignore it unless a parent complains
D. Adjust the student grades without informing the teacher.

17. A staff member shares that they feel targeted due to their religious beliefs. What is the most ethical way to respond?

A. Ask them to avoid bringing religion into the workplace
B. Recommend they ignore the issue to keep peace
C. Initiate a respectful conversation, follow reporting procedures, and ensure a safe environment
D. Encourage them to take personal leave while tensions subside.

18. The principal is asked by a board member to share confidential evaluation information about a teacher. What should the principal do?

A. Share the information to maintain political favor
B. Decline to share and explain that it is confidential personnel information
C. Ask the teacher to waive their privacy
D. Provide a summary but omit the teacher's name.

19. A teacher witnesses a colleague using inappropriate language with a student but hesitates to report it. What is the principal's ethical responsibility?

A. Do nothing unless a parent complains
B. Wait to see if the behavior continues
C. Advise the teacher to ignore the situation to preserve staff morale.
D. Investigate the concern according to district protocol and take appropriate action

20. The principal discovers a mistake in the school's reporting of discipline data that paints the school in a more favorable light. What is the ethical action?

A. Leave the data as-is since it helps the school
B. Quietly adjust the data without reporting the mistake
C. Correct the error and notify the district with an explanation
D. Blame the mistake on office staff and move on

Answer Key Ethical Leadership 1-10

Question Number	1	2	3	4	5	6	7	8	9	10
Correct Solution	C	C	C	B	A	C	B	C	C	B

Answer Key Ethical Leadership 11-20

Question Number	11	12	13	14	15	16	17	18	19	20
Correct Solution	C	C	A	B	C	A	C	B	D	C

Domain V: Organizational Leadership

This domain focuses on the principal's role in managing the systems, operations, and resources that keep a school running effectively. Organizational leadership involves ensuring that schedules, budgets, facilities, and staffing align with the school's mission, vision, and goals. By creating efficient structures, maintaining safe and supportive environments, and allocating resources equitably, principals enable teachers to focus on instruction and students to focus on learning. Strong organizational leadership ensures that daily operations support long-term school improvement and success.

Organizational Leadership

Real-Life Scenario A: Managing operational systems

When Mrs. Sharon Lee became principal of Riverside Intermediate School, she inherited a building plagued by years of deferred maintenance, most urgently, a leaking roof in the 5th-grade wing. Every time it rained, ceiling tiles stained, buckets lined the hallway, and teachers scrambled to rearrange desks to avoid drips near students' workspaces.

The district had already maxed out its maintenance budget for the year, and Mrs. Lee was told that a full roof replacement wouldn't be possible for at least 18 months. However, she refused to let this become "just another facilities issue." Instead, she saw it as an opportunity to model ethical, student-centered operational leadership despite limited resources.

Mrs. Lee documented the damage in detail photos, water intrusion maps, and a log of safety hazards.

She compiled a data-driven facilities report and presented it to the district office to push the roof higher on the capital improvement priority list. To protect students and staff, Mrs. Lee, Temporarily relocated affected classrooms to other parts of the building. She worked with the district's facilities manager to schedule interim patching and tarp coverage. Arranged for weekly mold and air-quality checks to comply with health regulations. The school remained in compliance with local and state safety guidelines, even without a full roof replacement.

She created a shared Google Sheet for teachers and custodial staff to log leaks, odors, or water stains in real time. This reduced delayed maintenance responses and gave the facilities team better data for short-term repairs. Rather than hide the issue, Mrs. Lee addressed it openly with students and families:

She included updates to building in her weekly newsletter. At PTA meetings, she explained how facilities impact learning and how the school was responding with care and transparency.

"Every child deserves a safe, dry, distraction-free learning space. That's part of our mission and we're treating this as an equity issue, not just a facility issue." Mrs. Lee reached out to local businesses and the PTA for support. A local hardware store donated waterproof ceiling tiles and industrial tarps. The PTA funded weatherproof bins for student materials. She applied for an emergency facilities grant through the state education department.

Although the roof wasn't immediately fixed, Mrs. Lee demonstrated exceptional leadership by maintaining a safe environment, following policy, using data for advocacy, and staying transparent with stakeholders. Her creative and ethical management not only built trust but also resulted in Riverside being moved up on the district's facilities priority list.

Organizational Leadership

Real-Life Scenario B: Aligning and obtaining fiscal and human resources

At Brookstone Elementary School, Principal Mrs. Evelyn Ramos faced a difficult situation: the school's special education population had increased by 20% over two years, but staffing and intervention support had not kept pace. During her spring budget review, Mrs. Ramos realized the school could not continue offering quality services without restructuring resources. Instead of making cuts across the board, she led a collaborative budgeting process, involving teacher leaders, the child study team, and the school business administrator. Together, they analyzed IEP compliance data, staffing allocations, and intervention group sizes. Based on their findings, Mrs. Ramos made the difficult decision to postpone a planned Chromebook upgrade and instead reallocate Title I funds to hire an additional special education teacher and a part-time reading interventionist.

To ensure students had access to the best instructional support, she also worked with the district HR office to recruit candidates who reflected the school's cultural and linguistic diversity. One new hire was a certified bilingual special education teacher who could support students in both English and Spanish. To promote retention, Mrs. Ramos introduced a mentoring program for new staff, hosted quarterly check-ins, and worked with grade-level teams to ensure equitable distribution of instructional responsibilities. She also used student achievement and behavioral data to evaluate the impact of these decisions, adjusting group sizes and support schedules midyear.

By the end of the school year, students receiving targeted reading interventions showed marked growth, and staff reported improved workload balance and clarity in assignments. Through ethical stewardship, strategic planning, and inclusive leadership, Mrs. Ramos successfully aligned fiscal and human resources to address real student needs while building staff trust and strengthening the school's capacity to deliver equitable learning opportunities.

Real-Life Scenario C: Protecting the welfare and safety of students and staff

At Pineview Middle School, Principal Mr. Anthony Delgado took a proactive stance on student and staff safety after a series of regional school incidents raised concerns among parents and faculty. Recognizing the need for a clearly articulated, comprehensive approach, Mr. Delgado led to the development of an updated school safety and emergency response plan that complied with local, state, and federal guidelines. He involved a wide range of stakeholders such as teachers, the school nurse, the school resource officer, PTA leaders, and student representatives to ensure diverse perspectives were included. Together, they reviewed entry protocols, hallway supervision, fire drill procedures, and lockdown routines. Mr. Delgado also conducted a building safety audit, which revealed blind spots in camera coverage and inconsistent visitor check-in practices. He used this data to advocate for updated security cameras and an electronic visitor ID system, reallocating discretionary funds to support the changes.

Beyond physical safety, Mr. Delgado prioritized emotional well-being by expanding access to counseling and mental health services. He worked with the district's wellness coordinator to secure a part-time school psychologist and established a private referral system for staff experiencing burnout or stress. At the start of the school year, he held assemblies and parent forums to communicate safety expectations, including behavior guidelines, bullying prevention protocols, and anonymous reporting options. All communications were documented in newsletters, website updates, and call logs, and translated for families who spoke languages other than English.

To ensure readiness for emergencies, Mr. Delgado identified and posted contact details for key support personnel, including emergency responders and local mental health agencies. These were shared with faculty during monthly safety briefings and uploaded to the school's security portal. In collaboration with the transportation department, he also led a review of bus safety procedures and implemented mandatory ID checks for afternoon dismissals.

By taking a systems-level approach rooted in best practices, Mr. Delgado established not just compliance, but trust, transparency, and a culture of shared responsibility. Students and staff reported feeling safer and more supported, and the school saw a significant decline in incidents requiring disciplinary or emergency intervention.

How are plans developed for appropriate use of school facilities? Who is involved?

At Maple Hill High School, Principal Mrs. Elena Watkins noticed ongoing scheduling conflicts and growing tension over shared space usage. The gymnasium was frequently double-booked by athletic teams and after-school clubs. Meanwhile, outside organizations, like a local youth soccer league and a community choir, had started requesting weekend access often without clear approval or supervision. Recognizing the need for structure and equity, Mrs. Watkins led an initiative to develop a formal Facilities Use Plan aligned with district policy and designed to protect student learning time, maintain school property, and support safe community engagement.

To begin, Mrs. Watkins reviewed the district Board of Education policies which clarified that school-sponsored programs take priority and that external requests must go through both building-level review and district-level approval. Understanding this would require input from multiple perspectives, she formed a Facilities Use Planning Committee, which included:

- The Assistant Principal (who oversees the master schedule),
- The Athletic Director (responsible for team practice/game scheduling),
- The Head Custodian (who manages building access and maintenance),
- The PTA President,
- A student council representative,
- And a district facilities liaison (who grants final approval for external users).

Together, the committee identified key facility usage trends, reviewed maintenance and custodial capacity, and collected feedback from staff and local groups. Using this data, they developed a step-by-step process that outlined:

- Who may use the building: internal school programs, district academic services, and approved community-based organizations with proof of insurance.
- Priority of usage: instructional needs such as school extracurricular activities would be the first priority followed by district events, outside nonprofit organizations, and other public interest groups.
- Request procedure: All requests must be submitted through a digital form at least two weeks in advance, reviewed first by the principal, and then forwarded to the district's facilities office for confirmation. The form included time, location, type of activity, estimated attendance, supervision plans, and custodial support needs.
- Usage requirements: external groups had to agree to follow school conduct rules, pay custodial or security fees when needed, and leave facilities in good condition.

Mrs. Watkins hosted training sessions for school staff and informational meetings for local partners to explain the updated plan. She also launched a shared Google calendar to track usage and prevent overlaps. All communications and approvals were documented, and custodial staff used a digital log to report concerns or damages after each event.

The result was a fair, transparent, and sustainable system that not only reduced conflicts and confusion but also strengthened relationships between the school and community. Most importantly, it preserved facilities for student-centered use first, aligning with the school's core values and instructional mission.

Outline

Assessing School Needs and Usage Priorities

- Begin by evaluating how current space is used and what additional needs exist.
- *Example:* The principal conducts a facilities audit to determine whether classrooms, gym space, and common areas are being used efficiently.

2. Align Facility Use with the School's Mission and Goals

- Space planning should support instructional, extracurricular, and community priorities.
- *Example:* A school focused on STEM programs allocates lab space for robotics and project-based learning.

3. Involve Key Stakeholders in the Planning Process

- Effective facility planning is collaborative and includes multiple perspectives.
- *Example:* A planning committee includes administrators, custodians, teachers, parents, students, and district operations staff.

4. Follow District Policies and Regulatory Guidelines

- Plans must comply with fire codes, ADA requirements, safety standards, and board policies.
- *Example:* Before approving a new after-school program, the principal ensures occupancy limits and emergency access routes meet local regulations.

5. Prioritize Equity and Accessibility

- Facility use must consider the needs of all student groups, including those with disabilities or language barriers.
- *Example:* The school installs bilingual signage and ensures that events are held in ADA-accessible spaces.

6. Develop a Scheduling System for Shared Spaces

- Clear procedures prevent conflicts over gymnasiums, libraries, and cafeterias.
- *Example:* The principal uses an online scheduling tool and weekly planning meetings to coordinate space usage among departments and outside groups.

7. Consider Community Use and Partnerships

- Facilities can often serve both school and local community needs.
- *Example:* The school partners with a local nonprofit to use the auditorium for evening workshops while ensuring custodial coverage and safety protocols.

8. Monitor and Evaluate Facility Effectiveness

- Regular feedback ensures that the plan continues to meet the needs of the school and community.
- *Example:* The principal surveys staff each semester to assess whether space use supports instructional goals and adjusts as needed.

What type of safety regulations must a building administrator be aware of and who should be contacted if there is a problem?

At Bound Brook Elementary, Principal Mr. Chamberlin was conducting a routine building inspection when he noticed several red flags in the lower-level classrooms: a malfunctioning emergency exit sign near the art room, heating vents blowing inconsistent air, and clutter partially blocking the main hallway. Knowing that building safety is a non-negotiable responsibility of school leaders, Mr. Chamberlin acted immediately.

As the building administrator, he understood that he must be aware of and compliant with multiple local, state, and federal safety regulations, including:

- Fire and building codes (e.g., unobstructed exits, working alarm systems, posted evacuation maps),
- Environmental safety laws (e.g., indoor air quality standards, mold prevention),
- Occupational Safety and Health Administration (OSHA) requirements,
- ADA accessibility standards,
- Safe handling of materials and equipment, especially in art and science classrooms.

To address the problems, Mr. Chamberlin first contacted the district facilities manager to inspect and repair the HVAC system and ensure proper air flow. He submitted a maintenance work order for the faulty exit sign and followed up with the custodial team supervisor to immediately clear the blocked hallway and retrain staff on the policy for safe storage in corridors.

He then reported the issues and corrective actions taken to the district safety coordinator, documenting them in Bound Brook's safety log. Additionally, he consulted the local fire marshal to schedule a follow-up compliance walkthrough before the next state-mandated inspection.

To reinforce awareness, Mr. Chamberlin held a brief safety training during the next staff meeting, reviewing procedures for identifying and reporting hazards. He also re-circulated the district's Safety Compliance Checklist and reminded staff that any observed safety concern, no matter how minor, must be reported immediately.

By taking swift, informed, and collaborative action, Mr. Chamberlin ensured Bound Brook Elementary remained in compliance, prevented further risk, and modeled the kind of ethical, accountable leadership that protects both students and staff.

Outline

1. Fire Safety and Emergency Evacuation Regulations

- Schools must comply with local fire codes, evacuation procedures, and inspection schedules.
- *Example:* The principal ensures fire drills are held monthly and that exits are clearly marked and unobstructed.
- Contact: Local fire marshal or district facilities director for inspections and compliance.

2. Health and Sanitation Standards

- Schools must meet health department standards for cleanliness, food service, water quality, and restrooms.
- *Example:* The nurse reports a pest issue in the cafeteria, prompting a sanitation inspection.
- Contact: Local health department or school district environmental services coordinator.

3. Building Code Compliance and Structural Safety

- Facilities must meet state and local building codes related to occupancy, accessibility, and structural integrity.
- *Example:* A leaky roof or faulty HVAC system is identified during a routine inspection.
- Contact: District maintenance supervisor or facilities department.

4. Security and Crisis Response Procedures

- Schools are required to have emergency operations plans for intruders, lockdowns, and natural disasters.
- *Example:* The school practices active shooter drills and has secure entry systems in place.
- Contact: School resource officer (SRO), local police, or district security coordinator.

5. ADA (Americans with Disabilities Act) Accessibility Requirements

- Schools must ensure that facilities are accessible to individuals with disabilities.
- *Example:* The principal identifies that a ramp is too steep and does not meet ADA slope guidelines.
- Contact: District ADA compliance officer or facilities project manager.

6. Playground and Equipment Safety

- Outdoor play areas must meet safety standards for equipment, surfaces, and supervision.
- *Example:* Broken playground equipment is flagged during recess supervision.
- Contact: District facilities department or contracted playground safety inspector.

7. Indoor Air Quality and Environmental Safety

- Schools must address concerns related to mold, asbestos, and air filtration.
- *Example:* Teachers report a persistent musty smell in certain classrooms.
- Contact: District environmental health coordinator or facilities director.

8. Reporting and Responding to Safety Hazards Promptly

- Administrators must respond quickly to concerns reported by staff, students, or families.
- *Example:* A teacher reports a ceiling tile that's sagging due to a leak.
- Contact: Maintenance help desk or emergency repair contact, depending on severity.

What are the components of a well-structured acceptable use policy?

At Unity River Middle School, Principal Mrs. Olabisi began noticing a pattern of digital misuse. Students were gaming during instruction, visiting non-educational websites, and using chat features inappropriately during lessons. At the same time, some teachers expressed confusion about which digital tools were approved for classroom use. Recognizing the need to promote responsible technology use and comply with district and federal policies, Mrs. Olabisi made it a top priority to revise and implement a comprehensive Acceptable Use Policy (AUP).

She collaborated with the school's technology integration specialist to lead a committee including teachers, a parent representative, the media specialist, and a district IT coordinator. Together, they reviewed New Jersey state expectations and federal guidelines such as CIPA (Children's Internet Protection Act) and FERPA (Family Educational Rights and Privacy Act) to ensure the revised AUP was both compliant and effective.

The policy clearly outlined its purpose which is to support learning, protect users, and guide ethical digital behavior. It applied to all students, staff, and anyone using school networks or devices.

The Acceptable Use Policy, AUP detailed appropriate educational uses, including accessing online curriculum, conducting research, submitting assignments, and participating in digital discussions on district-approved platforms.

It prohibited accessing inappropriate content, bypassing firewalls, cyberbullying, plagiarism, unauthorized downloads, and misuse of artificial intelligence tools.

The policy promoted ethical online conduct, password security, intellectual property respect, and appropriate communication on school-approved platforms.

Users were reminded that device and network use could be monitored. Guidelines were provided for protecting personally identifiable information (PII) and maintaining district technology systems.

The AUP included a range of consequences aligned with the district code of conduct, from verbal warnings to loss of privileges and administrative action depending on the severity of the violation.

Staff were expected to model and reinforce the AUP during instruction. Administrators monitored compliance and responded to incidents consistently.

Families reviewed and signed the AUP at the start of the school year. The policy was also introduced during orientations and posted online for reference.

After implementation, Mrs. Olabisi ensured the policy was introduced through digital citizenship lessons across all grade levels. Staff received guidance on instructional tech integration, and regular reminders helped keep expectations clear. As a result, incidents of digital misuse declined. Students began demonstrating more responsible online behavior, and staff reported increased confidence in using educational technology effectively.

By updating and actively reinforcing the Acceptable Use Policy, Unity River Middle School strengthened its digital learning culture, aligned with both legal requirements and its educational mission.

Outline

1. Purpose and Scope of the Policy

- Clearly state the intent of the policy and who it applies to (students, staff, visitors).
- *Example:* "This policy outlines appropriate use of district-owned technology for all users on school premises and networks."

2. Definitions of Key Terms

- Include terms such as "user," "device," "network," "personal data," and "inappropriate content."
- *Example:* Define "network" as any district-provided internet, wireless, or cloud-based service.

3. Guidelines for Appropriate Use

- Provide examples of acceptable behaviors when using school technology and internet access.
- *Example:* "Users may access digital resources for learning, collaboration, and research related to school curriculum."

4. Prohibited Activities

- Outline specific unacceptable uses that violate policy or law.
- *Example:* "Users may not engage in cyberbullying, bypass filters, or access obscene, violent, or discriminatory content."

5. User Privacy and Monitoring Notice

- Clarify that school systems are monitored and that users should not expect full privacy.
- *Example:* "Emails, browser history, and device usage may be reviewed by authorized personnel."

6. Responsibilities of Users

- Set expectations for keeping passwords secure, respecting intellectual property, and reporting misuse.
- *Example:* "Students must not share login credentials and must credit online sources used in assignments."

7. Consequences for Violations

- Describe disciplinary actions or loss of access rights that result from non-compliance.
- *Example:* "Violations may result in restricted access, suspension of privileges, and disciplinary referrals."

8. Guidelines for the Use of Personal Devices (Bring Your Own Device, BYOD)

- Address whether personal devices are allowed and under what conditions.
- *Example:* "Personal devices must connect to the guest network and follow the same AUP standards."

9. Internet Safety and Digital Citizenship Education

- Reinforce that users will be taught responsible and safe online behavior.
- *Example:* "Students will receive instruction in recognizing phishing, managing online identity, and protecting personal data."

10. Signature of Agreement

- Request a signed acknowledgment from students, parents (if applicable), and staff to confirm understanding.
- *Example:* "All users must sign the AUP agreement form before receiving device access or credentials."

What are the standard criteria for evaluating the usefulness of a communication and/or information management system?

At Brookstone Middle School, Principal Ms. Delgado noticed that parent engagement had declined, and staff often complained about delays in receiving key updates. After several missed announcements and a handful of families reporting they didn't know about an upcoming literacy night, she decided it was time to evaluate the school's current communication and information management systems.

She collaborated with her leadership team to review the system using several key criteria. First, they assessed accessibility and user-friendliness. Many parents, especially multilingual families, found the platform difficult to navigate and only available in English. Next, they evaluated timeliness and efficiency, finding that staff announcements were often buried in lengthy email threads rather than delivered in real-time. The system also lacked integration with their student information system, requiring staff to copy and paste parent emails manually, an inefficient process prone to error.

Data security and confidentiality were also reviewed to ensure compliance with FERPA and district policies. Ms. Delgado found that the current platform lacked role-based access controls, posing a risk for unauthorized data exposure. On the technical reliability front, teachers had documented multiple outages during report card season, another red flag.

The leadership team also evaluated whether the system provided adequate customization and scalability, noting that it lacked the ability to filter communications by grade level or to support multimedia formats. Feedback from staff and families revealed confusion due to unclear messaging, indicating a need for communication clarity and translation features. Finally, they compared the cost-effectiveness of the current system against newer options, identifying alternatives with more robust features at similar pricing.

Based on this analysis, Ms. Delgado transitioned the school to a new system that supported multiple languages, real-time alerts, integration with their gradebook, and better data protection. Within a month, communication improved noticeably: families received updates in their home language, staff reported greater clarity, and event participation increased. The school's shift to a more effective system ultimately enhanced transparency, stakeholder trust, and overall school operations.

<u>Outline</u>

1. Accessibility and User-Friendliness

- The system should be easy to navigate and useable by all stakeholders (staff, families, students).
- *Example:* A communication app offers multilingual support and mobile access for families without computers.

2. Efficiency and Timeliness

- The system should streamline workflows and allow timely sharing and retrieval of information.
- *Example:* Teachers can instantly post announcements and updates to parents via a shared platform.

3. Integration with Existing Systems

- It should integrate with other district tools such as SIS (Student Information System), LMS (Learning Management System), and HR platforms.
- *Example:* A principal accesses attendance, grades, and parent contact info all within one dashboard.

4. **Security and Data Privacy Compliance**
   - The system must protect sensitive information and comply with laws like FERPA and HIPAA (if applicable).
   - *Example:* Only authorized users can view IEP documents, with multi-factor authentication required.

5. **Reliability and Technical Support**
   - The platform should be stable, with minimal downtime and responsive customer support.
   - *Example:* A help desk resolves system errors within 24 hours and offers live troubleshooting.

6. **Customization and Flexibility**
   - It should allow for school-specific needs such as custom alerts, templates, or reporting features.
   - *Example:* A school can create behavior incident reports that align with their PBIS program.

7. **Communication Reach and Engagement Tracking**
   - The tool should monitor who has received, read, or responded to messages or updates.
   - *Example:* The platform shows that 85% of parents viewed the school newsletter within 48 hours.

8. **Scalability and Future Growth Potential**
   - The system should support additional users, schools, or modules as the district grows, or needs evolve.
   - *Example:* A district expands the platform to include staff onboarding and digital PD tracking.

9. **Cost-Effectiveness and Value**
   - The benefits of the system should justify its cost in terms of saved time, improved communication, or efficiency.
   - *Example:* Switching to a unified communication platform saves the school $10,000 annually in printing and postage.

10. **Feedback and Continuous Improvement Capability**
    - The system should collect user feedback and offer updates based on user experience.
    - *Example:* After staff input, the vendor adds a feature to flag unread parent messages.

Essential Questions #5 — Organizational Leadership

What recent federal laws have had the most impact on plant operation, accessibility, and safety?

At Silverwood Intermediate School, Principal Dr. Hart was preparing for the district's annual facilities audit when she realized her school had fallen behind on several compliance updates. As she reviewed her building operations plan, she worked closely with the facilities manager, school nurse, and district operations director to ensure Silverwood met current federal mandates related to plant operation, accessibility, and safety.

One major focus was compliance with the Americans with Disabilities Act (ADA). Dr. Hart noticed that although ramps had been installed at the main entrances, several interior doorways were too narrow for students in wheelchairs, and the auditorium lacked accessible seating. She initiated a building walkthrough with a district ADA coordinator, and together, they developed a phased plan to widen doorframes, update signage to include Braille, and retrofit bathrooms with appropriate support bars, ensuring that the building met ADA accessibility standards for students, staff, and community members.

Dr. Hart also worked to ensure compliance with Occupational Safety and Health Administration (OSHA) guidelines, particularly those related to indoor air quality and emergency preparedness. With increased awareness of airborne illnesses and allergens, she led efforts to upgrade the school's HVAC filtration system and implemented a new cleaning protocol using EPA-approved disinfectants. These changes were guided in part by recommendations from the Centers for Disease Control and Prevention (CDC) and supported through federal funding allocated under the Elementary and Secondary School Emergency Relief (ESSER) Act, which helped schools improve safety during and after the COVID-19 pandemic.

Additionally, Dr. Hart reviewed the school's compliance with the Asbestos Hazard Emergency Response Act (AHERA). The district conducted inspections, but no recent awareness training was provided to staff. She arranged for a certified specialist to train custodians and classroom teachers on recognizing and reporting potential hazards.

Finally, she revisited the school's emergency preparedness plan to align with the, Every Student Succeeds Act (ESSA) requirement that schools maintain safe and supportive environments. Working with local law enforcement and the school crisis team, Dr. Hart organized lockdown drills, ensured that fire and safety inspections were current, and added a visible visitor management system at the main entrance.

By aligning school practices with federal regulations such as ADA, OSHA, AHERA, ESSER, ESSA, and guidance from the Centers for Disease Control and Prevention (CDC), Dr. Hart not only improved Silverwood's operational compliance but also enhanced safety, accessibility, and learning conditions for every student and staff member.

<u>Outline</u>

1. **ADA Title II & DOJ's New Digital Accessibility Rule (April 2024**)
    - Requires all public schools' websites and mobile apps to conform to WCAG 2.1 Level A/AA standards.
    - Implications:
        - Ensures digital inclusiveness for users with disabilities (screen readers, keyboard navigation).
        - Contracts with vendors must include web-accessibility guarantees.

2. **Amended Section 504 & ADA Regulations (Effective July 8, 2024)**
    - Expanded protections against disability discrimination in federally funded programs Federal Register.
    - Implications:
        - Schools must revisit facility modifications, aided technologies, and accommodation protocols.
        - ADA Title II and 504 now require consistent interpretation and implementation.

3. **Infrastructure Investment and Jobs Act (IIJA) – Accessibility Investments**
    - Allocates funding for transportation-related accessibility, including pedestrian infrastructure near schools U.S. General Services Administration.
    - Implications:
        - Provides support for retrofitting school-adjacent pathways, crossing signals, and ADA-compliant drop-off zones.

4. **PLAN for School Safety Act of 2023 (H.R. 6613)**
- Enhances federal grants and guidance for school safety equipment and facility upgrades.
- Implications:
  - Enables modernization of security systems, lockdown capabilities, lighting, and surveillance.

5. **Bipartisan Safer Communities Act (June 2022)**
- Focused on mental health supports and enhanced school safety programming Congress.gov
- Implications:
  - Encourages thoughtful design of safe, trauma-informed environments (e.g., secure entry, counseling spaces).

Who Should Be Contacted When Issues Arise

Issue Type	**Primary Contact(s)**
Fire/life safety	Local fire marshal; district facilities director
Digital accessibility issues	DOJ Civil Rights Division; district IT/data coordinator
Physical accessibility	District ADA compliance officer; state architect
Facility safety/structural	District maintenance/facilities department
Security and crisis readiness	School resource officer, district security coordinator
Disability compliance	Office for Civil Rights (DOJ/HHS) for Section 504/ADA

What strategies should a school leader use when faced with budget cuts?

At Maple Ridge Middle School, Principal Mrs. Foster received notice that her school would face a 10% reduction in operational funding for the upcoming school year due to district-wide budget constraints. Rather than make immediate cuts, Mrs. Foster approached the situation strategically to protect student learning and staff morale.

She began by forming a budget review committee that included the assistant principal, school business administrator, teacher leaders from each grade level, and a parent representative. Together, they conducted a line-by-line analysis of the existing budget, identifying fixed costs, contractual obligations, and discretionary spending.

To guide their decision-making, Mrs. Foster gathered and reviewed student achievement data, enrollment projections, and program usage reports. This data-driven approach allowed her team to prioritize spending that directly supported core instructional goals and equity. For example, they chose to protect funding for intervention programs supporting multilingual learners and students with IEPs, even while scaling back on less-used extracurricular activities.

She also solicited input from staff and the school community, hosting a town hall and using surveys to ensure transparency. This helped build trust and generate creative ideas, such as switching to digital subscriptions in the library and consolidating some elective offerings into interdisciplinary courses to reduce staffing overlap.

Next, Mrs. Foster examined alternative funding sources, including local grants, Title I allocations, and partnerships with community organizations. She successfully partnered with a local nonprofit to provide after-school tutoring at no cost to the school.

In terms of human resources, rather than layoffs, Mrs. Foster restructured schedules and offered voluntary transfers and shared staffing between schools. She worked with HR to protect the school's diverse hiring goals and maintain staff morale.

Throughout the process, she communicated frequently and clearly with stakeholders, explaining why certain decisions were made and how they aligned with the school's mission. She also committed to revisiting the midyear budget to adjust if additional funds became available.

By focusing on collaboration, data, transparency, and equity, Mrs. Foster not only navigated the budget cuts effectively but also reinforced a school culture of shared responsibility, innovation, and resilience.

Outline

1. Prioritize Core Instructional Programs and Student Needs

- Protect the integrity of teaching and learning as the central mission.
- *Example:* Maintain funding for literacy and math interventions, even if enrichment programs are temporarily scaled back.

2. Engage Stakeholders in Transparent Budget Conversations

- Involve staff, families, and community members in decision-making.
- *Example:* Hold town halls and advisory committee meetings to discuss trade-offs and gather input.

3. Conduct a Program and Cost-Effectiveness Audit

- Review current programs to identify what is yielding strong outcomes and what may need restructuring or elimination.
- *Example:* Use data to determine which after-school programs have the highest student impact relative to cost.

4. Explore Alternative Funding Sources

- Seek grants, partnerships, and donations to offset shortfalls.
- *Example:* Partner with local businesses to sponsor student competitions or technology resources.

5. Streamline Operations and Reduce Non-Essential Spending

- Cut or consolidate administrative expenses before impacting classrooms.
- *Example:* Reduce non-critical travel, subscriptions, or overtime pay.

6. Reallocate Staff Strategically Based on Enrollment and Need

- Use staffing models that align with student enrollment and identified priorities.
- *Example:* Combine sections with low enrollment and reassign personnel to high-need areas.

7. Communicate Early, Honestly, and Frequently

- Build trust by keeping the school community informed and prepared for changes.
- *Example:* Send regular budget updates via newsletters and staff meetings.

8. Preserve Morale and Support Staff Through Transitions

- Acknowledge challenges while focusing on shared values and purpose.
- *Example:* Recognize staff efforts and invite input on cost-saving ideas.

9. Phase in Cuts Gradually When Possible

- Spread adjustments over time to minimize disruption and allow for planning.
- *Example:* Reduce certain programs by half this year with a full phase-out next year if needed.

10. Advocate at the District and State Level

- Elevate the school's needs and advocate for equitable funding.
- *Example:* Submit impact statements to district officials and collaborate with other principals to present a united case.

What other resources are available to a school outside of budgeted allocations?

At Brookside Academy, Principal Mr. Carter faced a challenge when funding fell short for a much-needed after-school STEM enrichment program. Rather than abandon the initiative, Mr. Carter explored alternative resources beyond the school's allocated budget.

First, he identified grant opportunities at the local and state level. With the help of a district grant writer, Brookside applied for and received a Title IV, Part A grant, which supports well-rounded educational opportunities. This grant allowed the school to purchase STEM kits and pay teachers a stipend for leading the sessions.

Mr. Carter also leveraged community partnerships. He reached out to a nearby university's education department, which provided interns to support the after-school program as part of their service-learning requirement. Additionally, a local tech company donated refurbished laptops and sent volunteer engineers to mentor students once a month.

Recognizing the potential of in-kind donations, he partnered with the PTA and local businesses for supplies and snacks. The PTA hosted a fundraiser that brought in additional funds, while a neighborhood grocery store donated healthy snacks weekly, ensuring students had food before the sessions began.

To tap into district-shared services, Mr. Carter coordinated with the district's instructional technology team to borrow 3D printers and robotics equipment already housed at another school. By scheduling shared access, Brookside avoided duplicate purchases while expanding learning opportunities.

Lastly, Mr. Carter used volunteerism and service credits as a creative resource. Retired teachers and professionals in STEM-related fields volunteered their time to co-lead projects. High school students fulfilling service hour requirements also helped with tutoring and supervision.

By thinking beyond the budget, Mr. Carter activated a powerful network of grants, partnerships, donations, shared services, and volunteers, turning a financial limitation into a collaborative success story that enriched students learning far beyond what money alone could buy.

Outline

1. Grants and Competitive Funding Opportunities

- Schools can apply for federal, state, and private foundation grants.
- *Example:* A Title I school applies for an after-school program grant from the 21st Century Community Learning Centers initiative.

2. Community and Business Partnerships

- Local organizations can donate time, services, or materials to support school needs.
- *Example:* A neighborhood hardware store donates supplies for a school garden project.

3. Parent-Teacher Organizations (PTO/PTA)

- Parent groups can raise funds and provide volunteers for events, materials, or field trips.
- *Example:* The PTA funds new books for classroom libraries through a community book fair.

4. Volunteers and Interns

- Colleges, community members, and service organizations can offer skilled volunteers or student interns.
- *Example:* A local university sends education majors to assist with small group reading instruction.

5. Donations and In-Kind Contributions

- Schools can receive supplies, equipment, or services at no cost from individuals or businesses.
- *Example:* A tech company donates refurbished laptops for student use.

6. Educational Foundations and Alumni Networks

- School or district-specific foundations or alumni can offer targeted support.
- *Example:* A former graduate establishes a scholarship fund or donates instruments to the music program.

7. Shared Services Across Schools or Districts

- Schools can collaborate to reduce costs through shared staff, services, or equipment.
- *Example:* Several schools share a behavior specialist who rotates campuses.

8. Student-Led Initiatives and Fundraisers

- Students can contribute through service projects and fundraising campaigns.
- *Example:* A student council hosts a talent show to raise funds for new recess equipment.

9. Digital Resources and Open Educational Tool

- Many high-quality instructional materials are freely available online.
- *Example:* Teachers use open-source curriculum platforms like CK-12 or Khan Academy.

10. Local Government and Nonprofit Support Programs

- City and nonprofit agencies may offer youth programming, health services, or food assistance.
- *Example:* A local YMCA provides after-school supervision and tutoring at no cost to families.

Essential Questions #8 Organizational Leadership

What is an example of competing interests in terms of budget development?

At Oak Hill Middle School, Principal Mrs. Morgan began the annual budget planning process by surveying department heads and reviewing school performance data. Two major priorities quickly emerged: the special education department requested additional paraprofessional support due to increased IEP caseloads, while the science department advocated for upgraded lab equipment to align with the new state STEM curriculum standards.

Both requests were valid and directly supported student learning, but the school's discretionary budget only had room to fully fund one of them.

Mrs. Morgan convened her school leadership team, including department heads, the business administrator, and parent representatives, to analyze the impact of each proposal. The special education team shared data showing that some students were missing required support minutes, which posed legal and instructional risks. On the other hand, science teachers argued that without modern lab materials, they couldn't meet grade-level expectations or provide meaningful hands-on learning experiences especially for high-achieving students.

This created a clear tension between legal compliance and academic innovation, a classic case of competing interests in budget development.

After a collaborative discussion and review of enrollment and staffing data, Mrs. Morgan proposed a compromise: she would reallocate part of the funds to hire one additional paraprofessional for immediate IEP support and seek a STEM grant and community sponsorship to fund science lab upgrades midyear. She also committed to revisiting science needs in the next budget cycle.

By facilitating a transparent, data-informed process and prioritizing compliance without dismissing innovation, Mrs. Morgan helped resolve the competing interests in a way that upheld equity and preserved trust across departments.

Outline

1. Instructional Staffing vs. Extracurricular Programs

- School leaders often face difficult decisions when limited funds must be allocated between core academics and enrichment activities.
- *Example:* The school budget can either fund a full-time intervention teacher to support reading gaps or continue funding multiple extracurricular clubs and sports.

2. Academic Achievement vs. Building Maintenance

- Budget decisions may pit instructional improvements against facility upgrades.
- *Example:* Funds earmarked for a science lab renovation are redirected to purchase updated math curriculum materials.

3. Technology Expansion vs. Professional Development

- Both technology and teacher training are critical, but limited resources may force a choice.
- *Example:* The school can afford either a new set of Chromebooks or ongoing PD in culturally responsive teaching, not both.

4. Equity Initiatives vs. School-Wide Programs

- Leaders may face tension between targeted support for underserved groups and universal programming.
- *Example:* A proposal to fund bilingual aides for English learners is weighed against renewing a software license used school wide.

5. Stakeholder Preferences vs. Data-Driven Needs

- Parent, teacher, or board preferences can clash with evidence-based priorities.
- *Example:* Community members advocate for more arts programming, while data shows a pressing need for math intervention.

6. Short-Term Visibility vs. Long-Term Investment

- High-visibility projects may compete with foundational but less visible investments.
- *Example:* Replacing uniforms for school sports teams garners support, while early literacy intervention requires more investment with slower results.

7. Central Office Directives vs. Site-Based Needs

- Sometimes district-level mandates do not align with individual school priorities.
- *Example:* The district allocates funds for a new attendance system, but the school urgently needs classroom aides.

What are some ways in which the effectiveness of support staff impacts teaching and learning?

At Hawthorne Creek Elementary School, Principal Ms. Dana Ellis began noticing inconsistencies in student progress among classrooms that served high numbers of multilingual learners and students with IEPs. After reviewing walkthrough notes and assessment data, she realized that the quality and consistency of support staff including paraprofessionals, instructional aides, and clerical support were significantly affecting classroom instruction and student learning outcomes.

For example, in one third-grade classroom, an experienced paraprofessional who had been trained in behavior support strategies was able to keep a student with emotional needs calmly engaged in the lesson, allowing the teacher to continue whole-group instruction without disruption. In contrast, another class with a new, untrained aide experienced frequent interruptions and reduced instructional time, as the classroom teacher had to manage both the lesson and student behaviors without adequate help.

Ms. Ellis also observed that efficient front office staff played a key role in instructional time. Because office assistants managed attendance reporting, early dismissals, and parent inquiries smoothly, teachers were less likely to be pulled from class or interrupted which resulting in stronger classroom focus and continuity.

Recognizing these patterns, Ms. Ellis prioritized job-embedded training for support staff. She partnered with the district to offer monthly professional development in behavior management, small group instruction, and language acquisition strategies. She also clarified roles and expectations so that all staff felt valued and purposeful.

Within one quarter, both teachers and students reported improved learning conditions. Teachers noted that they could focus more on planning and instruction, while students received better-targeted assistance in real time. By investing in the professional growth and the coordination of support staff, Ms. Ellis created a more cohesive, responsive learning environment demonstrating how critical these team members are to the school's academic success.

Outline

1. Instructional Support Enhances Student Learning

- Paraprofessionals, instructional aides, and interventionists provide individualized or small-group support.
- *Example:* A math aide helps struggling students in a pull-out setting, allowing teachers to focus on core instruction.

2. Office Staff Improve Communication and School Operations

- Efficient front office staff ensure smooth information flow between home and school.
- *Example:* A responsive secretary keeps families informed about student absences, testing dates, and school events.

3. Custodians Maintain a Safe and Healthy Learning Environment

- Clean, well-maintained facilities promote student well-being and reduce distractions.
- *Example:* Custodians ensure classrooms are disinfected, contributing to lower absenteeism due to illness.

4. Counselors and Social Workers Support Emotional and Academic Growth

- Mental health professionals help address barriers to learning and create a supportive school climate.
- *Example:* A school social worker connects families with housing support, allowing students to return to school focused and ready to learn.

5. Technology Staff Enable Digital Learning and Instructional Access

- IT support staff keep devices, networks, and digital tools functioning smoothly.
- *Example:* A technician ensures that Chromebooks are repaired, and software is updated before testing season.

6. Security and Safety Personnel Foster a Climate of Trust

- Safety officers help students and staff feel secure, reducing stress and disruptions.
- *Example:* A school security guard builds positive relationships with students while maintaining safe entry procedures.

7. Food Services Ensure Students Are Ready to Learn

- Nutrition services provide healthy meals that support attention and academic engagement.
- *Example:* Breakfast programs ensure students are nourished and able to focus during morning lessons.

8. Library and Media Specialists Support Literacy and Research Skills

- Librarians curate resources and teach research, media literacy, and reading strategies.
- *Example:* The media specialist collaborates with teachers to support project-based learning and book access.

9. Bus Drivers and Transportation Staff Ensure Reliable Attendance

- Consistent, safe transportation directly impacts student attendance and punctuality.
- *Example:* A dependable bus driver builds rapport with students and ensures they arrive at school ready to learn.

10. Unified Collaboration Maximizes Impact

- When support staff are respected and included in school-wide efforts, the entire learning environment improves.
- *Example:* Principals involve all staff in school improvement planning, fostering ownership and alignment across roles.

Essential Questions #10 Organizational Leadership

What is the importance of establishing clear job qualification requirements before interviewing candidates for a position?

At Riverstone Charter Middle School, Principal Mr. Tyrone Glenn needed to hire a new math interventionist midyear due to a sudden resignation. In the rush to fill the role quickly, he skipped the usual process of updating the job description and clarifying specific qualifications. The posting simply read "math interventionist – grades 6–8," without outlining key requirements such as experience with data-driven instruction, co-teaching, or knowledge of Tier 2 and Tier 3 intervention strategies.

As a result, Mr. Glenn ended up interviewing a wide range of applicants some with only general math classroom experience and others with unrelated backgrounds, like tutoring or elementary math instruction. During the interviews, it became clear that none of the candidates fully met the school's needs, and valuable time was wasted clarifying expectations that should have been listed upfront.

After this setback, Mr. Glenn paused the process. He met with the RTI coordinator, instructional coach, and grade-level teachers to define the essential qualifications: experience with diagnostic assessments, comfort with middle school math content, ability to collaborate in PLCs, and a demonstrated track record of accelerating growth in underperforming students.

They updated the job posting to reflect these expectations and added "preferred qualifications" such as experience collaborating with multilingual learners and knowledge of progress monitoring tools like I-Ready.

The second round of candidates was far more aligned. Mr. Glenn hired a candidate with targeted intervention experience and strong references from a similar school. The new hire began implementing small-group pullouts within two weeks, and by the next benchmark assessment cycle, student scores in the intervention group had already begun to improve.

By first clarifying job qualifications, Mr. Glenn saved time, reduced mismatches, and ensured that hiring aligned with the school's instructional goals and student needs.

Outline

Ensures Fairness and Equity in Hiring

- Clear qualifications create a consistent standard that applies to all applicants.
- *Example:* All candidates for a teaching role must hold the same required certifications and experience to be considered.

2. Helps Identify the Best-Fit Candidates Efficiently

- Well-defined requirements allow leaders to quickly screen out applicants who do not meet baseline criteria.
- *Example:* Only candidates with experience in bilingual education advance to interviews for a dual-language program.

3. Aligns Hiring with School Goals and Needs

- Qualifications reflect the specific skills and expertise needed to support school priorities.
- *Example:* A school focused on STEM ensures candidates for a science teacher position have relevant coursework or prior teaching experience in the subject.

4. Prevents Bias and Subjectivity in the Selection Process

- A clear rubric reduces the influence of personal preference or unconscious bias.
- *Example:* Interview panels score candidates based on pre-established qualifications rather than personality or familiarity.

5. Supports Legal and Ethical Hiring Practices

- Documented qualifications help protect against discrimination claims and support transparency.
- *Example:* A rejected applicant challenges the decision, and the school can show they didn't meet the posted degree requirement.

6. Guides the Development of Interview Questions

- Targeted questions can assess specific competencies directly related to the job role.
- *Example:* If collaboration is a required skill, the interview includes a scenario question about working on an interdisciplinary team.

7. Sets Clear Expectations for the Role

- Candidates better understand the demands and scope of the job before they're hired.
- *Example:* Posting that the position requires evening family events prepares candidates for those responsibilities.

8. Streamlines Onboarding and Performance Evaluation

- Hiring based on defined qualifications sets the stage for aligned professional growth and support.
- *Example:* A new hire's PD plan builds on the instructional strategies noted as core job expectations.

Essential Questions #11 Organizational Leadership

What types of plans and strategies should a school leader have in place to protect staff and students and to monitor threats to their emotional security?

At Maple Valley Intermediate School, Principal Mrs. Serena Blake began the new academic year with a focused mission: to enhance both the physical and emotional safety of her school community. The previous year had been marked by an uptick in bullying incidents and a noticeable rise in student anxiety. Recognizing that emotional well-being is foundational to student success and staff morale, Mrs. Blake developed a multi-layered plan to protect emotional security and proactively monitor potential threats to it.

One of her first strategies was to implement a schoolwide Social-Emotional Learning (SEL) curriculum, which was delivered weekly during homeroom. These structured lessons focused on key topics such as empathy, managing emotions, peer relationships, and conflict resolution. To ensure consistency, teachers received training on how to integrate SEL practices into everyday instruction and classroom routines, helping students build emotional resilience.

To strengthen mental health support, Mrs. Blake assigned dedicated counselors to each grade level and arranged for small-group counseling sessions during non-instructional times. She also partnered with a local mental health agency to offer on-site counseling for students with more intensive needs. These steps have made mental health resources more accessible and visible, reducing stigma and encouraging early intervention.

To empower students and staff to report concerns confidentially, the school launched an anonymous reporting system available online. Students, parents, and staff could submit reports of bullying, emotional distress, or potential threats, which were then monitored daily by the school's safety and wellness team. This created a safe, structured channel for speaking up without fear of retaliation.

Mrs. Blake also reinforced the school's crisis response and risk assessment procedures. Her leadership team received specialized training in how to identify and respond to warning signs of emotional distress or aggression. In partnership with district security, the school conducted simulations and walkthroughs of threat response scenarios, ensuring all staff knew their role in maintaining a safe environment.

Recognizing that emotional safety applies to staff as well, Mrs. Blake has introduced several staff wellness initiatives. She launched a wellness committee, added calming "reset zones" in staff lounges, and provided monthly professional development on trauma-informed teaching, self-care, and de-escalation strategies. These steps helped reduce burnout and modeled the same care that staff were expected to extend to students.

To shift from a punitive to a restorative culture, the school implemented restorative circles as an alternative to traditional discipline. This practice encouraged accountability, peer-to-peer dialogue, and conflict resolution. To track the school's emotional climate, Mrs. Blake also rolled out quarterly climate surveys for both students and staff. Data from these surveys was used to identify trends, adjust strategies, and prioritize supports.

Through this comprehensive and proactive approach, Mrs. Blake transformed the emotional culture of Maple Valley Intermediate. The results spoke for themselves: conflict-related office referrals dropped significantly, climate survey scores improved, and students reported feeling safer and more supported in their classrooms. Most importantly, both staff and students knew that their emotional well-being mattered and that they were part of a caring, responsive school community.

<u>Outline</u>

1. Establish a Comprehensive School Safety and Mental Health Plan

- Integrate emotional well-being into the school's safety protocols.
- *Example:* The school's crisis response plan includes procedures for mental health emergencies, grief support, and trauma response.

2. Provide Access to Mental Health Professionals

- Ensure students and staff can access qualified counselors, social workers, or psychologists.
- *Example:* A full-time school counselor is available for both individual and group support sessions.

3. Implement Regular Social-Emotional Learning (SEL) Programs

- Integrate SEL into the curriculum to build resilience, empathy, and self-regulation.
- *Example:* Weekly SEL lessons are embedded into advisory periods or morning meetings.

4. Monitor School Climate Through Surveys and Feedback Tools

- Use climate surveys to assess emotional safety, belonging, and trust.
- *Example:* Students and staff complete anonymous climate surveys twice a year; data is used to adjust supports.

5. Train Staff to Recognize and Respond to Signs of Distress

- Provide PD in trauma-informed practices, de-escalation, and mental health awareness.
- *Example:* Teachers receive training on how to spot early warning signs of anxiety, depression, or withdrawal.

6. Create Safe, Inclusive Physical and Virtual Environments

- Ensure that students feel emotionally safe in classrooms, hallways, and online spaces.
- *Example:* Classroom agreements promote respect and inclusion; online platforms are monitored for cyberbullying.

7. Establish Clear and Confidential Reporting Systems

- Enable students and staff to report concerns about emotional safety anonymously.
- *Example:* The school uses an online tip line and encourages students to report threats to well-being.

8. Foster Strong Relationships and a Positive School Culture

- Build trust between students, staff, and leadership through intentional connection.
- *Example:* Teachers greet students at the door each morning and conduct regular check-ins.

9. Partner with Families and Community Mental Health Agencies

- Extend emotional support systems beyond school walls.
- *Example:* The school refers families to community counseling centers and hosts wellness workshops for parents.

10. Review and Update Safety and Wellness Policies Regularly

- Continuously evaluate and improve plans based on emerging needs and feedback.
- *Example:* The principal convenes a wellness team each semester to review safety data and update procedures.

What are the components of a comprehensive safety and security plan and who should be considered key emergency personnel?

At Brighton Ridge Middle School, Principal Mrs. Ruiz led the school's annual review of its comprehensive safety and security plan in preparation for the new academic year. Her goal was not only to comply with district and state regulations but also to ensure that the plan reflected the real-time needs of students, staff, and the broader school community. She began by assembling a safety planning committee that included the assistant principal, the school nurse, a teacher representative, a school resource officer (SRO), the head custodian, the guidance counselor, and a parent liaison.

The first component of their plan focused on emergency preparedness, which included procedures for fire drills, lockdowns, evacuations, and shelter-in-place scenarios. These protocols were reviewed for clarity, and roles were assigned to specific staff members to lead students to safety in case of an emergency. Mrs. Ruiz ensured that the evacuation maps were updated and visible in all classrooms and common areas.

The second component addressed threat identification and prevention. The team evaluated data from last year's discipline referrals and student incident reports to identify high-risk areas, such as bathrooms and unsupervised hallways. In response, new hallway duty schedules and additional security cameras were added to monitor these zones. The school counselor and social worker also expanded their mental health screenings and check-ins with at-risk students as a proactive measure.

A third major component involved communication protocols. Mrs. Ruiz created a clear chain of command for emergency response, ensuring that every staff member knew who to report to and how information would be disseminated. The school adopted a mass notification system that allowed text, call, and email alerts to be sent to parents and staff during emergencies. Regular communication drills were held to practice these procedures.

Key emergency personnel were clearly identified and trained. This included the school nurse (for medical emergencies), the SRO (for safety threats), custodial staff (for managing building systems), the front office team (for emergency communications), and crisis counselors (for emotional support following a traumatic event). Each of these individuals had updated contact lists, clearly defined roles, and participated in tabletop exercises and live drills.

Finally, the safety and security plan addressed community partnerships, including contact with the local fire department, police, and emergency medical services (EMS). Mrs. Ruiz invited first responders to walk through the school quarterly to stay familiar with the layout and ensure rapid response in case of a real emergency.

By the end of the planning process, the school community felt confident and empowered. Teachers reported greater clarity in their roles, parents appreciated the transparency, and students participated in safety week activities to reinforce their own awareness and responsibility. Mrs. Ruiz had not only complied with policy, but she had also built a safety culture rooted in preparedness, prevention, and shared accountability.

Outline

1. Emergency Operations Plan (EOP) Framework

- A written plan detailing procedures for various emergency scenarios.
- *Example:* Includes response protocols for fire, lockdowns, severe weather, and medical emergencies.

2. Threat Assessment and Prevention Strategies

- Systems to identify, assess, and intervene in potential threats.
- *Example:* A trained threat assessment team evaluates reports of concerning behavior and determines appropriate action.

3. Crisis Communication Protocols

- Clear procedures for notifying staff, families, media, and emergency services.
- *Example:* A communication tree outlines who contacts whom in each type of emergency.

4. Evacuation, Lockdown, and Shelter-in-Place Procedures

- Specific instructions based on the nature of the threat.
- *Example:* Fire evacuation routes are posted; lockdown procedures are practiced each semester.

5. Reunification and Recovery Procedures

- Plans for reuniting students with families and restoring school operations post-crisis.
- *Example:* A reunification site is designated off-campus, with student release procedures in place.

6. Staff Roles and Responsibilities

- Every adult on campus should know their specific duties during an emergency.
- *Example:* Designated staff help sweep hallways during fire drills or check attendance post-lockdown.

7. Training and Drills

- Ongoing training ensures readiness for various situations.
- *Example:* Staff receive CPR, AED, and first aid certification; students practice fire, lockdown, and evacuation drills.

8. Collaboration with Local Emergency Services

- Establish working relationships with first responders and emergency management agencies.
- *Example:* Police and fire departments participate in joint drills with the school annually.

9. Mental Health and Trauma Response Plan

- Provide post-crisis emotional support for students and staff.
- *Example:* Crisis counselors are available for debriefing and referrals following traumatic events.

10. Building Security Measures and Access Control

- Physical safeguards to prevent unauthorized entry or harm.

Why is interagency cooperation important when dealing with safety and security concerns?

At Cedar Springs Intermediate School, Principal Mr. Jordan Mills faced an urgent challenge when a student made a vague but concerning statement on social media about "not wanting to be in school anymore" and referenced "finishing things once and for all." A fellow student saw the post and reported it to a teacher, who immediately alerted the school counselor and administration. Mr. Mills knew that responding quickly and effectively would require more than just school personnel. Addressing this issue would require intentional, coordinated efforts among multiple agencies working together.

Mr. Mills followed the district's threat assessment protocol and immediately contacted the local police department, who dispatched a school resource officer to speak with the student and conduct a preliminary safety check. At the same time, the district mental health crisis team was brought in to assess the student's emotional state and determine whether there was an imminent risk of harm. The child study team reviewed the students' records and coordinated with the Department of Child Protection and Permanency (DCPP) to assess for any concerns at home.

Later that afternoon, a joint meeting was held at the school with representatives from all agencies involved: the local police, the crisis intervention team, the student's parents, a school social worker, and Mr. Mills. This multi-agency collaboration allowed for a clear understanding of the situation from every angle mental health, home environment, school history, and legal responsibility. Each group contributed a unique perspective, and together, they built a comprehensive safety plan that included immediate counseling support, temporary remote instruction, and ongoing home visits coordinated through a local youth services agency.

Through this cooperative response, the student received the support they needed without being criminalized or stigmatized. At the same time, the broader school community was reassured that the situation had been managed professionally, ethically, and safely.

Mr. Mills later shared with his staff during a faculty meeting that interagency cooperation had been crucial. "No single school leader, counselor, or teacher can manage these complex situations alone," he explained. "It takes a coordinated network, schools, law enforcement, mental health providers, and family services to keep students safe and supported."

Ms. Mills' action illustrates how interagency collaboration brings together multiple areas of expertise, ensures timely and appropriate action, protects students' rights, and promotes long-term safety both for the individual involved and the broader school community.

Outline

1. Enhances Preparedness Through Shared Expertise

- Different agencies bring specialized knowledge and training to emergency planning.
- *Example:* Police guide lockdown protocol development while fire departments advise on evacuation routes.

2. Improves Communication During Emergencies

- Real-time coordination helps reduce confusion and ensures faster response.
- *Example:* During a medical emergency, the school nurse and EMS communicate through pre-established channels to expedite care.

3. Aligns Roles and Responsibilities Across Responders

- Joint planning prevents duplication or gaps in responsibilities.
- *Example:* A reunification plan clearly outlines school staff tasks, law enforcement traffic control, and parent communication procedures.

4. Builds Trust and Relationships Before a Crisis Occurs

- Strong relationships increase confidence, collaboration, and efficiency during high-stress events.
- *Example:* Monthly safety meetings between school leaders and local agencies create a foundation for teamwork.

5. Ensures Compliance With Local, State, and Federal Safety Mandates

- Interagency collaboration ensures schools meet evolving legal requirements.
- *Example:* The district's safety plan is reviewed jointly by school personnel and municipal emergency managers to align with current laws.

6. Facilitates Resource Sharing in Crisis Response

- Schools benefit from agency tools, personnel, and expertise not available internally.
- *Example:* Local police provide training on threat assessment while the public health department assists with communicable disease protocols.

7. Supports Holistic Student Safety (Physical, Emotional, Digital)

- Agencies help address broader definitions of safety, including mental health and online security.
- *Example:* A partnership with the Department of Child Protection helps respond to abuse reports, while cybersecurity experts audit digital safety protocols.

8. Strengthens Post-Crisis Recovery and Support

- Interagency teams provide counseling, investigation, and recovery support after a crisis.
- *Example:* After a traumatic event, both school psychologists and county mental health professionals offer group counseling sessions.

Essential Questions #14 Organizational Leadership

How should/could a school leader deal with parents' concerns about unsafe conditions in their child's school?

At Jefferson Hills Elementary School, Principal Mrs. Carla Jennings began receiving emails and calls from a group of concerned parents whose children frequently reported slippery floors in the main hallway after lunch. One parent even shared that her child had slipped near the cafeteria doors, narrowly avoiding injury. Another parent voiced concern about dim lighting in the side stairwell, stating that her daughter felt unsafe walking through that area at dismissal.

Rather than dismiss the concerns or rely solely on custodial reports, Mrs. Jennings took immediate action. She organized a safety walkthrough with the head custodian, the school's safety officer, and a teacher representative. During the walkthrough, they observed that condensation from a nearby HVAC vent caused the tile floors near the cafeteria to become slick in the afternoons. They also noted that two fluorescent bulbs were out in the stairwell, significantly reducing visibility.

Mrs. Jennings documented the findings and immediately submitted a facilities maintenance request to the district to adjust the HVAC system and replace the lighting. She also ordered temporary non-slip mats for the cafeteria entrance and ensured that signage warning of wet floors was posted during lunch hours. To involve the community in the solution, she invited concerned parents to attend a School Safety Committee meeting, where she explained the actions taken and shared the plan for ongoing monitoring.

In the weeks that followed, Mrs. Jennings implemented a reporting protocol allowing students and staff to anonymously report facility safety issues. Custodial staff received refresher training on daily safety inspections, and school safety was added as a standing agenda item at monthly PTA meetings.

By taking the concerns seriously, responding transparently, and involving families in the solution process, Mrs. Jennings reaffirmed trust and strengthened the school's safety culture. Her leadership demonstrated that when parents speak up, school leaders listen and act.

Outline

1. Acknowledge Concerns with Empathy and Professionalism

- Create a safe space for parents to express their fears and frustrations.
- *Example:* A principal begins the conversation by thanking the parent for raising the concern and validating their desire to protect their child.

2. Gather Specific Details About the Concern

- Ask clarifying questions to understand the scope, timing, and nature of the safety issue.
- *Example:* A parent reports broken lighting in the parking lot; the leader confirms location, time of day, and any prior incidents.

3. Investigate Promptly and Thoroughly

- Conduct a site check, interview staff, review video, or consult logs as appropriate.
- *Example:* After a parent alleges bullying in a hallway, the principal checks camera footage and speaks with the student and supervises adults.

4. Communicate the Findings and Next Steps

- Report back to the parent with transparency while maintaining confidentiality for others.
- *Example:* The principal shares that supervision during recess will be increased and outlines steps taken to address a reported issue.

5. Implement Immediate Safety Measures if Needed

- Take swift, visible actions to reduce risk and demonstrate responsiveness.
- *Example:* If a gate is found to be broken, maintenance is called immediately, and temporary fencing is placed until repair is complete.

6. Engage Parents as Partners in Safety

- Involve families in safety committees or invite their feedback in policy discussions.
- *Example:* The school forms a parent advisory group to review emergency protocols and suggest improvements.

7. Review and Reinforce Safety Procedures With Staff and Students

- Revisit expectations for supervision, behavior, and reporting to prevent future concerns.
- *Example:* After a complaint about unsafe hallway behavior, the principal reminds staff of duty expectations and re-teaches transitions to students.

8. Maintain Open and Ongoing Communication

- Keep families informed of changes, improvements, and ongoing efforts to create a safe environment.
- *Example:* A follow-up message is sent to families highlighting recent facility upgrades and new safety procedures.

Essential Questions #15 Organizational Leadership

Under what circumstances would a school leader contact a child protective agency? Law enforcement agency? District legal counsel?

During lunch duty at Hamilton Ridge Middle School, a teacher observed a student, Jordan, rushing to eat an entire week's worth of snack items taken from other students' lunchboxes. When questioned privately, Jordan stated he hadn't eaten at home for the past few days and didn't have food in the house. The student also disclosed that he often stayed up late taking care of younger siblings while his parents were "out."

The teacher reported the incident to Principal Mrs. Tanya Powell, who gathered basic details without asking leading questions. Based on the information, lack of access to food, caregiving responsibilities beyond age-appropriate expectations, and possible neglect, Mrs. Powell determined that there was reasonable suspicion of neglect and promptly contacted the Division of Child Protection and Permanency (DCPP) to file a report, as required by state law.

Later that week, a different teacher found a private notebook containing threatening language about harming another student. The writing included names and specific after-school locations. Mrs. Powell contacted the school resource officer (SRO) to assess the potential threat and notify the local police department for further investigation. The student's parents were notified after consultation with law enforcement.

Finally, during the investigation, the student's guardian raised legal objections regarding how the school searched the student's backpack and questioned the handling of the notebook. To ensure compliance with school policy and student rights, Mrs. Powell consulted with the district's legal counsel before releasing any further information or conducting additional searches.

Below are the criteria for reporting

- Child Protective Agency (DCPP): Contacted when there is suspicion of neglect (e.g., lack of food, inappropriate caregiving responsibilities).
- Law Enforcement: Contacted when there is a potential threat of violence or student safety concern.

- District Legal Counsel: Contacted when legal questions arise about student rights, searches, parent challenges, or possible litigation.

Outline

1. Contacting a Child Protective Agency (e.g., Child Protective Services - CPS)

School leaders are mandated reporters and must contact child protection services when:

- **Suspected abuse or neglect is disclosed, observed, or reasonably suspected**
  - *Example:* A student arrives with unexplained bruises and confides that a parent caused them.
- **There are signs of abandonment or inadequate supervision**
  - *Example:* A young student reports being left home alone for multiple days.
- **A child reveals exposure to domestic violence or unsafe living conditions**
  - *Example:* A student shares details about ongoing physical altercations in the home.

    Note: Reporting must occur even if the details seem uncertain reasonable suspicion is enough.

2. Contacting a Law Enforcement Agency (e.g., Local Police or School Resource Officer)

Law enforcement should be contacted when:

- **There is an immediate or credible threat to safety (violence, weapons, intruders)**
  - *Example:* A student is reported to be in possession of a weapon on school grounds.
- **Criminal activity occurs on or near campus**
  - *Example:* Vandalism, theft, or physical assault occurs during school hours.
- **An incident requires crowd control or school evacuation**
  - *Example:* A bomb threat or active shooter alert is triggered.
- **Student involvement in illegal activity requires investigation**
  - *Example:* A student is caught selling drugs or engaging in cybercrime.

3. Contacting District Legal Counsel

A school leader should consult legal counsel when:

- **Faced with a complex personnel issue involving contracts, termination, or grievance**
  - *Example:* A staff member files a legal complaint alleging discrimination or retaliation.
- **Parental/legal guardianship disputes impact student safety or records access**
  - *Example:* A non-custodial parent demands to pick up a child despite a court order.
- **Responding to subpoenas, FERPA requests, or legal notifications**
  - *Example:* An attorney requests access to a student's discipline file.
- **Uncertainty exists about how to apply a district policy in a sensitive situation**
  - *Example:* A teacher posts controversial content online, and the principal seeks guidance on next steps.
- **Before issuing statements related to potential legal matters**
  - *Example:* A serious incident is under media attention, and public response is being crafted.

Essential Questions #16 Organizational Leadership

How can a school leader stay current with regulations related to student and staff safety (e.g., fire codes, immunizations, precautions against infectious disease)?

At Maple Crest Middle School, Principal Mrs. Douglas made it a priority to stay up to date with all safety regulations impacting students and staff. Each month, she attended the district's school leader meetings, where representatives from the local health department and Office of Emergency Management reviewed any updates to fire safety codes, immunization mandates, and public health protocols, especially those related to COVID-19 and seasonal flu prevention.

To ensure her school's practices were aligned with current law, Mrs. Douglas regularly collaborated with the district facilities supervisor, who kept her informed of inspection timelines and building code changes. After a routine fire inspection revealed outdated emergency lighting in two stairwells, she immediately submitted a maintenance request and ensured her custodial team followed the updated requirements outlined in the report.

On the health front, she collaborated closely with Nurse Bellamy, the school nurse, to track student immunization records and respond to guidance from the Centers for Disease Control and Prevention (CDC) and the New Jersey Department of Health. When a new infectious disease advisory was issued, Nurse Bellamy briefed Mrs. Douglas, who then coordinated with her leadership team to adjust hygiene protocols and communicate changes to staff and families.

To promote consistency, Mrs. Douglas scheduled quarterly School Safety Committee meetings, which included staff, the PTA president, a student representative, and the school's security officer. This group reviewed regulations, safety drills, and facility updates and provided input on revisions to the school's annual safety plan.

By staying connected to district resources, engaging health and safety professionals, and fostering a collaborative approach, Mrs. Douglas ensured that Maple Crest remained fully compliant and ready to protect its students and staff year-round.

Outline

1. Subscribe to State and Local Education Agency Updates

- Regular updates from Departments of Education, Health, and Safety provide timely regulation changes.
- *Example:* A principal subscribes to the NJDOE and local health department email alerts to receive notifications on new health mandates and policy changes.

2. Participate in Professional Associations and Networks

- Join national or state-level organizations that provide policy briefs, training, and alerts.
- *Example:* Membership in the National Association of Secondary School Principals (NASSP) gives access to federal policy updates, legal trends, and leadership webinars.

3. Attend Compliance and Safety Training Workshops

- Engage in district- or state-sponsored professional development specific to safety codes and legal responsibilities.

- *Example:* A school leader attends an annual district training on OSHA updates, infectious disease response, and emergency preparedness.

4. Maintain Regular Contact With District Safety or Legal Personnel
- Collaborate with specialists within the district for clarification and support.
- *Example:* The principal schedules quarterly check-ins with the district's risk management officer or legal counsel to discuss safety protocols and compliance reviews.

5. Develop a Compliance Calendar or Checklist
- Track deadlines and review periods for key safety areas such as fire drills, immunization records, and staff certifications.
- *Example:* A shared Google calendar alerts school leaders to renewal dates for fire safety inspections and required staff training.

6. Collaborate With Local Agencies and First Responders
- Partner with fire marshals, health departments, and police to stay aligned with evolving standards.
- *Example:* The school nurse and principal meet with the local public health officer to review immunization updates and infectious disease protocols.

7. Monitor Updates From CDC, OSHA, and Other Regulatory Bodies
- Use reputable national agencies as go-to sources for health and safety guidance.
- *Example:* During a flu outbreak, the school leader uses CDC school toolkits to update building protocols.

8. Conduct Routine Safety Audits and Policy Reviews
- Periodic internal reviews help ensure that all procedures align with current regulations.
- *Example:* A safety committee performs monthly checks of AED devices, first aid supplies, and fire extinguisher logs.

9. Encourage Staff to Share Regulatory Updates and Concerns
- Create a culture where teachers, nurses, and custodial staff report changes or compliance issues.
- *Example:* A custodian notifies the principal that new fire safety signage requirements were posted in the facilities bulletin.

10. Document Training, Inspections, and Policy Implementation
- Keeping accurate records ensures compliance and helps during audits or inspections.
- *Example:* A principal maintains a binder with certificates of training, inspection reports, and updated safety protocols.

Essential Questions #17 Organizational Leadership

What impact do scheduling and staffing decisions have on student learning?

At Mapleville Middle School, Principal Mrs. Douglas noticed a troubling trend: students in Grade 7 were underperforming in math compared to other grade levels. After reviewing assessment data and teacher feedback, she discovered that the current master schedule placed math at the very end of the day after lunch and elective periods when students were most distracted and mentally fatigued. Additionally, one of the math sections was overcrowded due to uneven teacher assignments, with one teacher managing 32 students while another taught just 18.

Recognizing how scheduling and staffing decisions directly affect instructional quality and student engagement, Mrs. Douglas initiated a full review of the school's master schedule. She collaborated with her leadership team and department heads to analyze enrollment patterns, instructional blocks, and teacher strengths. Together, they implemented the following changes:

- Moved core subjects like math and ELA to morning blocks when students were more alert and focused.
- Balanced class sizes by redistributing students based on data and ensuring equitable teacher loads.
- Assigned the teacher with stronger student growth outcomes to the inclusion class with more diverse learning needs.
- Built common planning time into the schedule for math teachers to collaborate on lesson design, data review, and differentiation strategies.

By midyear, classroom observations showed increased student participation, and benchmark data reflected a 17% improvement in math scores across Grade 7. Teachers reported greater satisfaction with their schedules, and students were more engaged during core instruction.

Staffing and scheduling decisions aren't just logistical; they shape when and how students learn. Strategic alignment of time, teacher assignments, and instructional priorities can dramatically impact student outcomes, especially when grounded in data and collaborative planning.

Outline

1. Ensures Equitable Access to High-Quality Instruction

- Strategic staffing places the most effective teachers where they're most needed.
- *Example:* A school ensures that experienced math teachers are assigned to grades with historically low performance.

2. Affects Time-on-Task and Academic Engagement

- Scheduling determines how much instructional time students receive in core content areas.
- *Example:* A block schedule allows students extended time for science labs and collaborative math problem-solving.

3. Influences Class Size and Differentiation Capacity

- Thoughtful staffing prevents overcrowding and supports manageable teacher-to-student ratios.
- *Example:* Hiring an additional reading interventionist allows for smaller guided reading groups in early grades.

4. Shapes Opportunities for Targeted Intervention and Enrichment

- Scheduling intervention blocks or push-in support can close achievement gaps.
- *Example:* A master schedule includes a 30-minute daily WIN ("What I Need") period for personalized learning.

5. Affects Teacher Collaboration and Instructional Planning

- Common planning time enables data analysis, vertical alignment, and interdisciplinary units.
- *Example:* Grade-level teams have shared prep periods to co-plan lessons and analyze student work.

6. Impacts Student Support Services Delivery

- Scheduling determines when and how students receive services like counseling, speech, or ESL.
- *Example:* ELL students are scheduled to receive language support without missing core instruction.

7. Influences School Climate and Student Behavior

- Balanced schedules reduce transitions and unstructured time that often lead to behavioral issues.
- *Example:* Staggered lunch and recess schedules help maintain supervision and reduce disciplinary referrals.

8. Affects Staff Morale and Retention

- Fair and flexible scheduling contributes to a positive work culture and instructional consistency.
- *Example:* A teacher with a dual certification is scheduled within one subject area to avoid burnout and promote quality instruction.

9. Determines Student Access to Electives and Specialized Programs

- Creative scheduling broadens learning opportunities beyond core academics.
- *Example:* Rotating elective schedules allow all students to experience music, art, and STEM each semester.

10. Influences Continuity and Learning Progression

- Strategic assignment of teachers to grade levels or content areas builds program coherence.
- *Example:* A middle school retains subject-specific teachers across multiple years for improved student-teacher rapport and academic continuity.

Organizational Leadership Quiz

1. **A principal discovers that multiple teachers are using outdated versions of the curriculum. What is the best first step to improve instructional consistency?**
   A. Require teachers to submit weekly lesson plans
   B. Conduct classroom walkthroughs and provide curriculum refresh sessions
   C. Purchase new textbooks for every subject
   D. Send an email asking teachers to update their materials

2. **During a budget planning meeting, the leadership team is debating whether to prioritize funding for technology upgrades or hiring an additional counselor. What is the most appropriate leadership action?**
   A. Decide based on last year's priorities
   B. Choose the option with the least cost
   C. Analyze student performance and needs data to determine alignment with school goals
   D. Post a staff poll to vote on the options

3. **A school is experiencing frequent disruptions during transition periods. What should the principal implement first?**
   A. Establish clear hallway procedures and increase adult supervision
   B. Increase security camera coverage
   C. Cancel passing periods and keep students in block classes
   D. Add hall passes to track student movement

4. **A district audit reveals inconsistencies in how attendance is tracked across classrooms. What is the principal's most effective response?**
   A. Remind teachers to take attendance daily
   B. Conduct a training on district attendance procedures and monitor compliance
   C. Assign the attendance clerk to check all rosters
   D. Ask department heads to review their teams

5. **Due to rising maintenance costs, the school's operating budget is strained. What leadership action demonstrates sound operational management?**
   A. Freeze all spending until the end of the quarter
   B. Eliminate extracurricular activities
   C. Conduct a line-item review of the budget and explore cost-saving alternatives
   D. Request more money from the district without justification

6. **Staff express frustration with the school's master schedule, stating that collaboration time is limited and unevenly distributed. What is the best approach?**
   A. Tell staff to meet during their lunch periods
   B. Restructure the schedule to ensure common planning time across grade levels
   C. Extend the school day by 30 minutes
   D. Rotate duty assignments weekly

7. **A fire drill reveals that some staff members do not follow emergency protocols. What should the principal do next?**
   A. Send a memo reviewing procedures
   B. Ignore the issue since no one was harmed
   C. Post evacuation maps in every classroom
   D. Provide targeted retraining and conduct another drill for accountability

8. **A principal wants to promote greater efficiency in daily operations. What strategy best supports this goal?**
   A. Automate attendance and lunch orders through an integrated data system
   B. Allow staff to choose their own classroom supplies
   C. Increase the number of daily announcements
   D. Schedule more meetings to check in with every department

9. **Teacher turnover has increased and exit surveys cite lack of support and unclear expectations. What should the principal do to address this trend?**
   A. Offer incentives to teachers who stay longer
   B. Eliminate staff meetings to reduce workload
   C. Ask remaining teachers to cover additional classes
   D. Revise onboarding processes and improve communication about school procedures

10. The **school's front office receives frequent complaints from parents about delayed responses. What action best reflects effective organizational leadership?**

A. Extend office hours to include weekends
B. Review communication procedures and retrain office staff on timely, respectful engagement
C. Post a sign explaining staff limitations
D. Assign students to assist the office

11. A principal notices that student transitions between classes are chaotic and often lead to tardiness. What is the most effective first step?

A. Increase hallway supervision and gather data on transitions
B. Shorten passing time to minimize student movement
C. Implement automatic detentions for tardy students
D. Hold a schoolwide assembly about the importance of punctuality

12. During a staff meeting, the principal shares that student achievement data shows no improvement. What is the best way to lead a solution-oriented conversation?

A. Ask teachers to defend their scores
B. Highlight the challenges and emphasize external causes
C. Facilitate collaborative data analysis and action planning by grade level teams
D. Assign new curriculum materials to teachers immediately

13. A school experiences high teacher turnover each year. What should the principal do to increase retention?

A. Offer exit interviews only to those who resign mid-year
B. Build a mentoring and coaching program for new and veteran teachers
C. Provide weekly PD on classroom management
D. Avoid long-term planning until staffing stabilizes

14. The principal wants to improve instructional consistency across grade levels. What is the most effective leadership action?

A. Require all teachers to use the same lesson plans
B. Observe lessons and provide general feedback at the end of the semester
C. Develop collaborative planning time and peer observation structures
D. Create a school-wide pacing guide with no teacher input

15. A new curriculum initiative is being rolled out. How should the school leader ensure a smooth transition?

A. Provide training, resources, and follow-up support based on staff needs
B. Allow each teacher to interpret the curriculum on their own
C. Monitor implementation only through standardized test scores
D. Wait to introduce changes until the next school year

16. The school's support staff feel excluded from decision-making. What is the best way to build a more inclusive environment?

A. Host a meeting to explain the leadership hierarchy
B. Increase support staff duties to boost involvement
C. Invite support staff to serve on school committees and recognize their contributions
D. Leave support staff out of committees to avoid additional burden

17. Budget reductions are expected for the upcoming school year. What should the principal do first?

A. Eliminate all non-instructional programs
B. Reduce teacher planning time to cut costs
C. Avoid discussing the cuts until details are final
D. Communicate transparently with staff and involve stakeholders in Planning

18. The master schedule consistently results in unequal class sizes. What leadership strategy best addresses this issue?

A. Randomly assign students to balance numbers
B. Review scheduling processes and use data to improve equity
C. Avoid changing the current schedule to prevent confusion
D. Ask teachers to manage the issue on their own

19. Several teachers report technology failures during online testing. What is the principal's most appropriate response?

A. Blame the district IT department
B. Suspend testing until the state provides new devices
C. Work with staff and IT to troubleshoot, document issues, and ensure backup plans
D. Tell teachers to complete testing manually

20. The school's facilities are outdated, with multiple maintenance issues affecting learning. What is the best next step for the principal?

A. Submit repeated requests to the district without follow-up
B. Wait for the next budget cycle before taking action
C. Instruct teachers to adjust to the conditions
D. Create a facility audit with input from staff and prioritize issues for repair

Answer Key Organizational Leadership

Question Number	1	2	3	4	5	6	7	8	9	10
Correct Solution	B	C	A	B	C	B	D	A	D	B

Answer Key Organizational Leadership

Question Number	11	12	13	14	15	16	17	18	19	20
Correct Solution	A	C	B	C	A	C	D	B	C	D

Domain VI: Community Engagement Leadership

This domain focuses on the principal's role in building strong partnerships with families, community organizations, and stakeholders to support student success. Community engagement leadership involves creating open lines of communication, valuing diverse voices, and fostering collaborative relationships that extend learning beyond the classroom. By prioritizing authentic engagement, principals strengthen trust, enhance resources, and create a supportive network where students and families feel connected and empowered.

Community Engagement Leadership

Real-Life Scenario A: Collaborate with families and other community members

At Riverside Heights Elementary School, Principal Mrs. Grant had noticed a widening gap in student achievement among multilingual learners and economically disadvantaged families. Parent engagement was low, especially for families who spoke languages other than English or worked evening jobs that made it difficult to attend traditional school events.

Recognizing that removing barriers to learning required strong family and community partnerships, Mrs. Grant launched a "Connected Communities" initiative aimed at strengthening collaboration with families and neighborhood organizations.

She began by hosting bilingual listening sessions held in the school library during both mornings and evenings to gather input from families about their challenges and aspirations. Parents expressed concerns about limited access to after-school tutoring, unclear communication about their children's progress, and difficulty navigating the special education referral process.

In response, Mrs. Grant partnered with a local community center and church to create free evening tutoring programs and parenting workshops. She also collaborated with the school counselor and Title I coordinator to provide interpreters at IEP meetings and translated all key communications, including newsletters, report cards, and announcements, into the top three home languages.

To improve communication, she trained staff in two-way communication techniques and created a school-wide communication plan that included regular updates through Remind texts, social media posts, and a family-friendly section on the school website. Celebrations like "Culture and Curriculum Night" and monthly "Student Success Spotlights" were added to highlight student achievement and promote community pride.

She also made it a priority to include parents in school decisions. When revising the school's behavior policy, she formed a family advisory committee that reviewed data and provided feedback. Parents felt respected, heard, and invested in the school's direction.

By the end of the year, family survey responses showed a 40% increase in parents who felt welcomed and informed. Student attendance and performance also improved, especially among students whose families had previously been disengaged.

Through inclusive outreach, multilingual communication, community partnerships, and shared decision-making, Mrs. Grant built a bridge between school and home. Her approach demonstrated how school leaders can remove barriers to learning and foster a collaborative, student-centered community that uplifts every child.

Community Engagement Leadership

Real-Life Scenario 2 B: Community interests and needs

At Crescent Hill Middle School, Principal Dr. Amina Riley noticed growing tensions between faculty and families regarding proposed changes to the school's dress code and discipline policy. Teachers wanted stricter enforcement, citing classroom disruptions, while parents especially from immigrant and culturally diverse backgrounds expressed concern that the policies unfairly targeted their children's cultural expression.

Understanding the need to identify competing perspectives among staff, students, parents, and community members, Dr. Riley organized a series of structured community forums and listening circles, with translators on hand to ensure full participation. She used anonymous surveys and small-group discussions to collect honest feedback from all stakeholders, including student representatives.

To engage with the local community proactively, she attended neighborhood events, visited local religious centers, and met with community organizers to learn more about the values and concerns of the families they served. Dr. Riley made a point to be visible not just at school events, but also at Saturday food drives, youth sports games, and community cleanups.

Realizing that traditional engagement strategies weren't reaching all families, she used research-based communication methods, like partnering with local radio and WhatsApp groups in multiple languages, to keep families informed. She also conducted a student-led focus group to better understand how policies were affecting peer relationships and mental well-being.

Dr. Riley invited diverse voices into the decision-making process by creating an Equity Leadership Team that included local faith leaders, school alumni, a representative from the local youth justice organization, and parents from various backgrounds. This team helped co-create a revised student handbook with culturally responsive practices and a restorative discipline framework.

By the end of the school year, Crescent Hill saw improved family-school trust, fewer student suspensions, and higher attendance at parent-teacher conferences. Teachers also reported feeling more supported and informed about the cultural needs of their students.

By recognizing diverse viewpoints, engaging in the broader community, and intentionally including underrepresented voices, Dr. Riley built a school culture rooted in shared responsibility, cultural competence, and mutual respect ultimately improving outcomes for all students.

Community Engagement Leadership

Real-Life Scenario C: Maximizing community resources

At Westview Community School, Principal Mrs. Carla Bennett noticed an increase in chronic absenteeism and health-related barriers to learning, particularly among students from low-income families. Many parents reported challenges accessing basic medical care, mental health support, and consistent meals issues that directly impacted student achievement and classroom behavior.

Mrs. Bennett knew that overcoming these barriers required more than just school-based solutions. She began by collaborating with local community agencies, including a nearby health clinic, a behavioral health provider, and the Department of Children and Families. Together, they created an in-school wellness program that offered weekly counseling sessions, vision and hearing screenings, and a mobile health van parked on campus every Friday.

Recognizing that shared resources could benefit the whole community, Mrs. Bennett entered into partnerships with local organizations. She worked with a neighborhood church to host after-school homework help, with a local food pantry to operate a weekend backpack program, and with the recreation department to offer family fitness nights on the school's playing fields. These partnerships were equitable and transparent, with all participating groups included in a shared-use agreement reviewed by the district's legal team.

To ensure community resources directly supported student learning, she regularly met with partner organizations to evaluate their impact. This included reviewing attendance records, parent participation rates, and changes in academic performance among supported students. When one tutoring program showed limited results, she replaced it with a mentorship initiative run by a nearby college.

To sustain and grow this support, Mrs. Bennett led outreach efforts that included publishing a quarterly community impact report, highlighting student success stories tied to specific partnerships. She met with city council members and the school board to request expanded funding and access to mental health professionals. She also hosted community forums to gather input and educate families about available services.

Finally, Mrs. Bennett consistently advocated education and student needs, both locally and at the state level. She joined a coalition of principals who met regularly with policymakers to push for more equitable school funding and increased social-emotional support in public schools. At every opportunity, she made the case that strong schools create strong communities, and that investing in students' well-being is a shared responsibility.

By intentionally cultivating partnerships, evaluating resource impact, and advocating for her school's needs, Mrs. Bennett demonstrated how a school leader can transform community connections into meaningful support systems enhancing student learning, family stability, and community pride.

Essential Questions #1 Community Engagement Leadership

In what types of situations can family and community stakeholders be helpful?

A well-run school functions much like a busy train station, where students are the passengers traveling toward their future. At a major hub like New York's Penn Station, it takes more than just train conductors to keep things running. There are information desk agents, MetroCard attendants, food service workers, and transit police officers, all ensuring that passengers stay safe, informed, and on schedule.

Similarly, a school's success relies on a network of family and community stakeholders who work behind the scenes to keep students on track. These include:

- **Families and caregivers** who provide emotional grounding and advocate for student needs
- **Community health workers** who offer physical and mental wellness services
- **Local business owners** who sponsor events, offer internships, or donate supplies
- **Faith-based leaders** who provide mentorship, support, and moral guidance
- **Nonprofit partners** who assist with food distribution, housing needs, or after-school tutoring
- **Law enforcement and safety officers** who support safe routes to school and restorative practices

When students face delays whether academic, emotional, or environmental. These partners step in to:

- **Redirect traffic** (e.g., mentoring, counseling, translating school materials),
- **Provide nourishment** (e.g., food pantries, health screenings),
- **Repair tracks** (e.g., tutoring, behavior interventions, attendance initiatives),
- Or simply cheer students on at the platform (e.g., awards nights, cultural events, college signing days).

Family and Community Stakeholders Be Helpful by:

1. Removing Barriers to Learning
Stakeholders can provide direct services or interventions that address issues preventing students from accessing instruction such as hunger, housing, mental health, or transportation.
Example: A local food pantry partners with the school to deliver weekly weekend meal kits to families experiencing food insecurity.

2. Decision-Making & Policy Development
Schools can involve families and community members in site-based planning teams, advisory councils, and committees to help shape key policies.
Example: Parents and community leaders sit on the school's strategic planning team to revise the student discipline policy, ensuring it reflects restorative practices and cultural sensitivity.

3. Communication & Outreach
Community partners can help reach families through culturally appropriate, multilingual, and multimodal communication channels, improving transparency and trust.

Example: A local cultural center translates report cards and conducts parent workshops in Spanish and Haitian Creole to support engagement.

4. Resource Integration

Leaders can coordinate with community agencies to provide services or materials that the school cannot offer alone creating a more equitable environment for students.

Example: A school teams up with a mobile dental clinic to provide free checkups and cleanings during school hours.

5. Health & Social Services

By working with health clinics, hospitals, or nonprofit service providers, schools can address physical and emotional health needs that impact learning.

Example: A partnership with a local behavioral health agency allows a licensed therapist to provide in-school counseling one day a week.

6. Advocacy

Stakeholders can raise awareness of school needs at the local or state level and speak on behalf of students and educators during budget hearings or legislative discussions.

Example: Community leaders attend a city council meeting to advocate for funding to maintain school nursing positions in all district schools.

7. Public Engagement & Accountability

Schools can share performance data and plans with the community, encouraging feedback and co-ownership of student outcomes.

Example: A principal hosts a town hall with parents and faith leaders to review NJSLA results and develop community-based tutoring programs to close gaps.

8. Cultural Competence

Stakeholders help ensure that school practices respect students' cultural backgrounds, languages, traditions, and values leading to better engagement and equity.

Example: A Somali parent liaison helps staff understand culturally appropriate communication styles, improving relationships between teachers and families.

9. Media Communication

During events, emergencies, or celebrations, stakeholders, especially those in media or public relations, can help share accurate, timely information.

*Exampl***e:** A school partners with a local radio station to publicize its STEM fair and highlight student projects, increasing community pride and visibility.

10. Crisis & Population Response

During emergencies or demographic shifts, community stakeholders can respond quickly to support affected students and families.

After a fire displaces several families, a local nonprofit organizes a drive to provide uniforms, school supplies, and temporary housing assistance.

11. Use of School Facilities

School leaders may develop partnerships with community groups to responsibly use school buildings for non-instructional purposes like adult education, health clinics, or recreational events.

Essential Questions #2 Community Engagement

What guidance do various laws, policies, and regulations provide for determining when family or guardians have input to educational decisions?

A school is like a homeowner who wants to remove a wall in their house. While it may seem quicker and easier to tear down the wall without anyone knowing, the homeowner must first get a permit from the town ordinance. The permit exists to ensure that any structural change is safe, legal, and aligned with regulations.

In everyday school settings, family input isn't just appreciated. It's legally required at key points. For example, when a student is being evaluated for special education services under IDEA, school leaders must involve parents in the IEP team meeting to discuss support and placement options. A real-life situation might involve a 4th grade student struggling with reading comprehension. The school's Child Study Team schedules a meeting with the parents to review evaluation results and collaboratively draft an IEP that includes small-group instruction and speech therapy.

Similarly, under Section 504, if a student is diagnosed with Type 1 diabetes, school staff must meet with the parents to develop 504 Plan outlining accommodations like snack breaks and nurse access.

Under FERPA, school leaders are required to get parent consent before sharing student records externally for instance, before forwarding discipline reports to a private therapist or outside agency. ESSA further strengthens the role of families by requiring their input in Title I school planning. A school might host a family forum to revise its parent compact, asking families to give feedback on how the school can better support home learning and communication. Finally, in accordance with state law, a school considering retaining a 3rd grader due to below-grade reading scores must consult and obtain the parent's written consent. In all these scenarios, school leaders demonstrate legal compliance and build trust by treating families as essential partners in student success.

Similarly, when schools make significant decisions such as changing a student's placement, providing accommodations, sharing records, or initiating evaluations. They must seek input and obtain consent from the parent or guardian. Just as towns protect houses, federal laws like IDEA, Section 504, FERPA, and ESSA protect students and families ensuring educational changes are made with consent, transparency, and accountability

Outline

Key Laws & When Family Input is Required

1. IDEA – Individuals with Disabilities Education Act

- **Requires family input** for:
  - Evaluations & reevaluations
  - IEP development
  - Educational placement
  - Manifestation Determination Reviews

2. Section 504 – Rehabilitation Act of 1973

- **Requires parental notification and input** for:
  - Initial evaluations
  - Plan development
  - Significant program/service changes

3. FERPA – Family Educational Rights and Privacy Act

- Grants families:
    - The right to access and review education records
    - The right to request corrections
    - The right to consent before information is shared outside the school (except under limited exemptions)

4. ESSA – Every Student Succeeds Act

- Requires **meaningful family involvement** in:
    - Title I school-parent compacts
    - School improvement planning
    - Family engagement policies

5. State and Local Laws

- Often require family input for:
    - Early grade retention
    - Literacy interventions
    - Health decisions (e.g., immunizations, wellness plans)

Essential Questions #3 Community Engagement

Under what conditions and situations should a school leader involve the local media?

School leaders should involve the local media strategically, not impulsively. The goal is to build trust, promote transparency, celebrate success, and respond appropriately to crises while protecting student privacy and upholding district policies. Leaders must balance timely communication with legal and ethical responsibilities, especially under FERPA, state reporting laws, and board-approved protocols.

Engaging with the media is comparable to clicking "post" on social media once the information is shared, it becomes permanent and public. It is no longer under the speaker's control and may be interpreted, amplified, or used in ways never intended.

The same principle applies in school leadership. Once a statement is made to the media, it cannot be taken back. For this reason, school leaders must follow district communication policies, which typically include:

- Verifying the accuracy of all information before releasing it
- Consulting with the superintendent or communications director before issuing any public statements
- Complying fully with FERPA and student/staff confidentiality laws
- Evaluating the message for tone, timing, and potential long-term impact

A school leader who communicates with the media without careful preparation risks undermining trust and credibility. Public messaging should never be reactive. It must be deliberate, strategic, and compliant with district expectations to protect the integrity of the school and the well-being of its students

The Media should be contacted to celebrate success by Highlighting academic achievement, school improvement, student accomplishments, or community partnerships. For example, a school leader invites the local news to cover a district robotics team winning a state championship.

They should be contacted to inform the community about public events such as promoting open houses, parent forums, or school initiatives open to the public. For example, the media is invited to cover the launch of a new bilingual literacy program serving immigrant families.

They should be contacted during a crisis or emergency such as during a weather-related school closure or safety lockdown, the district office and principal collaborate on a statement for the media.

Another way that the media should be contacted is to correct misinformation. When false or misleading narratives are circulating that could damage the school's credibility or cause panic. For example, a school leader addresses rumors of poor water quality by issuing a media release with test results and a safety plan.

<u>When to Involve the Media</u>

1. To Celebrate Success

- Highlight academic achievement, school improvement, student accomplishments, or community partnerships.
- Example: A school leader invites the local news to cover a district robotics team winning a state championship.

2. To Inform the Community About Public Events

- Promote open houses, parent forums, or school initiatives open to the public.
- Example: The media is invited to cover the launch of a new bilingual literacy program serving immigrant families.

3. During a Crisis or Emergency

- Share verified, essential information when the public needs to be informed—following district crisis communication protocols.
- Example: During a weather-related school closure or safety lockdown, the district office and principal collaborate on a statement for the media.

4. Correct Misinformation

- When false or misleading narratives are circulating that could damage the school's credibility or cause panic.
- Example: A school leader addresses rumors about contaminated water by issuing a media release with test results and a safety plan.

Essential Questions #4 Community Engagement Leadership

What strategies are effective for communicating school and student success to families and the community?

Imagine a nonprofit organization opening a food bank stocked with fresh produce, essential supplies, and volunteers eager to help the community. Everything is in place to serve those in need. A few flyers are dropped off at local businesses, and a single post is made on a social media page that hasn't been updated in months. No follow-up, no translation, no outreach to trusted community spaces, just a minimal effort to get the word out.

As a result, the shelves stay full. The food goes untouched. The service exists, but it's invisible to the people who need it most.

Schools face a similar challenge. A school may be doing incredible work offering academic support, student celebrations, and community programs, but if the message is inaccessible, inconsistent, or culturally disconnected, families remain on the outside looking in.

Effectively communicating school and student success requires more than just newsletters or announcements, it demands a strategic, intentional, and inclusive approach. School leaders must ensure that messages are accessible, culturally responsive, celebratory, and transparent.

When families and community stakeholders feel informed and involved, they are far more likely to support student learning, advocate for school needs, and trust leadership.

That's why school communication isn't just about broadcasting, it's about building relationships. Just as a food bank must communicate clearly and inclusively to fulfill its mission, schools must ensure that every family sees the invitation, understands the message, and feels empowered to engage. Strong communication is the sign on the building, the open door, and the bridge that turns good work into shared success.

Effective school leaders use a variety of strategic methods to communicate success and build trust with families and the broader community. These approaches include multimedia celebrations such as sharing photos and videos of student events on social media and school websites, and personalized messaging like sending individual notes or certificates to recognize student growth. Hosting community events and highlights allows families to engage with student work firsthand, while public recognition through local media or board meetings elevates achievements beyond the school walls.

Leaders also use data transparency with a human touch, pairing academic data with student stories to make information more relatable. Ensuring translation and cultural responsiveness helps families receive success communications in their home languages, fostering inclusiveness. Celebrating partnerships with community organizations shows how collaboration supports student learning. Schools also empower students through student-led communication, such as peer-hosted videos and announcements. Finally, schools create feedback loops to hear from families and maintain consistent communication schedules, like weekly newsletters, so that families know when and how to stay connected to their child's success.

Outline

1. Share Success Through Multiple Communication Channels

- Use a variety of platforms to reach different audiences and increase accessibility.
- *Example:* Post student achievement highlights on the school website, social media, and newsletters in multiple languages.

2. Host Family and Community Recognition Events

- Celebrate students and school accomplishments in public forums that promote pride and engagement.
- *Example:* Organize a "Student Success Night" to highlight academic projects, awards, and extracurricular achievements.

3. Include Student Voices in the Messaging

- Let students articulate their own progress to build authenticity and ownership.
- *Example:* Students lead presentations at board meetings or share learning goals during student-led conferences.

4. Use Data Visuals to Highlight Academic Growth

- Display progress with clear, user-friendly visuals to show impact over time.
- *Example:* Share charts showing increases in reading scores or attendance at parent forums or on digital dashboards.

5. Highlight Success Stories in Local Media and Community Forums

- Promote positive narratives beyond the school walls to elevate visibility and public trust.
- *Example:* Submit articles or student profiles to local newspapers, education blogs, or community newsletters.

6. Develop Monthly or Quarterly Success Spotlights

- Establish a consistent routine for sharing good news with families.
- *Example:* A monthly "Principal's Post" highlights a staff member, a student, and a school goal reached.

7. Involve Families in Celebrations of Learning

- Create authentic opportunities for families to see progress firsthand.
- *Example:* Host "Family Walkthrough Days" where parents visit classrooms and observe instruction in action.

8. Recognize Staff Contributions to Student Success

- Publicly affirm the efforts of teachers and support staff in school-wide achievements.
- *Example:* Feature a "Teacher of the Month" in communications and tie it to a student success outcome.

9. Use Feedback Loops to Improve and Expand Messaging

- Gather input from families to ensure messages are meaningful and effective.
- *Example:* Conduct a quick survey asking families how they prefer to receive updates and what information matters most to them.

10. Align Messaging With the School's Vision and Goals

- Reinforce strategic objectives to build coherence and shared purpose.
- *Example:* A newsletter section called "Vision in Action" links recent accomplishments to school-wide goals like improving literacy or fostering belonging.

Essential Questions #5 Community Engagement Leadership

How can a school leader involve families in decision making about their children's education?

Just like a driver needs directions to reach a new destination, a school needs guidance and input from parents to help a child succeed.

Imagine driving somewhere unfamiliar, and suddenly, the GPS stops working. The driver can't see detours, traffic jams, or safer alternate routes. The trip becomes stressful, confusing, and inefficient.

This mirrors what happens when schools operate without parental input. When parents don't share key information about a child's learning style, emotional needs, cultural background, or home situation the school may choose a route that doesn't work for the student. The teacher may misread behaviors, miss opportunities to intervene early, or apply strategies that don't align with the student's needs.

But when schools and families stay connected, communicate frequently, and adjust the route together, the educational journey becomes more efficient, more responsive, and more supportive for the student who matters most.

A school leader can involve families in decision-making by creating inclusive systems that invite their voices and honor their perspectives. This includes offering flexible, accessible IEP and RTI meetings with interpretation when needed, creating family advisory councils to give input on school policies, and using two-way communication tools like Talking Points to hear feedback. Leaders can also host workshops that explain support services and invite families to co-create goals during student-led conferences. By showing families how their input shapes real decisions, like changing homework policies or discipline practices, leaders build trust and strengthen partnerships that support student success. Finally, shared decision-making should be embedded in daily school culture, not just reserved for formal meetings. One school does this by adding a "Family Insight" segment to staff meetings, where a parent shares a strategy that supports their child's learning. These practices not only build trust, but they also create a culture where families feel like valued partners in their child's education.

Outline

Strategies for Involving Families in Decision-Making

Collaborative Planning Meetings

- Involve families meaningfully in IEP, 504, RTI, and goal-setting conferences.
- *Example:* Ask families for input on what strategies have worked at home during a child's IEP meeting.

2. Create Family Advisory Groups

- Invite diverse families to participate in advisory councils or school-based teams.
- *Example:* Form a family voice committee that provides input on school culture, discipline, and academic planning.

3. Conduct Surveys and Listening Sessions

- Ask families about their preferences and concerns before making major changes.
- *Example:* Survey families in multiple languages before revising the school's homework policy.

4. Empower Families with Knowledge

- Provide workshops or one-pagers explaining school processes, intervention systems, and their rights.
- *Example:* Host a Saturday session explaining how Tier 2 reading support works and what role families play.

5. Invite Families to Early Intervention Teams

- Include families in problem-solving conversations before special education is considered.
- *Example:* At an MTSS meeting, the school shares reading data and asks parents for context and suggestions.

6. Respect Cultural and Linguistic Needs

- Offer interpretation, flexible scheduling, and culturally responsive practices.
- *Example:* Schedule evening virtual IEP meetings with interpreters available to ensure equitable participation.

7. Student-Led Goal Conferences

- Let students and families co-create personal goals in conferences.
- *Example:* During student-led conferences, students reflect on strengths, families offer insight, and goals are set together.

8. Two-Way Communication

- Use tools like Remind, Talking Points, or home-school liaisons to gather feedback.
- *Example:* A bilingual liaison regularly contacts families of English learners to hear their concerns and offer updates.

9. Celebrate Family Input

- Close the loop by publicly acknowledging how parent feedback has been used.
- *Example:* After families suggest more outdoor time, the principal sends an update showing how recess was extended.

-

Essential Questions #6 Community Engagement Leadership

What strategies could a school leader use to communicate with parents and the community when English is not the primary language or where many languages are spoken?

At a kindergarten graduation, more than half the families in attendance were not proficient in English. While the event was well-organized, all materials, including the graduation program and the entire celebration were presented only in English, with no translation or interpretation provided. As a result, many families were unable to fully understand or engage with the proceedings.

Situations like this demonstrate how language can be a barrier to meaningful engagement. When school communication is not designed to be accessible, it unintentionally excludes families and limits their ability to support student learning or participate in school culture.

To promote equity and engagement, school leaders must adopt communication strategies that are linguistically appropriate, culturally responsive, and community driven. When families are informed in a language they understand, they are more likely to be involved, ask questions, provide input, and feel connected to the school's mission.

To effectively communicate with families when English is not the primary language or when many languages are spoken, school leaders should use a range of inclusive strategies. First, they can ensure all important documents and meetings are supported by professional translation and interpretation services, avoiding reliance on students or untrained individuals. Tools like Talking Points or Parent Square provide two-way, multilingual messaging for daily updates. Hiring bilingual staff or cultural liaisons helps families navigate the school system and feel supported. Hosting multilingual events with live interpretation and translated signage ensures equitable participation. Leaders should also use visual aids and clear, simple language to make written communication more accessible. Surveys and feedback tools should be translated into families' home languages to encourage inclusive input. Finally, partnering with trusted community organizations can strengthen outreach efforts and build cultural bridges. These strategies help ensure that all families, regardless of language, are informed, engaged, and empowered to support their children's education.

Outline

Communicating Across Languages

1. Use Professional Interpretation and Translation Services

- Translate essential documents (newsletters, IEPs, notices) into families' home languages.
- Use trained interpreters, not students, for formal communication.

2. Adopt Multilingual Communication Tools

- Use apps that offer two-way, automatic translation.
- Ensure your website and school platforms have multilingual options.

3. Hire Bilingual Staff and Cultural Liaisons

- Employ staff or liaisons who speak the dominant non-English languages in the school community.
- A Spanish-speaking family liaison supports families with enrollment, events, and parent meetings.

4. Host Multilingual and Culturally Inclusive Events

- Provide live interpretation at school events or use translation headsets.
- Offer simultaneous translation during meetings or open house.
- Host a family engagement night with translation in multiple languages and multilingual signage.

5. Use Visual Aids and Clear Language

- Combine written messages with icons, pictures, and plain language to support comprehension.
- Use infographics to explain grading policies or behavior expectations in multiple languages.

6. Translate Feedback Tools

- Provide surveys and response forms in multiple languages to ensure broad participation.
- Translate a school climate survey into home language and distribute both print and digital versions.

7. Partner with Community Organizations

- Work with cultural centers, faith-based organizations, and local nonprofits that have existing trust with multilingual families.
- Collaborate with a Korean community organization to co-host a back-to-school night for Korean-speaking families.

Essential Questions #7 Community Engagement Leadership

What policies should be in place for communicating with and responding to the media?

At Lincoln Heights Middle School, a student was injured during a science lab experiment. Within hours, local news outlets began calling the school for details. Some staff were unsure whether they could respond and what information they could share.

Fortunately, Principal Rivera had already established a school media communication policy. The policy required that all media inquiries be directed to the district communications office, with no teacher or staff member authorized to speak on behalf of the school. It also included procedures for crafting a consistent message in collaboration with district leaders and legal counsel.

Principal Rivera immediately contacted the district's communications director. Together, they prepared a brief, accurate statement that confirmed the incident occurred, reassured the public that the students received medical attention, and emphasized that safety protocols were being reviewed. No student names or personal details were shared to comply with FERPA.

In addition, Rivera informed staff not to post or comment about the incident on social media, as outlined in the district's social media and confidentiality policy. A letter was sent home to families the same day, summarizing the incident in clear, non-alarming language and explaining the steps being taken.

<u>Outline</u>

1. Designate a School or District Spokesperson

- Only authorized personnel (usually the principal or communications director) should communicate with the media.
- **Why:** Prevents mixed messages or unapproved information from being released.

2. Require Media Requests to Go Through Central Office

- All interviews, filming, or coverage requests should be routed through district channels.
- **Why:** Ensures legal compliance, parental consent, and message consistency.

3. Adopt a "No Surprise" Rule

- The school board and district leadership should be notified before any media release involving sensitive topics (e.g., student incidents, school safety).
- **Why:** Keeps leadership informed and protects institutional credibility.

4. Establish Media-Response Protocols for Crisis Situations

- Define who speaks, what can be shared, and what must remain confidential.
- **Why:** Minimizes misinformation and protects student/staff privacy

5. Provide Media Training for School Leaders

- Principals and assistant principals should receive training on speaking to the press and preparing statements.
- **Why:** Enhances confidence and professionalism under pressure.

6.Train Staff on Media Protocol

- Offer professional development or written guidelines on how to handle media interactions.
- **Why:** Empowers staff to respond professionally, even under pressure.

7. Include Student Privacy Guidelines

- Media releases should never share identifiable student information without parental consent (in accordance with FERPA).
- **Why:** Protects student rights and complies with federal law.

8. Develop Pre-Approved Messaging Templates

- Keep prepared statements for common topics (e.g., weather closures, test results, school events).
- **Why:** Speeds up response time and ensures tone/wording is appropriate

9. Set a Review Process for Public Announcements

- All press releases should be reviewed by district legal/communications staff before publication.
- **Why:** Reduces legal risk and aligns with district values.

:

Essential Questions #8 Community Engagement

How does a school leader, new to a school and/or area, identify appropriate stakeholders?

Starting at a new school as a leader is like walking into the middle of a group project that's already halfway done. The materials are spread out, some people are leading without titles, others are waiting to be heard, and there's unspoken tension about how things have been handled before. If the new person walks in and immediately starts changing everything without asking questions, the group won't move forward, it'll fall apart.

That's why the most effective school leaders begin by learning who is already holding the school together. They listen to teachers who've weathered the storms, staff who know every corner of the building, and parents who've watched decisions ripple into their homes. They don't confuse volume with values. Sometimes the most powerful stakeholders are the quiet ones who stay late, mentor others, or run the morning drop-offline with precision.

Stakeholder identification is less about titles and more about trust. For a new leader to lead well, they need to understand who's already leading quietly and work alongside them, not over them.

<u>Outline</u>

<u>Identify appropriate stakeholders</u>

1. Start With the People in the Building

- Internal culture isn't always defined by titles, it's shaped by those who show up early, stay late, and earn trust through consistency.
- **Example:** A new principal attends team meetings and observes classroom dynamics before proposing changes.

2. Review Documentation That Tells a Story

- Past School Improvement Plan (SIP)parent outreach records, and teacher-led initiatives show who's been actively involved and who might've been left out.
- **Why it matters:** It honors the past and builds future plans with context.

3. Ask and Listen Through Verbal Communication

- One-on-one conversations or small listening groups can surface honest insights that wouldn't be captured on a form.
- **Example:** A leader asks, "What's something about this school you hope never changes?" to identify values and influencers.

4. Engage Families and Community Voices

- Stakeholders extend beyond staff parent advocates, local nonprofits, and community liaisons often bridge gaps the school can't.
- **Example:** A leader attends a community board meeting or joins a local cultural celebration to meet families outside of school walls. Presence is power not just for supervision, but for trust. People open up when they see leadership involved, not just informed.

Essential Questions #9 Community Engagement

What conflict-resolution strategies would be helpful in resolving differences between competing groups to work for the best interests of the school and students?

Resolving school-based conflicts is like trying to get a group of musicians to play the same song when everyone's playing a different tune, it sounds like chaos, not collaboration. One group might be focused on test scores, another on student mental health, another on resource equity and all of them might be right in their own way. But without shared rhythm, harmony is impossible.

The job of a school leader isn't to silence disagreement, it helps groups recognize that they're all part of the same band, working toward the same performance: student success. When a leader brings empathy, clarity, and structure to the conversation, tension can turn into teamwork.

True conflict resolution requires more than compromise, It demands understanding, reframing, and reminding all parties of the common goal: what's best for students.

Outline

Conflict-Resolution Strategies That Work in Schools

1. Start With Shared Purpose

- Reframe the conflict around a unifying question: What's best for students?
- *Example:* A principal opens a tense meeting by having everyone list what they want students to gain from the decision.

2. Listen Without Defensiveness

- Give each group space to share their perspectives without immediate rebuttal.
- Use neutral language to summarize their concerns.
- *Why:* People are more willing to collaborate when they feel heard, not dismissed.

3. Clarify Misunderstandings

- Many school conflicts stem from miscommunication, assumptions, or misinformation.
- *Strategy:* Ask, "Can we pause to check what we *think* we heard before we respond?

4. Use a Structured Mediation Process

- Implement clear steps:
    - Define the issue
    - Identify interests (not positions)
    - Explore common ground
    - Generate options
    - Agree on next steps
- *Why*: Structure reduces emotional escalation.

5. Appoint a Neutral Facilitator (When Needed)

- For high-stakes or emotionally charged conflicts, bring in a neutral party like a counselor, coach, or district leader to guide the process.
- *Why:* It removes perceived bias and helps keep focus.

6. Set Norms for Respectful Dialogue

- Before any discussion, set ground rules: no interruptions, assume good intent, speak from your own experience, etc.
- *Example*: A shared norms poster is displayed in every meeting space.

7. Focus on Interests, Not Egos

- Move from "I want" to "What our students need."
- *Strategy:* Use sentence frames like "I'm advocating for this because I've seen how it impacts learning..."

8. Use Data as a Neutral Anchor

- Ground the discussion in student performance, climate survey results, or attendance data.
- *Why:* Numbers can shift the focus from emotion to action.

9. Acknowledge Emotion Without Letting It Derail

- Emotions are valid but must be guided productively.
- *Strategy:* "This appears to be important to you. Let's make sure we put that into a solution."

10. Celebrate Resolution Publicly

- When opposing groups reach consensus, highlight that as a model of adult collaboration.
- *Why:* Reinforces a culture of teamwork, not tribalism.

Essential Questions #10 Community Engagement

What criteria should be considered in developing programs, committees, or activities that include the community?

Creating meaningful community involvement in schools is like planning a potluck, you don't just bring what you like to eat; you think about who's coming, what they care about, and how to make everyone feel welcome. If the same three people bring all the food and no one else gets a seat at the table, the event won't feel inclusive. It will feel like a performance.
In the same way, school leaders must intentionally design committees, programs, and activities that reflect the full diversity of the school community, not just the loudest voices or the most available volunteers. That means considering who's typically invited, who's consistently left out, and what barriers exist that might prevent full participation.

The goal isn't just to check a box for "community involvement", it's to build authentic partnerships that strengthen the school's work for students. That only happens when the criteria for inclusion are equitable, strategic, and welcoming.

Outline

Criteria for Meaningful Community Involvement

1. Representation That Reflects the Community

- Programs should include voices from all major demographic, linguistic, cultural, and economic groups.
- *Example:* A school creates a bilingual parent advisory committee after realizing Spanish- and Haitian-Creole-speaking families weren't attending PTA meetings.

2. Equity in Access and Participation

- Consider schedules, transportation, childcare, language access, and digital literacy.
- *Example*: A school offers hybrid committee meetings, one in person and one virtual at varied times to accommodate working families.

3. Purpose-Driven Engagement

- Don't invite people just to "have a parent there." Clarify the role, responsibility, and impact their input will have.
- *Why:* People show up more when they feel their presence matters.

4. Clear and Transparent Selection Process

- Avoid cliques or "invite-only" committees. Allow open applications or nominations.
- *Example:* A school publicizes all committee openings and explains the criteria for joining.

5. Student-Centered Mission

- Activities must always tie back to improving student experiences, support, or outcomes.
- *Example*: A family-school partnership is formed to brainstorm more inclusive after-school clubs for students with disabilities.

6. Capacity Building for Participants

- Provide training or support for those who join (especially families who haven't been involved before).
- *Why:* When people understand how schools work, they're better able to contribute meaningfully.

7. Ongoing Feedback and Adaptation

- Gather regular feedback about what's working and what needs adjusting.
- *Example:* After hearing that new families feel intimidated in committee meetings, the school adds a co-facilitator role for a parent ambassador.

8. Celebration and Visibility of Community Contributions

- Make sure efforts are recognized and celebrated schoolwide, not just tucked into a newsletter.
- *Why*: It affirms that the community is part of the school's identity, not an outsider audience.

Essential Questions #11 Community Engagement Leadership

What Cultural or Socioeconomic Factors Exert the Most Influence on Student Learning?

Understanding the cultural and socioeconomic influences on student learning is like analyzing the full context of a movie not just the scene that's playing. If you walk into a theater midway, you might misunderstand a character's actions without knowing what came before. The same is true with students. You can't fully understand their academic performance or behavior without knowing the broader circumstances shaping their lives.

Some students come to school carrying stress from poverty, language barriers, unstable housing, or trauma. Others may face cultural disconnects between home values and school expectations. These factors don't determine a student's potential, but they do shape the support they need.

Leaders and educators who recognize these contextual factors are better positioned to teach with empathy, adapt instruction, and remove systemic barriers so that every student has a fair opportunity to succeed.

Outline

Key Cultural and Socioeconomic Factors Influencing Learning

1. Poverty and Financial Instability

- Impacts health, nutrition, attendance, homework completion, and access to supplies or technology.
- *Example:* A student without reliable internet struggles to complete online assignments but is often assumed to be unmotivated.

2. Parental Education and Schooling Experience

- It affects how comfortable families feel navigating school systems or helping with academic work.
- *Example:* A family may deeply value education but be unfamiliar with American grading systems or teacher expectations.

3. Language Differences and Multilingual Households

- It can create communication gaps between home and school; students may struggle to bridge linguistic demands in academic settings.
- *Strategy:* Offer translation tools, visual support, and vocabulary scaffolding.

4. Cultural Values and Norms

- Influence student behavior, participation, and attitudes toward authority, competition, and collaboration.
- *Example:* Some students may avoid speaking out in class out of respect, not disengagement.

5. Access to Academic Enrichment and Learning Resources

- Students in under-resourced communities often have fewer extracurriculars, books, or tutoring.
- *Solution:* Schools can offer free clubs, loaner devices, and equitable enrichment.

6. Unstable Housing or Food Insecurity

- It affects sleep, concentration, and emotional regulation.
- *Example:* A student acting out may be coping with hidden stress from living in a shelter or food insecurity.

7. Community Safety and Trauma Exposure

- Exposure to violence or instability can lead to chronic stress, impacting memory, focus, and behavior.
- *Solution:* Trauma-informed classrooms and strong SEL support are critical.

8. Representation in Curriculum and Staff

- Students engage more when they see themselves reflected in content and leadership.
- *Example:* Including culturally relevant literature and hiring diverse educators improves belonging and motivation.

Essential Questions #12 Community Engagement

How would developing cultural sensitivity help a school leader to engage diverse groups in school planning and improvement efforts?

Engaging diverse families without cultural sensitivity is like bringing bacon to a gathering hosted by a family that doesn't eat pork. The guest may have good intentions, and the dish might be delicious, but it unintentionally signals a lack of awareness and respect. The result? The host feels unseen, and the guest's effort misses the mark.

In the same way, school leaders who make decisions or invite participation without understanding families' cultural values, beliefs, and needs may unintentionally exclude or offend. Cultural sensitivity helps leaders move from assumption to intention from outreach to partnership.

By developing cultural sensitivity, school leaders become more effective at building trust, creating inclusive spaces, and inviting authentic input into school planning and improvement. When people feel respected and understood, they are more likely to contribute, collaborate, and commit to the work of school transformation.

Outline

How Cultural Sensitivity Supports Inclusive School Planning

1. Builds Trust with Marginalized or Underserved Communities

- Acknowledges historical exclusion and invites relationship-building.
- **Example***:* A principal holds community forums in different languages to listen and learn before proposing changes.

2. Improves Communication and Reduces Misunderstandings

- Awareness of cultural norms prevents missteps in tone, timing, and method.
- **Example***:* Avoiding evening meetings during religious observances or fasting periods.

3. Fosters Meaningful Inclusion in Decision-Making

- Respecting cultural customs allows for more authentic input and collaboration.
- **Example***:* Using focus groups led by trusted community members to guide improvement plans.

4. Aligns School Improvement Goals with Real Needs

- Planning based on family lived experiences ensures relevance and equity.
- **Example***:* Prioritizing translation services after learning language access is a barrier to participation.

5. Prevents Tokenism

- Cultural sensitivity moves leadership beyond symbolic inclusion to shared ownership.
- **Example:** Co-creating parent engagement strategies instead of appointing a "diverse representative."

6. Strengthens Community Relationships

- Families who feel seen and respected are more likely to remain engaged and invested.
- *Solution:* Increased collaboration, volunteerism, and support for school goals.

What methods are effective for keeping abreast with the dynamics, changes, and trends in a community?

Keeping up with changes in a school community is like being the head chef in a restaurant with a rotating menu and seasonal ingredients. If the chef doesn't check what's fresh, what's running low, or what customers are asking for, the kitchen will keep preparing the same meals even if they no longer satisfy the guests.

Similarly, a school leader who assumes that last year's community needs still apply may overlook new populations, rising concerns, or untapped resources. To serve effectively, school leaders must "check the ingredients" often by listening, observing, and partnering regularly with families, staff, and local organizations.

Whether it's a change in housing patterns, new immigrant families, shifts in employment, or health concerns, leaders who stay engaged with evolving dynamics are better positioned to lead with relevance, responsiveness, and equity.

Outline

Effective Methods for Staying Informed About Community Trends

1. Maintain Ongoing Two-Way Communication

- Use multilingual surveys, listening circles, town halls, and family focus groups.
- *Example:* A biannual survey reveals growing interest in after-school childcare.

2. Collaborate with Local Organizations and Agencies

- Faith groups, clinics, housing agencies, and nonprofits often have frontline insights.
- *Example:* A local food bank director reports a spike in family demand, prompting weekend meal planning.

3. Conduct School Leader Walk-Throughs and Neighborhood Visits

- Seeing the environment firsthand offers a deeper understanding of student experiences.
- *Why:* A walk-through reveals new apartment developments bringing in multilingual families.

4. Analyze Local Data and Reports

- Use census updates, school enrollment trends, and city council meeting minutes.
- *Example:* City data shows an increase in refugees settling in the district's west side.

5. Encourage Feedback from Staff Who Live in the Community

- Teachers, secretaries, and aides often hear concerns before they reach formal channels.
- *Strategy:* Host monthly "community pulse" meetings with staff volunteers.

6. Engage Cultural and Community Liaisons

- Trained liaisons can identify subtle shifts and build bridges

Essential Questions #14 Community Engagement Leadership

How can a school leader advocate for the school within the greater community?

Advocating for a school in the greater community is like a coach speaking at a press conference after a big game. The players (students and staff) put in the effort, made progress, and achieved important wins but it's the coach's responsibility to explain the strategy, celebrate growth, and make the case for what's needed next. If the coach stays silent, the team may go unnoticed, underfunded, or misunderstood.

Likewise, school leaders serve as advocates who elevate their school's successes and challenges to external audiences such as local organizations, civic leaders, elected officials, and community members. They tell the story of student achievement, teacher innovation, and program impact, while also advocating for resources, partnerships, and policy changes that support the work.

Strong advocacy isn't just about pride, it's about purpose. Leaders who amplify their school's voice build the understanding and support needed to sustain meaningful, equitable progress.

Outline

How School Leaders Advocate for Their Schools

1. Build Strategic Partnerships with Local Organizations

- Form alliances with nonprofits, businesses, civic groups, and colleges.
- *Example:* A local company sponsors STEM supplies after visiting a school robotics demo.

2. Communicate School Successes with Authenticity and Purpose

- Use newsletters, town halls, and social media to spotlight staff and student efforts.
- *Example:* Sharing a teacher-led math fair and student testimonials with the local news.

3. Engage Elected Officials and Policymakers

- Invite them to campus events, student exhibitions, or advisory meetings.
- *Example:* Hosting a "State of the School" event where legislators meet students and teachers.

4. Leverage Media and Public Platforms Responsibly

- Write op-eds, create media kits, and share compelling visuals and stories.
- *Example:* A principal writes a letter to the editor highlighting student-led civic engagement.

5. Attend Community Meetings and Forums

- Participate in town halls, planning boards, and neighborhood association events.
- *Why:* These spaces allow leaders to listen, inform, and advocate directly.

6. Create and Share a Clear, Compelling School Narrative

- Combine student data, community context, and personal stories to build public understanding.
- *Example:* A video series shares how a dual-language program helps multilingual learners thrive.

7. Empower Students and Families as Advocates

- Equip them to speak publicly, join delegations, or share stories with funders.
- *Result:* Community hears directly from those impacted by school efforts.

How would a school be affected by a dramatic increase in a special population (e.g., English learners or students requiring special education services)?

A dramatic increase in a special population is like an airline discovering mid-boarding that a third of its passengers now require wheelchair access or language support. The plane and crew weren't originally staffed or equipped for this change and without immediate adjustments, the journey could be delayed, stressful, or even unsafe.

In the same way, a school facing a sudden rise in English learners, students with disabilities, or other specialized populations must rapidly respond with staffing, training, communication, and infrastructure. The shift affects instruction, resources, scheduling, and family engagement and demands a collaborative, equity-centered response.

The goal is not just to accommodate the new needs but to adapt the system, so all students receive high-quality, inclusive education, without compromising the support already in place for others.

Outline

School Impact of a Dramatic Shift in Special Populations

1. Instructional Needs Increase
- Teachers must adapt content, pace, and delivery to meet diverse learning needs.
- *Example:* An influx of EL students prompts the addition of visual aids, scaffolded vocabulary, and sentence frames in general ed classrooms.

2. Staffing Adjustments Are Required
- The school may need to hire or reassign ESL teachers, case managers, aides, or interventionists.
- *Challenge:* Hiring shortages may delay service delivery or increase teacher workload.

3. Professional Development Becomes Urgent
- General education staff must be trained in inclusive practices, co-teaching, and differentiation.
- *Example:* PD sessions on WIDA standards, IEP implementation, and trauma-informed instruction.

4. Schedule and Program Modifications Are Needed
- Additional small-group, pull-out, or co-taught settings may need to be added.
- *Impact:* School schedules, support blocks, and resource room availability may be reshuffled.

5. Family and Community Communication Must Expand
- Outreach must be linguistically accessible and culturally responsive.
- *Example:* Translating all school materials, hiring interpreters, and using home visits for trust-building.

6. Resources and Materials Must Be Reallocated or Expanded
- Need for adapted curriculum, assistive technology, sensory tools, or bilingual texts.
- *Budget challenge:* Funding may need to shift from other areas.

7. School Climate and Equity Considerations Emerge
- Inclusion must be intentional to avoid stigma or isolation of the new population.
- *Example:* Peer buddy systems and schoolwide cultural celebrations.

Essential Questions #16 Community Engagement Leadership

Under what circumstances should an administrator look to outside resources in assisting students and their families?

Supporting students and families is like being a first responder: school leaders can stabilize many situations, but sometimes the emergency requires calling in additional help. Just as a firefighter might call paramedics for medical care or engineers for structural hazards, school leaders must recognize when student or family needs go beyond what the school can provide.

Outside resources become critical when needs exceed the school's legal, financial, or professional capacity, such as in cases of homelessness, food insecurity, mental health crises, immigration support, abuse, or medical emergencies. The role of the administrator is not to "fix everything," but to connect families to the appropriate services with dignity, urgency, and respect.

By partnering with community agencies, health providers, housing programs, and social service networks, school leaders become advocates and connectors ensuring students have the external support needed to fully access their education.

Outline

When and Why Administrators Should Use Outside Resources

1. When Student Needs Exceed School Capabilities

- *Example:* A student experiencing trauma shows signs of PTSD. The school counselor can provide support, but long-term therapy must come from a licensed provider.

2. In Cases of Health, Housing, or Safety Emergencies

- *Example:* A family faces eviction. The administrator contacts a local housing authority or legal aid service to provide immediate support.

3. When Families Experience Language or Legal Barriers

- *Example:* A newly arrived immigrant family needs legal services, translation, and cultural navigation help. The school partners with refugee and immigrant support centers.

4. To Address Chronic Absenteeism or Behavioral Issues Rooted in Home Stress

- A student's repeated absences are linked to unstable housing and family illness. The administrator connects them to a community outreach case manager.

5. To Provide Wraparound Services

- Partnering with a hospital or food pantry to bring mobile services to campus.

6. When Parent Engagement Is Low Due to External Barriers

- A family doesn't attend meetings due to fear of deportation or mistrust of institutions. Community liaisons or nonprofits can help rebuild trust.

7. To Comply with Mandated Reporting or Legal Obligations

A teacher notices a student with unexplained bruises who confides they are afraid to go home, the teacher immediately reports the concern to child protective services and the school principal, ensuring the child's safety and fulfilling legal obligations.

Essential Questions #17 Community Engagement Leadership

What laws and regulations govern the use of school facilities?

Managing the use of school facilities is like running a community center that's also in a secure government building. It must remain welcoming to the public but also operate under strict policies that protect its primary purpose and users. Schools are public institutions, and their facilities, classrooms, gyms, auditoriums, and fields are valuable assets. But opening them up to outside use requires careful alignment with laws, liability protections, and district policies.

The primary legal and regulatory considerations include ensuring that facility use doesn't interfere with the school's educational mission, that it complies with nondiscrimination laws, that religious and political access is handled neutrally, and that health, safety, and liability standards are met. Administrators must also follow board policies that regulate when, how, and by whom spaces can be used and ensure equitable access for all community groups.

A school leader's role is to balance community engagement with legal and operational responsibility, ensuring that school property is used safely, fairly, and in line with educational values.

<u>Outline</u>

<u>Laws and Policies Governing School Facility Use</u>

1. Local Board of Education Policies

- Most districts have facility use policies that include application procedures, fee structures, and supervision requirements.
- *Example:* A community dance group must submit a request and pay a facilities fee for after-hours gym use.

2. Equal Access Act (EAA)

- Public secondary schools must provide equal access to all student groups, including religious and political clubs, if they allow other noncurricular groups.
- *Implication:* A Bible study group cannot be denied access if a chess or drama club is allowed.

3. First Amendment Protections

- Schools cannot promote or inhibit religion. Facilities must be available on a content-neutral basis if open to the public.
- *Example:* A religious group can rent the auditorium under the same terms as a secular nonprofit.

4. Title IX and Nondiscrimination Laws

- Use of school facilities must comply with civil rights laws prohibiting discrimination based on race, gender, disability, religion, or national origin.
- *Implication:* Facilities must be accessible (ADA compliance) and offered to all qualified groups.

5. Safety, Supervision, and Liability

- Districts may require insurance, adult supervision, or custodial fees to minimize risk.
- *Example:* An athletic league using the gym must provide proof of liability insurance.

6. Restricted Use During School Hours

- Most laws prioritize student instruction and restrict community use during instructional hours.
- *Policy:* Facility use may be limited to evenings or weekends unless it's a school-sponsored event.

7. Maintenance and Cost Recovery

- Districts may charge fees for utilities, staffing, and wear-and-tear.
- *Example:* A theater group pays a custodial fee to use the auditorium on weekends.

8. Emergency or Political Use

- In some states, schools must open facilities as emergency shelters or polling places.
- *Requirement:* May include temporary closures or access modifications under state emergency laws.

Essential Questions #18 Community Engagement Leadership

How can the community be helpful in identifying and supplying resources for the school and school programs?

A school is like a thriving community garden; it cannot reach its full potential without the collective effort of those around it. Community members work together to plant seeds, tend the soil, water the crops, provide nutrients, and protect the plants from pests and disease each playing a vital role in helping the garden flourish. Similarly, local businesses, nonprofits, health agencies, families, and cultural organizations contribute unique knowledge, materials, expertise, and networks to support schools. These partners can help school leaders identify hidden challenges such as food insecurity or limited access to technology and provide essential tools, mentorship, or funding. When schools cultivate authentic relationships with these partners, resources flow more naturally, and programs become more relevant, equitable, and sustainable.

A strong school-community partnership doesn't just address gaps; it creates a shared investment in the success of every child.

Outline

Community Roles in Identifying and Supplying Resources

1. Community Insight Reveals Hidden Needs

- Community members may observe gaps schools don't immediately see.
- *Example:* A food pantry reports a rise in family visits, prompting a school meal expansion.

2. Local Businesses Can Provide Financial and Material Support

- Donations, sponsorships, and internships align businesses with student goals.
- *Example:* A tech company donates tablets for a 1:1 device program.

3. Faith-Based and Nonprofit Organizations Offer Wraparound Services

- These groups support needs beyond academics (meals, clothing, aftercare).
- *Example:* A nonprofit funds weekend backpacks of food for students.

4. Families and Alumni Offer Volunteerism and Expertise

- Parents, grandparents, and graduates can support instruction and school culture.
- *Example:* An alumnus offers resume workshops for high school seniors.

5. Cultural Organizations Add Relevance and Representation

- Museums, libraries, and cultural groups help schools offer diverse, inclusive programming.
- *Example:* A local museum co-develops curriculum on Latinx heritage.

6. Civic Groups Help Identify Safety and Health Needs

- Police, social workers, or public health officials may offer insights and funding.
- *Example:* The town health department partners on a mental wellness campaign.

7. Ongoing Feedback Channels Help Align Resources

- Surveys, advisory groups, and community forums help match offerings to needs.
- *Example:* A bilingual parent group identifies the need for translated school forms.

8. Community Partnerships Sustain Enrichment Programs

- Provide funding, mentorship programs, internships, and career exposure opportunities for students.

Essential Questions #19 Community Engagement Leadership

How can a school leader use community resources to support student learning?

Using community resources to support student learning is like a conductor leading an orchestra. Each instrument brings a different sound, and together they create harmony. The conductor (school leader) doesn't play every note but understands how to bring in the right instruments (community partners) at the right time to elevate the performance (student achievement).

Just as a conductor listens carefully and aligns each section's contribution to the overall piece, a school leader must identify student needs and strategically coordinate partnerships such as mental health agencies, local businesses, libraries, cultural institutions, and parents to strengthen and enrich learning. The most powerful performances happen when everyone is coordinated.

When community resources are used purposefully, they don't just accompany instruction, they transform it into something more powerful and lasting.

How School Leaders Use Community Resources to Support Student Learning

1. Identify Specific Student Needs

- Start with data: academic gaps, attendance, social-emotional needs, or resource shortages.
- *Example:* Low attendance and disengagement in a 9th grade cohort may signal a need for mentoring or career exploration.

2. Map Available Community Assets

- Take stock of existing partnerships, local businesses, universities, service agencies, and cultural institutions.
- *Example:* A nearby tech company, library, and arts nonprofit could each support different student learning outcomes.

3. Align Community Support with Instructional Goals

- Ensure resources enrich core learning rather than distract from it.
- *Example:* A science teacher partners with a local nature center to provide hands-on learning tied to NGSS standards.

4. Facilitate Authentic, Long-Term Partnerships

- Don't just bring in one-time speakers build sustained programs with mutual benefit.
- *Example:* A local college runs a semester-long writing lab for middle schoolers.

5. Engage Families as Learning Partners

- Leverage parents' skills, cultures, and networks to co-create learning experiences.
- *Example:* Bilingual parents host story time in students' home languages.

6. Address Barriers to Learning Through Community Wraparound Services

- Learning is limited if basic needs are unmet partner with agencies to provide food, health care, and mental health supports.
- *Example:* A health center provides vision screenings, helping students access learning more clearly.

7. Create Pathways for Real-World Learning

- Use internships, service learning, job shadowing, or guest speakers to connect academics to life beyond school.
- *Example:* A local architect leads a geometry-based design project.

8. Evaluate Impact and Adjust

- Track student outcomes are linked to partnerships to ensure effectiveness.
- *Example:* After partnering with a nonprofit organization that provides music education or programs to support student learning, reading scores improve in early grades, showing the value of the integration.

Essential Questions #20 Community Engagement Leadership

What guidelines/restrictions would normally be in place when a school enters into a relationship with an outside party (e.g., local business, health service, law enforcement agency)?

Partnering with an external organization is similar to choosing vendors for a community event. The event coordinator, the school leader can't just choose anyone. They must ensure that every vendor or partnership is qualified, follows rules, aligns with the event's purpose, and contributes to a safe, successful experience. Hiring a food vendor without permits, or a security firm with no training or a speaker with a political agenda, would compromise the event.

Similarly, schools must be selective, compliant, and strategic when building relationships with outside parties. Whether partnering with local businesses, health agencies, or law enforcement, school leaders must protect student safety, data privacy, instructional integrity, and legal compliance. That means background checks, written agreements, alignment to educational goals, and equity in access.

The goal is not just to bring in support but to bring in the right support, under the right conditions.

Outline

Key Guidelines and Restrictions for External Partnerships in Schools

1. Clear Educational Purpose

- All partnerships must directly or indirectly support the school's mission and student success.
- *Example:* A local business offering internships must tie experiences to learning goals, not just free labor.

2. Written Agreements (MOUs or Contracts)

- Define roles, responsibilities, duration, supervision, access to students, and liability coverage.
- *Example:* A health agency providing on-site services signs an MOU outlining service scope, scheduling, and reporting.

3. Background Checks and Student Safety

- Anyone interacting with students must pass criminal history and fingerprint checks per district/state law.
- *Example:* Mentors from a community center undergo background checks before starting a lunch program.

4. FERPA and Data Privacy Compliance

- Partners must not have access to student records unless explicitly authorized under FERPA guidelines.
- *Example:* A tutoring company cannot access grades or IEPs without parent consent and district approval.

5. Neutrality and Non-Endorsement

- Schools cannot promote or endorse religious, political, or commercial interests.
- *Example:* A political group cannot distribute campaign material through a school club.

6. Equity in Access

- Partnerships should not exclude students based on ability, income, or identity.
- *Example:* A club funded by a local nonprofit must be open to all interested students, not just high achievers.

7. District and Board Approval

- Larger or long-term partnerships often require school board approval, especially if involving funding or school property use.
- *Example:* Leasing space to a mental health agency must be approved by the board and reviewed by legal counsel.

8. Monitoring and Evaluation

- Schools should assess partner effectiveness and alignment to goals annually or at designated intervals.
- *Example:* A college access program is evaluated based on student participation, feedback, and college enrollment data.

Community Engagement Leadership Quiz

1. **A principal notices that parent attendance at back-to-school nights is significantly lower among multilingual families. What is the most effective first step?**
   A. Send a second reminder flyer home in English
   B. Ask the PTA to reach out to families informally
   C. Record the event and post it online afterward
   D. Provide interpretation services and translated invitations

2. **During a school improvement planning session, only a few parents attended, and they all represent the same neighborhood. What should the principal do to ensure diverse community input?**
   A. Use the feedback from attendees to finalize the plan
   B. Reschedule the meeting for another day
   C. Offer transportation, childcare, and outreach in multiple languages
   D. Ask teachers to encourage their students' parents to attend

3. **A school leader wants to develop a community service program that strengthens ties between students and local stakeholders. What is the most appropriate first step?**
   A. Assign teachers to develop service projects
   B. Survey families and community organizations to identify shared priorities
   C. Require each student to complete 10 hours of service
   D. Invite only high-performing students to participate

4. **A parent approaches the principal about starting a family literacy night to support reading at home. What leadership response best models shared decision-making?**
   A. Politely thank the parent and file the idea for later
   B. Ask the parent to run the event without school input
   C. Partner with the parent to co-develop the program and invite staff to participate
   D. Refer the parent to the PTA to discuss logistics

5. **A new apartment complex opens nearby, and the school sees an influx of families unfamiliar with school routines. What is the best leadership strategy to engage these families?**
   A. Post a flyer in the lobby of the new building
   B. Create a welcome orientation in multiple languages and offer family liaisons
   C. Ask existing families to welcome newcomers
   D. Send home extra copies of the student handbook

6. **The school's community partnership with a local college has stalled. Meetings are infrequent, and the college has pulled back involvement. What should the principal do?**
   A. Let the partnership end and seek a new one
   B. Publicly blame the college for lack of commitment
   C. Meet with the college liaison to clarify goals and renew shared expectations
   D. Send the college a list of student needs

7. **A principal receives feedback that community members feel disconnected from the school's decision-making. What is the most effective leadership response?**
   A. Hold a public relations event to highlight school success
   B. Begin publishing board meeting minutes in the newspaper
   C. Establish a community advisory council that meets regularly
   D. Send out a one-time survey asking for suggestions

8. **A school leader wants to involve more families in academic goal setting. What is the most impactful strategy?**
   A. Host student-led conferences where families help co-develop goals
   B. Send home report cards with written goals from teachers
   C. Share generic learning goals at a school-wide meeting
   D. Provide test score reports and offer interpretation

9. **A school serving a linguistically diverse population is redesigning its website. What feature is most important to ensure equitable communication?**
   A. A rotating slideshow of student events
   B. A weekly principal blog
   C. Multilingual navigation and translation options
   D. A teacher directory with email addresses

10. **A community organization offers to support the school's after-school tutoring program. What should the principal do first?**
    A. Ask for a financial donation instead
    B. Review the organization's mission and confirm alignment with school goals
    C. Accept immediately and schedule tutors
    D. Let the teachers decide how to use the support

11. **A principal notices that parent attendance at school events is low, especially among families who speak a language other than English. What is the most effective step to improve engagement?**
    A. Require teachers to contact all parents before each event
    B. Offer interpretation services and culturally relevant programming at events
    C. Move all events to daytime hours for easier access
    D. Send more flyers home in English and hope for a better turnout

12. **A school wants to develop a mentoring program with local businesses. What is the most appropriate first step?**
    A. Assign teachers to cold-call nearby companies
    B. Create a flyer and send it to the community
    C. Meet with business leaders to co-create a vision aligned with school goals
    D. Launch the program with current resources and add partners later

13. **A group of families expresses concern that their cultural holidays are not represented in school activities. What should the principal do first?**
    A. Ask teachers to celebrate every culture
    B. Review the school calendar and invite parent input on inclusive representation
    C. Explain that school time is limited, and holidays can't all be acknowledged
    D. Suggest families host their own celebrations at home

14. During a school board meeting, a parent criticizes the school for not addressing bullying. What is the best leadership response?

A. Publicly deny the issue to protect the school's image
B. Thank the parent for their input and follow up with them privately to investigate
C. Ask the parent to submit their concern in writing
D. Shift blame to student behavior and discipline policy

15. The school is planning a community clean-up day. What strategy best encourages broad participation?

A. Make attendance mandatory for students
B. Personally invite local leaders, families, and student organizations to participate
C. Have only the student council organized the event
D. Plan it during a school holiday for greater convenience

16. A principal wants to improve communication with families who don't often attend in-person meetings. What is the best approach?

A. Eliminate in-person meetings and use only email
B. Send paper surveys home with students
C. Post important updates on the school bulletin board
D. Offer virtual options and flexible times for family meetings

17. A new school leader wants to build stronger relationships with underserved community groups. What is the most important first step?

A. Create a promotional video showcasing school accomplishments
B. Attend cultural and community events outside the school
C. Email a school newsletter to all families
D. Wait until parent-teacher conferences to connect

18. Parents at a Title I school feel uninformed about how funds are used. What is the most transparent leadership action?

A. Share a summary of Title I spending and invite families to review and give feedback
B. Post the district's Title I plan on the school website
C. Hold a staff-only meeting about Title I updates
D. Refer families to the state education department's website

19. A school's advisory board is made up entirely of English-speaking parents from the PTA. How should the principal address this imbalance?

A. Dissolve the board and start a new one
B. Require the current board to translate meeting notes for others
C. Limit board decisions to school staff only
D. Invite multilingual families and community representatives to join and co-lead

20. Community members have skills to offer but feel unsure how to contribute. What should the school leader do?

A. Post a list of needed roles and match volunteers to their interests
B. Ask teachers to assign volunteers to random tasks
C. Limit volunteer opportunities to field trips only
D. Wait until volunteers ask for assignments

Answer Key Community Engagement Leadership #1-10

Question Number	1	2	3	4	5	6	7	8	9	10
Correct Solution	D	C	B	C	B	C	C	A	C	B

Answer Key Community Engagement Leadership #11-20

Question Number	11	12	13	14	15	16	17	18	19	20
Correct Solution	B	C	B	B	B	D	B	A	D	A

Domain VII: Analysis Constructed Responses

This section focuses on the principal's role in interpreting student work to evaluate mastery, guide instruction, and promote continuous learning. Analysis of constructed responses involves reviewing open-ended tasks, performance assessments, and written explanations to determine not only what students know, but how they think and apply their knowledge. By using clear rubrics, identifying patterns in errors, and providing targeted feedback, principals ensure that teachers can adjust instruction to address misconceptions and deepen understanding. By prioritizing thoughtful analysis of student responses, school leaders create the conditions where students develop higher-order thinking skills and teachers refine instructional practices.

Score	Criteria
3 – Proficient	Fully addresses all parts of the prompt with clarity, depth, and specificity. Demonstrates strong understanding of school leadership principles. Uses logical steps, strategic insight, and realistic actions. Clear writing, well-organized, with examples or justifications.
2 – Basic	Addresses most aspects of the prompt but may lack depth or detail. Reasonable understanding of leadership practices but may miss key steps. Writing is clear but could be more precise or cohesive.
1 – Limited	Superficial or incomplete response. Minimal understanding of leadership practice. Key points are missing or unrealistic. Writing may be disorganized or vague.
0 – Off-topic/No response	Does not address the prompt, or response is missing or irrelevant.

Analysis Constructed Response Prompt #1

Scenario Prompt

Unity Heights Middle School (UHM) is a suburban school serving grades 6–8. The district requires all students to take quarterly benchmark assessments in each core subject, aligned with state standards and the district pacing guide. These assessments measure mastery of the instructional content taught up to that point.

Ms. Ramirez, the new principal, reviews the most recent benchmark data and notices that while most seventh-grade teachers show expected growth in science scores, Mr. Green's students have demonstrated significantly lower progress. Mr. Green is a veteran teacher who is well-liked by students and parents but has expressed resistance to recent curriculum updates.

To better understand the situation, Ms. Ramirez conducts three classroom walkthroughs over two weeks, reviews Mr. Green's lesson plans, and examines formative assessments. She notes that instruction appears heavily textbook-driven, with limited opportunities for student engagement, hands-on activities, or checks for understanding.

Ms. Ramirez decides to address the situation through a coaching and support plan with the goal of improving instructional effectiveness and student learning outcomes.

Documents Provided:

- **Document A**: 7th-grade science benchmark data
- **Document B**: Principal's walkthrough notes on instructional practice and lesson design

Document A – Benchmark Data Snapshot

Teacher	Q1 Score	Q2 Score	Growth (Q1→Q2)
Ms. Lee	68%	82%	+14%
Mrs. Pa tel	72%	84%	+12%
Mr. Green	65%	67%	+2%
Ms. Chen	70%	83%	+13%

Document B – Principal Ramirez's Walkthrough Summary

- Lessons are aligned to the pacing guide, but lectures are heavy.
- Minimal opportunity for hands-on inquiry or student collaboration.
- Checks for understanding are infrequent rare use of exit tickets or formative questioning.
- Student engagement is low, with passive note-taking and limited questioning.

Analysis Constructed Responses #1

Constructed-Response Question

Using the information from Documents A and B, craft a response addressing the following:

1. Describe two instructional concerns evident from the data and observations.
2. Propose two actions Principal Ramirez should take to support Mr. Green's growth.
3. Explain how data should be used to monitor improvement.
4. Outline a process for accountability and the next steps.

Analysis Constructed Responses #1

Sample Outline

1. Instructional Concerns

- Limited Academic Growth: Mr. Green's students show just a +2% gain from Q1 to Q2—well below peers (+12–14%), indicating slow mastery.
- Restricted Pedagogical Practices: Walkthroughs reveal a reliance on lectures and few student-centered strategies or formative checks, which correlates with low engagement and learning.

2. Recommended Actions

- Instructional Coaching & Modeling: Partner Mr. Green with a peer or coach to co-plan and model lessons incorporating hands-on labs, small-group inquiry, and formative tools like exit tickets.
- Professional Learning Opportunities: Arrange targeted PD sessions on inquiry-based science instruction, formative assessments, and student engagement strategies allowing Mr. Green to explore and apply new approaches.

3. Data-Informed Monitoring

- Benchmark Analysis: Continue to track Mr. Green's benchmark scores quarterly and compare gains to growth targets and peer performance.
- Formative Assessment Tracking: Implement weekly formative assessments, quizzes, ticket-out-the-door, discussion probes and monitor for improved student understanding and participation.

4. Accountability and Follow-Up Process

- Develop a clear, measurable improvement plan with specific goals (e.g., improve benchmark gains to match school average +10%; implement 2 formative checks per week).
- Schedule bi-weekly coaching sessions and monthly walkthroughs to observe implementation and provide feedback.
- Review progresses each quarter using data from Document A and formative trends and revise the support plan as needed.
- Recognize and affirm improvements and consider broader sharing of successful strategies in staff meetings.

Unity Heights Middle School – Constructed Response Scoring Samples

Sample Score Point: 3 (Full Credit Response)

Two major instructional concerns are evident. First, Mr. Green's students demonstrate minimal academic growth on benchmark assessments, only 2% increase compared to his peers, indicating instructional effectiveness is lacking. Second, walkthroughs show that instruction is primarily lecture-based with limited engagement, hands-on learning, or formative checks key strategies in science instruction.
To address this, Principal Ramirez should implement targeted instructional coaching with Mr. Green, focusing on student-centered strategies such as inquiry-based labs and daily checks for understanding. Additionally, she should connect him with a high-performing colleague for peer modeling and co-planning sessions.
To monitor improvement, they should track ongoing formative assessments and analyze student work weekly, along with quarterly benchmark data to measure content mastery. A written improvement plan should include specific goals (e.g., use of two engagement strategies per week) and be reviewed bi-weekly through coaching sessions and classroom walkthroughs. This ensures accountability and offers the support needed for sustained growth.

Score Point: 2 (Partial Credit Response)
Response:
Mr. Green's students are not growing as much as others based on the data. He also seems to be using traditional lecture-style teaching instead of hands-on or engaging strategies.
Principal Ramirez should provide support by helping him try new ways to teach science, such as group work or labs. She could also help him plan lessons that include more student participation.
They can look at test scores and student work to see if things are improving. It would help to check in with him regularly to see if the new strategies are working.

Score Point: 1 (Limited Response)
Response:
The scores in Mr. Green's class are low. He needs to improve.
The principal can tell him to do more group work. Maybe that will help.
They can look at the test scores again later to see if there's a change.

Score Point: 0 (No Credit Response)
Response:
Mr. Green is not doing a good job. The students need to do better. The principal should fix it.

Analysis Constructed Response — Prompt #2

Essay Prompt 2 – Instructional Leadership

Prompt:
You have just reviewed mid-year data that shows significant underperformance in math for students in Grades 3–5. Teachers express that students lack problem-solving stamina and have difficulty explaining their thinking. Some teachers blame parents; others cite a flawed curriculum.

As the principal, write a plan detailing how you would:

- Diagnose the root cause of the issue
- Engage teachers in improving instruction
- Support consistent implementation of instructional changes
- Monitor student progress over time

Sample Answer

To address the mid-year data revealing math underperformance in Grades 3–5, I would lead a multi-step, data-driven action plan focused on diagnosing the root cause, building teacher capacity, supporting implementation, and monitoring progress.

Diagnosing the Root Cause:
The first step would be to conduct a structured data analysis session with grade-level teams and instructional coaches. We would disaggregate data by standard, item type, and subgroup to pinpoint where students are struggling (e.g., multistep word problems, math vocabulary, explaining reasoning). In parallel, I would organize classroom walkthroughs using a math-specific look-for tool focused on rigor, discourse, and cognitive demand. Additionally, student focus groups would help uncover student perspectives around confidence, engagement, and task difficulty. This triangulated data approach would help separate surface-level complaints from actionable root causes.

Engaging Teachers in Improving Instruction:
Rather than allow finger-pointing to continue, I would reframe the conversation by establishing a shared problem of practice: "How do we build students' mathematical reasoning and stamina?" Grade-level professional learning communities (PLCs) would be tasked with identifying and trying research-based strategies, such as number talks, math journals, or scaffolded open-ended tasks. I would partner with the math coach to model lessons, co-plan, and provide in-the-moment feedback. Teacher voice would be central: we would host solution circles to identify instructional shifts that feel both effective and feasible.

Supporting Implementation:
Consistency requires clear expectations and support. I would create a 6-week math instructional focus plan across Grades 3–5, identifying one core strategy (e.g., requiring students to "justify their reasoning") to implement schoolwide. I would ensure time in staff meetings and coaching cycles is aligned to this focus. Resources such as sentence stems, anchor charts, and student exemplars would be created collaboratively and posted in classrooms. Teachers would be given time to reflect, share artifacts, and revise their practices during grade-level release time.

Monitoring Student Progress:
To measure progress, I would implement short-cycle formative assessments tied to the targeted standards. Teachers would use common rubrics to assess student explanations, with data shared biweekly in PLCs. Walkthrough tools would be aligned to the focus strategy, and I would track trends across classrooms. At the student level, we would set personal math goals and celebrate gains, no matter how small. If needed, we would provide targeted intervention for students still struggling, including after-school or small-group support.

By focusing on collaborative problem-solving, instructional alignment, and consistent feedback loops, this plan not only addresses the current data but also builds long-term teacher capacity and student confidence in mathematics.

Essay Prompt 3 – Equity and Culture

Prompt:
Your school serves a diverse student population, including English learners and students from low-income backgrounds. The school climate survey reveals that students from marginalized groups feel disconnected and less supported by staff.

As the leader, describe how you will:

- Promote equity and cultural responsiveness among staff
- Create a culture of care and inclusion
- Involve families and community members to support the plan

Essay Prompt 3 – Equity and Culture

3-Point Sample Essay Response

Addressing the math underperformance in Grades 3–5 requires a strategic, inclusive, and evidence-based leadership approach grounded in instructional equity and continuous improvement.

Diagnose the Root Cause:
I would begin with a structured data review involving disaggregated math performance by standard, item type, and student subgroup. This would be paired with non-evaluative classroom walkthroughs using a calibrated observation tool focused on rigor, student discourse, and use of formative assessment. I would also facilitate student and teacher feedback sessions to better understand both learning and instructional barriers. These combined insights would help distinguish between gaps in curriculum delivery, student engagement, or instructional practices.

Engage Teachers in Instructional Improvement:
Blame-based mindsets must be redirected toward collaboration. I would establish a shared instructional focus across Grades 3–5, such as "developing problem-solving stamina through academic discourse." Professional learning communities (PLCs) will be allocated dedicated time and follow established protocols to examine student work, collaboratively plan lessons, and assess the efficacy of newly implemented strategies. I would partner with the math coach to provide demonstration lessons, embedded coaching, and opportunities for teachers to observe each other using practices like number talks and open-ended tasks.

Support Consistent Implementation:
Sustainable change requires structure. I would implement a schoolwide six-week math improvement cycle with clear observable indicators, such as requiring students to justify answers using sentence frames or visual models. Teachers would receive consistent support through coaching, check-ins and resource sharing. A shared Google folder with anchor charts, student exemplars, and recorded mini lessons would ensure equity of access. Leadership team members would conduct calibrated instructional rounds to provide real-time, non-threatening feedback and surface bright spots for celebration and replication.

Monitor Student Progress:
Progress would be monitored through common formative assessments aligned to problem-solving standards. Teachers would use a shared rubric to score student explanations and track growth over time. Results would be reviewed biweekly in PLCs and used to adjust instruction, provide intervention, or refine strategies. I would also track trends from walkthrough data and student engagement surveys to ensure both academic and affective growth. By empowering students to set and monitor personal goals, we create a culture of ownership and progress.

Through collaborative leadership, targeted professional learning, and a commitment to instructional consistency, we can shift both teacher practice and student outcomes in math.

Essay Prompt 4 – Family and Community Engagement

Prompt:
You've been asked to increase family and community engagement at your school. However, only 25% of families attend events, and most communication is in English, even though 60% of your families speak other languages.

Write a strategy explaining how you would:

- Assess and remove barriers to engagement
- Improve two-way communication with all families
- Develop partnerships with community groups that reflect your student body

Essay Prompt 4 – Family and Community Engagement (PSEL Standard 8)

3-Point Sample Essay Response

Effectively engaging families and community partners requires more than hosting events or sending home fliers. It demands intentional, inclusive systems that reflect the lived experiences of the school's population. My strategy would center on removing systemic barriers, improving two-way communication, and building culturally responsive partnerships.

Assess and Remove Barriers to Engagement:
I would begin by conducting a multilingual family engagement survey offered digitally, on paper, and through phone calls to understand why many families aren't participating. The survey would ask about preferred communication methods, event timing, childcare needs, and language support. I would also hold listening sessions with parent focus groups, using translators as needed, to hear directly from underrepresented voices. From this input, we could address root barriers such as offering evening events, providing transportation, offering childcare during meetings, and ensuring interpreters are available at all major gatherings. All events would be co-planned with family representatives from various language and cultural groups to ensure inclusivity.

Improve Two-Way Communication with All Families:
To promote authentic relationships, I would shift from one-way announcements to two-way, culturally responsive communication. This includes using platforms like TalkingPoints or ClassDojo, which translate messages into multiple languages, and setting expectations that teachers initiate periodic outreach beyond academics (e.g., celebrating student progress, not just concerns). We would train staff on how to communicate with cultural sensitivity and offer parent workshops on how to access school tools (e.g., PowerSchool, Google Classroom) in their home language. A multilingual family liaison would serve as a bridge between home and school, proactively supporting families and surfacing concerns or needs.

Develop Community Partnerships that Reflect the Student Body:
I would identify organizations faith-based groups, cultural centers, health clinics, immigrant support services, and small businesses that serve our families and invite them to collaborate with us. These groups could help co-host culturally affirming events (e.g., heritage nights, resource fairs), provide language-specific support services, and serve as ambassadors for school participation. By meeting families in familiar spaces and through trusted messengers, we build deeper connections. I'd also create a Family & Community Advisory Council composed of parents and community leaders representing our school's cultural diversity, to help shape ongoing school initiatives and ensure shared decision-making.

Through this plan, family engagement becomes not just an initiative, but a relational and inclusive culture rooted in trust, access, and mutual respect.

Essay Prompt 5 – School Improvement and Shared Vision (PSEL Standards 1 & 10)

Prompt:
Your district has given your school autonomy to create a three-year improvement plan. Staff are burned out and skeptical of new initiatives. Morale is low, and student achievement has plateaued.

Explain how you would:

- Lead a collaborative process to develop a shared vision and goals
- Use data to prioritize areas for improvement
- Build staff ownership of the school improvement process

Essay Prompt 5 – School Improvement and Shared Vision (PSEL Standards 1 & 10)

3-Point Sample Essay Response

Creating a meaningful three-year improvement plan requires more than data analysis, it requires trust, collaboration, and a vision that resonates. Given the low morale and skepticism around new initiatives, I would lead with transparency, empathy, and a deep commitment to collective ownership.

Lead a Collaborative Process to Develop a Shared Vision and Goals
I would begin by convening a representative Visioning Task Force made up of teachers, support staff, students, parents, and community members. The process would begin with small-group dialogues where participants reflect on what they believe students need most to thrive. We would revisit our school's core values, reflect on what's working, and co-construct a future-focused vision that reflects the hopes of our entire learning community. The goal would be to articulate a vision statement and 3–5 high-impact goals that are aspirational, measurable, and anchored in our mission. Every staff member would have a voice either through surveys, suggestion walls, or focus groups so no one feels "done to" or left behind.

Use Data to Prioritize Areas for Improvement
To ensure our goals are rooted in reality, we would conduct a comprehensive data audit that includes student achievement data (e.g., NJSLA, I-Ready), attendance trends, discipline referrals, and survey feedback from students, families, and staff. Disaggregating this data by grade level, subgroup, and domain (academic, behavioral, social-emotional) would allow us to spot equity gaps and systemic breakdowns. We would use this data to identify 2–3 priority areas with the greatest potential for impact such as increasing math proficiency, reducing chronic absenteeism, or strengthening Tier 1 instruction. These areas would become the backbone of our plan.

Build Staff Ownership of the School Improvement Process
To overcome initiative fatigue, I would frame this plan as an opportunity to simplify and focus not add more. Grade level and department teams would develop action steps aligned to each goal, allowing staff to lead the "how" of the work. I would establish regular shared planning time and cross-grade collaboration to promote peer learning and idea exchange. We'd use data cycles and brief improvement protocols (like Plan-Do-Study-Act) to give teams a safe, structured way to test small changes and see results quickly. Wins would be celebrated publicly, and feedback would be used to refine our plan in real-time. I would also implement quarterly "pulse checks" to ensure staff voice remains central throughout the 3-year implementation.

In doing so, the school improvement plan becomes more than a document. It becomes a culture shift rooted in shared vision, meaningful data, and empowered leadership at all levels.

Train Your Brain Refresher

This section is designed to feel like reviewing your notes before a big test. Its purpose is to give your brain a clear snapshot of the information so that, on exam day, even if every detail doesn't come to mind, you'll still recognize which answer makes sense. You know that intuitive feeling you sometimes get when something seems right, even if you can't explain exactly why? That's the kind of confidence this section helps you build for the exam.

1. A principal wants to ensure long-term improvement in literacy instruction. What is the best first step?
Conduct a needs assessment using student achievement data and teacher input to identify strengths and gaps in literacy instruction.

2. After a community forum reveals a disconnect between the school and non-English-speaking families, what is the best leadership response?
Provide translation/interpretation services, improve multilingual communication, and intentionally include these families in decision-making.

3. The school's improvement plan calls for increased inquiry-based instruction in science. Which strategy best supports this instructional goal?
Offer professional development and coaching on inquiry-based methods, followed by classroom walkthroughs and feedback to support implementation.

4. A school leader wants to build a culture of trust among staff. What is the best way to start?
Model transparency, actively listen to staff concerns, and follow through on commitments.

5. A student with an IEP is excluded from a field trip due to behavioral concerns. What is the principal's most appropriate action?
Ensure compliance with the IEP, provide accommodations or support, and work with staff to include the student in the field trip.

6. A teacher expresses frustration that students are disengaged during lessons. What should the instructional leader do first?
Observe the classroom to gather evidence, then collaborate with the teacher to adjust instructional strategies and increase engagement.

7. A principal notices that only a few parents attend school events. What is the best way to improve family engagement?
Survey families for input on timing, format, and needs; then adjust events to be more accessible and inclusive.

8. The school nurse reports that many students come to school without breakfast. What is the most ethical and strategic response?
Partner with community resources or implement a school breakfast program to ensure all students have access to healthy meals.

9. Several staff express confusion about new grading policies. What is the most effective leadership response?
Provide clear training and guidance, allow staff to ask questions, and ensure consistent communication about expectations.

10. A principal wants to improve special education compliance after noticing several overdue IEPs. What should the leader do first?
Review compliance data, meet with the special education team to identify causes of delays, and establish a system to track and meet deadlines.

Train Your Brain Refresher Set B

1. A newly hired teacher reports feeling isolated. What is the best action for supporting this teacher?
Assign a mentor and include them in a professional learning community for support and collaboration.

2. Data shows disciplined referrals disproportionately involve students of color. What should the principal do first?
Analyze referral practices, engage staff in equity-focused professional development, and review policies for bias.

3. A fire drill revealed staff confusion about evacuation roles. What is the best leadership response?
clarify roles, revise the safety plan as needed, and provide additional training and practice drills.

4. The school's vision includes "preparing all students for college and careers." What's the best way to embed this into daily practice?
Align instruction and programs with college- and career-readiness standards and provide real-world learning opportunities.

5. A school board member asks for student discipline data about a specific student. What should the principal do?
Protect student confidentiality and provide only aggregate data, in compliance with FERPA.

6. A student threatens to harm themselves during class. What is the principal's first ethical responsibility?
Ensure the student's immediate safety by following crisis protocols and contacting appropriate mental health professionals.

7. A school leader wants to reduce teacher burnout. What strategy best supports this goal?
Promote work-life balance by protecting planning time, limiting unnecessary meetings, and recognizing teacher contributions.

8. A veteran teacher resists using the district's new learning management system. What is the best way to support them?
Provide targeted training, peer support, and opportunities to practice until they feel confident with the system.

9. The superintendent asks for a presentation on school progress. What should the principal focus on?
Highlight student achievement data, progress toward goals, and strategies implemented to improve outcomes.

10. A school improvement goal is to increase 8th-grade math scores. What action best reflects instructional leadership?
Support teachers with professional development, collaborative planning, and data-driven instructional adjustments.

Train Your Brain Refresher — Set C

1. Families express concern about bullying during recess. What is the principal's most appropriate response?
Investigate concerns, increase supervision, and implement clear anti-bullying strategies with staff and students.

2. Teachers report unclear communication from leadership. What is the most strategic next step?
Establish consistent communication channels (e.g., weekly updates, agendas, feedback loops) and clarify expectations.

3. The parent of a student with a disability says their child was excluded from a club. What is the most appropriate leadership response?
Ensure compliance with IDEA by addressing the exclusion, providing equal access, and educating staff on inclusion.

4. To support strategic scheduling, what is the best practice when building the master schedule?
Prioritize student needs first, ensuring equitable access to core classes, interventions, and enrichment opportunities.

5. A principal wants to strengthen community-school relationships. What is an effective strategy?
Develop partnerships with local organizations, host family engagement events, and create advisory opportunities for stakeholders.

6. A principal wants to ensure alignment between classroom instruction and school goals. What is the most effective leadership action?
Conduct classroom walkthroughs, provide feedback, and monitor that instruction aligns with the school's vision and goals.

7. A student expresses anxiety about feeling excluded due to their gender identity. What is the principal's most appropriate response?

Listen, provide support, ensure anti-discrimination protections, and foster an inclusive environment for all students.

8. A district policy mandates that each school conduct at least two emergency drills per month. What is the principal's legal responsibility?
Ensure drills are conducted as required, documented properly, and reviewed for safety compliance

9. A veteran teacher consistently posts outdated grades, causing parent complaints. What should the principal do first?
Meet with the teacher to review grading expectations, clarify policy, and provide support for timely updates.

10. A school is launching a new dual-language program. What is the best way for the principal to ensure community support?
Engage families and community stakeholders early through information sessions, outreach, and opportunities for input.

Train Your Brain Refresher — Set D

1. A new assistant principal wants to build credibility with staff. What is the most effective first step?
Listen actively, observe classrooms, and build relationships before making major changes.

2. After a controversial policy decision, the school experiences increased tension among stakeholders. What should the principal do to refocus attention on student learning?
Recenter discussions on the school's mission and vision, highlight student outcomes, and create forums for constructive dialogue.

3. Teachers express frustration over inconsistent behavior referrals. What leadership strategy promotes fairness and consistency?
Develop and train staff on a clear discipline policy with shared expectations and consistent implementation.

4. The district is transitioning to a standards-based report card. What should the principal prioritize to support staff?
Provide professional development, collaborative planning time, and clear communication with families and staff.

5. A school leader notices students with disabilities are underrepresented in gifted programs. What is the appropriate first step?
Review identification practices for bias and ensure equitable screening and referral processes.

6. A parent group is concerned about a lack of cultural representation in the curriculum. What is the most effective response?
Engage parents and staff in curriculum review, and incorporate diverse, culturally responsive materials.

7. The principal wants to increase transparency around decision-making. Which approach is best?
Share data, explain rationales, and include stakeholders in the decision-making process.

8. Data shows students who transfer mid-year have lower achievement. What should the principal do?
Implement transition support such as orientation, peer mentoring, and targeted academic interventions.

9. A student violates the dress code but claims the policy is culturally biased. What should the principal do?
Review the policy for equity, address the student respectfully, and engage stakeholders in revising if bias is present.

10. A teacher resists using student data to guide instruction. What is the most effective leadership response?
Provide coaching, model effective data use, and show how it improves instruction and student outcomes.

Train Your Bain Refresher Set E

1. A teacher wants to pilot a new project-based learning unit that aligns with standards but differs from the current pacing. What should the principal do?
Support the pilot with clear parameters, monitor results, and share findings with staff to inform practice.

2. Student surveys show that many students do not feel emotionally safe at school. What is the most appropriate leadership response?
Address climate concerns by implementing SEL supports, anti-bullying strategies, and student voice opportunities.

3. A local organization offers to fund a school art program if they can place ads on campus. What is the most ethical course of action?
Decline advertising in exchange for funding and seek partnerships that align with school values and policies.

4. A teacher expresses discomfort using a culturally responsive curriculum adopted by the district. What is the best leadership response?
Provide training, coaching, and dialogue to build understanding and ensure fidelity to district expectations.

5. An emergency situation arises, and the principal is unavailable. What leadership practice ensures continuity?
Establish and train staff on a clear chain of command and emergency protocols in advance.

6. A school's English Learner (EL) population is increasing rapidly. What is the most strategic leadership move?
Expand EL supports through staffing, professional development, and culturally responsive instructional strategies.

7. A parent wants to opt their child out of assessments required by state law. What is the principal's legal responsibility?
Inform the parent of state requirements and ensure compliance with testing mandates.

8. During an observation, a principal notices a lack of student voice and engagement in classroom discussion. What is the best next step?
Provide feedback with strategies for increasing student engagement and model best practices if needed.

9. A school leader wants to make the teacher evaluation process more meaningful. What action best supports this goal?
Focus evaluations on growth by providing actionable feedback, coaching, and professional learning opportunities.

10. Community members complain that students are loitering outside stores after school. What is the best leadership response?
Collaborate with families, community partners, and staff to create safe, structured after-school options for student

School Leadership Vocabulary

Key Vocabulary and Best Practices for School Leaders

The following terms and concepts frequently appear on principal licensure exams. Knowing these definitions and how they connect to real-world leadership practice will strengthen your preparation.

Leadership and Vision

- **Mission Statement** – A school's purpose, describing why it exists.
- **Vision Statement** – A forward-looking goal for what the school community aspires to achieve.
- **Core Values** – Guiding beliefs and principles that shape decisions and culture.
- **Strategic Plan** – A long-term, data-driven plan aligning resources, people, and goals to the vision.
- **Continuous Improvement** – An ongoing cycle of goal setting, monitoring, reflection, and refinement.

Ethics and Equity

- **Equity** – Ensuring fair treatment, access, opportunities, and advancement for all students by removing systemic barriers.
- **Cultural Responsiveness** – Respecting and incorporating students' backgrounds, languages, and experiences in teaching and leadership.

- **Implicit Bias** – Unconscious attitudes or stereotypes that can influence decisions and interactions.
- **Ethical Leadership** – Decision-making guided by fairness, transparency, and professional norms.
- **Restorative Practices** – Approaches to discipline that focus on repairing harm and restoring relationships rather than punishment.

Curriculum, Instruction, and Assessment

- **Formative Assessment** – Ongoing checks for understanding during instruction to guide teaching.
- **Summative Assessment** – Evaluations of learning at the end of a unit, course, or year (e.g., standardized tests).
- **Data-Driven Decision Making** – Using multiple sources of evidence (achievement, attendance, climate surveys) to guide actions.
- **Professional Learning Communities (PLCs)** – Collaborative teacher groups that analyze data, share strategies, and align instruction.
- **Differentiation** – Adapting instruction to meet the diverse learning needs of students.
- **Tiered Interventions (MTSS/RTI)** – Multi-level systems of support for academic and behavioral needs.

School Culture and Climate

- **School Climate** – The overall quality and character of school life as experienced by students, staff, and families.
- **School Culture** – The shared beliefs, values, and traditions that shape behavior and expectations.
- **Social-Emotional Learning (SEL)** – Instructional practices that develop self-awareness, self-management, social skills, and responsible decision-making.
- **Inclusive Practices** – Strategies that ensure students with diverse abilities and backgrounds are supported in the general education environment.
- **Trauma-Informed Practices** – Teaching and leadership approaches that recognize the impact of trauma on learning and behavior.

Professional Capacity and Community

- **Instructional Leadership** – The principal's role in guiding curriculum, teaching, and assessment to improve student achievement.

- **Mentoring and Induction** – Systems of support for novice teachers and new staff.
- **Distributed Leadership** – Sharing leadership responsibilities with teacher-leaders, staff, and stakeholders.
- **Reflective Practice** – Continuous self-assessment and professional growth by educators.
- **Collective Efficacy** – The shared belief of educators in their ability to positively affect student outcomes.

Family and Community Engagement

- **Stakeholder Engagement** – Actively involving students, families, staff, and community partners in school decisions.
- **Two-Way Communication** – Reciprocal, transparent dialogue between schools and families, not just one-way announcements.
- **Community Partnerships** – Collaborations with local organizations, businesses, and nonprofits to support student success.
- **Family Engagement vs. Involvement** – Engagement implies active collaboration and shared decision-making, while involvement may be more limited to participation in events.
- **Culturally Responsive Engagement** – Outreach strategies that honor languages, traditions, and cultural perspectives of families.

Operations and Management

- **Resource Allocation** – Ensuring staffing, schedules, and budgets align with school goals and equity priorities.
- **Facilities Management** – Maintaining safe, healthy, and effective school environments.
- **Crisis Management** – Responding to emergencies with proactive planning and equity-focused decisions.
- **Accountability Systems** – Policies and processes for monitoring performance and ensuring compliance with district/state standards.
- **Instructional Time Protection** – Minimizing disruptions and maximizing engaged learning time.

School Improvement

- **Root Cause Analysis** – A systematic method to identify underlying causes of problems.

- **SMART Goals** – Goals that are Specific, Measurable, Achievable, Relevant, and Time-bound.
- **Improvement Cycle (Plan-Do-Study-Act)** – Continuous improvement model for testing and refining initiatives.
- **Progress Monitoring** – Regular assessment of student performance to inform instruction and interventions.
- **Change Management** – Leadership strategies for implementing and sustaining meaningful reforms.

Key Federal Laws

1. **FERPA (Family Educational Rights and Privacy Act)**
   Protects the privacy of student education records; gives parents certain rights.
2. **IDEA (Individuals with Disabilities Education Act)**
   Ensures students with disabilities receive Free Appropriate Public Education (FAPE) in the least restrictive environment (LRE).
3. **Section 504 of the Rehabilitation Act**
   Prohibits discrimination based on disability; provides accommodations and modifications in school.
4. **ADA (Americans with Disabilities Act)**
   Prohibits discrimination against individuals with disabilities in all public places, including schools.
5. **Title I (Every Student Succeeds Act - ESSA)**
   Provides financial assistance to schools with high percentages of children from low-income families.
6. **Title II (ESSA)**
   Supports effective instruction through professional development.
7. **Title IX of the Education Amendments of 1972**
   Prohibits sex-based discrimination in any school receiving federal funds.
8. **McKinney-Vento Homeless Assistance Act**
   Ensures educational stability and support for homeless students.
9. **Civil Rights Act of 1964 (Title VI)**
   Prohibits discrimination on the basis of race, color, or national origin in programs receiving federal funding.

10. **Equal Educational Opportunities Act (EEOA)**
    Requires schools to take action to overcome barriers to students' equal participation.

11. **No Child Left Behind Act (NCLB)** *(replaced by ESSA but still referenced)*
    Emphasized accountability and standardized testing.

12. **Protection of Pupil Rights Amendment (PPRA)**
    Regulates the administration of surveys and collection of information from students.

13. **Child Find Mandate** (under IDEA)
    Requires schools to identify, locate, and evaluate all children with disabilities.

Glossary of Laws and Key Terms

Leadership & Curriculum Terms

Core guiding principles that define the purpose and direction of the school.

1. **Coherence**
   Alignment between vision, curriculum, assessment, and instruction.

2. **Backward Design**
   Curriculum planning method where instruction starts with the end goals.

3. **Formative Assessment**
   Ongoing checks during instruction to inform teaching and learning.

4. **Summative Assessment**
   Evaluation at the end of an instructional period to measure outcomes.

5. **MTSS (Multi-Tiered System of Supports)**
   Framework to support all students' academic, behavioral, and social-emotional needs.

6. **RTI (Response to Intervention)**
   Tiered approach to identifying and supporting struggling learners.

7. **PBIS (Positive Behavioral Interventions and Supports)**
   Proactive approach to establishing behavioral supports and a positive school climate.

8. **Instructional Rounds**
   A practice where educators observe peers to improve instructional practices.

9. **Equity vs. Equality**
   Equity means giving each student what they need; equality means giving everyone the same.

10. **Culturally Responsive Teaching**
    Recognizing and honoring students' cultural references in instruction.

11. **Inclusive Practices**
    Ensuring students with disabilities learn alongside peers in general education settings.

12. **Differentiated Instruction**
    Tailoring teaching to meet individual needs of students.

13. **Data-Driven Decision Making**
    Using student performance data to guide instructional and organizational decisions.

14. **Stakeholder Engagement**
    Involving families, staff, and community members in school decision-making.

Human Resources & Ethics

1. **Collective Bargaining**
   Negotiation of employment terms between school boards and teacher unions.

2. **Due Process**
   Legal requirement that individuals are given fair procedures (important in suspensions, dismissals).

3. **Ethical Leadership**
   Making decisions that are morally and professionally sound.

4. **Conflict of Interest**
   Situation where personal interests might interfere with professional duties.

5. **Mandated Reporting**
   Legal obligation to report suspected child abuse or neglect.

6. **Professional Learning Communities (PLCs)**
   Teams of educators working collaboratively to improve teaching and learning.

7. **Instructional Supervision**
   Ongoing support and feedback provided to improve teaching practices.

8. **Observation & Feedback Cycles**
   Structured evaluation processes to support teacher development.

About the Author

Ingrid Fullerton is a certified supervisor and accomplished educator with more than 16 years of experience in instruction, curriculum design, and school leadership. She holds a Bachelor of Arts in Mathematics and a Master of Arts in Curriculum and Instruction, along with certifications from the New Jersey Department of Education in Elementary Education and a Middle School Mathematics Endorsement.

Throughout her career, Ingrid has served diverse student populations, with a strong focus on multilingual learners (MLLs), English language learners (ELLs), and students performing below grade level. Her recent mSGP score of 3.5 is a testament to her effectiveness in advancing the growth of even the most academically vulnerable learners.

As a curriculum designer, Ingrid brings deep expertise in aligning instructional strategies with standards-based goals. She specializes in developing responsive, equitable curriculum frameworks that enhance student engagement and learning outcomes. Her leadership approach is rooted in data-driven decision-making, culturally responsive pedagogy, and inclusive instructional models that affirm the potential of every student.

Ingrid is also the founder of NJ Learning for All, an initiative committed to promoting equity, access, and academic excellence for students who learn differently. When she couldn't find a leadership study guide that reflected her learning style, she wrote her own. That guide has since helped a growing number of aspiring school leaders prepare with confidence, clarity, and purpose.

Made in the USA
Middletown, DE
23 September 2025

17257677R00139